Cal Thomas
Grand Rapids
Jan. 1875.

# DÖDERLEIN'S HAND-BOOK

OF

# LATIN SYNONYMES.

TRANSLATED BY

REV. H. H. ARNOLD B.A.

WITH

AN INTRODUCTION

BY

S. H. TAYLOR, LL. D.

ANDOVER:
WARREN F. DRAPER,
MAIN STREET.
1874.

STEREOTYPED AND PRINTED BY
W. F. DRAPER, ANDOVER.

# INTRODUCTION

TO

# THE AMERICAN EDITION.

---

Dr. Ludwig Döderlein, the author of this work, was born in 1791, and became Professor in the University of Erlangen. He is an eminent philologist, and the author of several valuable philological works. The most important of these are: "The Formation of Latin Words;" "A Homeric Glossary;" "Handbook of Latin Etymology;" "Latin Synonymes and Etymologies," in six volumes; on this he labored more than twelve years, the first volume appearing in 1826, the last in 1828. From this latter work, the volume here presented was prepared by the author, and first published in 1840. After a familiarity of several years with most of the best manuals on Latin Synonymes, we find this superior to any of them, and better adapted to the wants of the student. It shows an intimate and comprehensive acquaintance with the language, and a nice discrimination between the significations of words having a greater or less similarity of meaning. The distinctions are generally well founded, and clearly stated. While at times the distinction may seem to be too refined and subtle, careful observation and more extended study will usually correct such an impression. The difference between related words may proceed from a variety of sources. It may be that of genus and species; or it may be historical, one being used at one time and the other at a different one; or one is abstract, the other concrete; one is literal, the other figurative; one is the more common expression, the other the more elegant; one is a prose word, the other poetical; one belongs to one kind of poetry, and the other to another. The difference also consists in the point of view which the writer takes. *Quies* is rest; *requies* also is rest; but the latter word shows that the writer has in mind a previous state of *unrest.* There are other differences also growing out of the essential nature of the words.

The advantages of the study of synonymes in a classical course, are too great to be neglected. A knowledge of them gives to the student a fulness and precision of his author's meaning otherwise unattainable. The point of a sentence often turns upon a delicate shade of thought conveyed by a particular word, which another of similar signification would not give; if this delicate shade is not appreciated, the writer's thought is either misapprehended, or but imperfectly understood.

Again, the habit of observing the proper use

of words related to each other in meaning, as whether one is generic, and the other specific, one abstract, the other concrete, one literal, the other figurative, or whatever be the ground and nature of the difference, is one of the essential benefits of classical study. The whole process of such study, when rightly conducted, is that of "arbitrating between conflicting probabilities;" and the closest power of arbitration is often requisite in determining the particular idea conveyed by related words. Or, if the distinctions are drawn out, as they are in a treatise on synonymes, the mind of the student is trained to close and discriminating observation, in being required to note and fix these distinctions, and to give a definite form to them in his own mind, and to express them in his own language.

Besides the more direct advantages resulting from the study of synonymes, an increased interest will thereby be given to classical studies

There is a natural fondness in the youthful mind for the process of comparison, for tracing resemblances and differences. This element should not be neglected when it can be turned to so good account. It will help to relieve the tedium and barrenness of classical study, as too often conducted, and to give some living features to languages which are too generally looked upon as "dead."

The meaning of a particular word is often given more distinctly by stating its opposite. The relation, or shade of thought, which cannot be conveyed fully by a direct definition, nor perhaps, indeed, by words at all, is made clear and distinct by showing to what it is opposed. This valuable means of elucidation, the author has used with great success in this work.

While the author has "omitted all detail in the treatment of Greek synonymes" in this compend, he has very wisely sought out the nearest corresponding Greek expression, and placed it with the Latin word to be explained. Thus the Greek word, to the more advanced scholar, will often throw light upon the Latin, and the Latin in turn upon the Greek. In this way the work is indirectly valuable in elucidating Greek synonymes.

The present edition of this work is reprinted from the second London edition, which is essentially the same as the first, with a few corrections and improvements.

S. H. T.

ANDOVER, JANUARY, 1858.

THE

# AUTHOR'S PREFACE.

---

THE wish has been expressed to me from different quarters, and particularly by several respectable schoolmasters, to see the essential results of my larger work on Latin Synonymes and Etymologies compressed into a Hand-book. Although within the twelve years since I began to work at the long-neglected study of Latin Synonymes, the market has been almost glutted with works of the same sort, in the form of hand-books, by Habicht, Ramshorn, Jentzen, and Schmalfeld, I have not, on that acount, the least hesitation in complying with the wish expressed to me, by publishing the present Abridgment; for, in asserting that my method and the arrangement of my materials are totally distinct from what have been adopted by those deserving authors, I trust that I am neither extolling myself, nor underrating them. The Abridgment which I here submit to the Public contains, I hope, all that is essential in my larger work; — to effect which object I have omitted certain things of less direct importance; namely, —

First, — All etymological deductions. Not wishing, however, entirely to renounce my principle of associating the etymology with the synonyme, I have inserted it between parentheses, whenever it was not either so obvious as to make the insertion unnecessary, or so far-fetched as to make the etymology doubtful. Many instances of this sort will and must, especially to him who is not conversant with etymological researches, appear singularly uncouth; but it would have led me too far to refer, in every instance, to the principles established in the Treatise on the Formation of Latin Words, which I have subjoined to my larger work as a Supplement. I must, therefore, entreat those readers and critics into whose hands my treatise has not fallen, to ignore (if I may use a law term) the words included between parentheses, or to suspend their verdict concerning them.

Secondly, — I have omitted all parallel passages, and such as have an affinity with each other, without possessing any stringent force as proofs. On the other hand, I have given at length those passages in the classics in which the ancients, in the course of speech, and not by means of grammatical reflections, have introduced synonymes in contrast with each other, and thus taught their differences; and where such passages were wanting, I have frequently brought into juxta-position several passages from one and the same author, in which he seems to have indicated some peculiar force in a particular expression.

Thirdly, — I have omitted all critical and exegetical discussions. The more scientific form of my larger work not only afforded me the opportunity, but imposed the obligation of entering upon such discussions; but in the present Abridgment I have thought it best, except in a very few cases, to omit them altogether.

Fourthly,—I have omitted all detail in the treatment of the Greek synonymes. Nevertheless, I have thought it of essential importance to search for the nearest corresponding expression, both in the Greek and German languages, and place them by the side of the Latin synonyme; and at the same time to ascertain, and make intuitive, as it were, the precise meaning and extent of the Latin expression, by the introduction of such words as are strictly in opposition to it.

Fifthly,—I have omitted the views of other writers on synonymes. In my larger work I introduced, often only as literary curiosities, distinctions derived from the Latin grammarians, Varro, Cicero, Agrætius, Pseudo-fronto, and Pseudo-palæmon; and I also quoted, whether agreeing with or differing from me, the modern writers on synonymes, Popma, Hill, Dumesnil, Smitson, Habicht, Ramshorn, Jentzen, and others. Instead of which I must here content myself with merely referring to such quotations as are contained in my larger work; and have therefore added, at the end of each article, the volume and page of that work in which these quotations are to be found.

Sixthly,—I have omitted such synonymes as are of very rare occurrence, and distinguished from each other by a very slight difference. In my larger work I have treated as synonymes many expressions, *ἅπαξ εἰρημένα*, that occur but once, and whose differences, on that very account, cannot be deduced from the general usage of the language, but can merely be guessed at from etymology and other sources. Such expressions are of no importance with reference to the object of this Handbook. The same may be said of many synonymes which can be distinguished, as it were, only by a microscope. Such synonymes are found throughout my larger work in great numbers, and have drawn upon me the reproach of "hair-splitting." The fact I must acknowledge, but cannot admit it to be a reproach; for surely it is the proper vocation of a scientific writer on synonymes, not so much to distinguish words that merely resemble each other in meaning, as those that are apparently equivalent. The greater their apparent equivalence, the more difficult it is to grasp their essential difference, and the more indispensable the aid of a guide to synonymes. If, therefore, it be admitted, that words identical in meaning do not exist, and that it is morally impossible, if I may use the expression, that they should exist, the only questions are, whether, in such cases, it is worth while to search out their differences, and whether it is possible to find them out. Science will answer the first question, without hesitation, in the affirmative; and with respect to the second, there can at least be no presumption in making the attempt. A distinction is soon obtained when several words are contrasted with the word under consideration; and if these contrasted words are also synonymous with each other, it must follow, that the affinity of the several words in meaning is so close, as to permit their interchange, as synonymes, under all circumstances. Their differences are altogether unimportant with reference to speaking and writing, but highly important as far as the intimate and more refined knowledge of the language itself is concerned. It is on this account that hair-splitting is allowable. Can there be a doubt that a distinction will be slight in proportion as it has its origin in the individual feelings of those by whom a language is used? Such distinctions in synonymes are, consequently, most felt in one's native language; it is only necessary that the feelings in which they have their origin should not be vague and unformed. In the introduction to the fourth part of my work I have evinced, I hope, sufficient liberality and tolerance with regard to the obligation of conforming to these hair-breadth distinctions, and selecting one's expressions accordingly. So much in justification of those reprobated hair-splittings; those discoveries of atoms, or, as my deceased friend Bremi expressed it, keen discernment of atoms, which in my larger work, more devoted to science than to instruction, found their proper place; but in the present Hand-book, intended for the use of schools, especially in the art of writing Latin, my predilection for such nice distinctions would be sadly out of place. Distinctions of that sort I have, therefore, for the most part, omitted, but not with the intention of silently retracting them.

I here submit a few observations to the notice of schoolmasters. For the purposes of instruction, synonymes may be divided into three classes; the first embraces those which the scholar cannot too quickly learn to distinguish, because their affinity is merely apparent, arising from their being translated by the same word in the mother-tongue; for instance, *liberi* and *infantes; animal* and *bestia; hærere* and *pendere; sumere* and *adimere; hostis* and *inimicus.* The interchange of such synonymes may be counted a blunder of the same sort as that which is called a solecism. To the second class belong those synonymes which may be distinguished from each other with ease and certainty, but which are, at the same time, so nearly related in meaning, that the ancients themselves use them, without hesitation, as interchangeable; for instance, *lascivus* and *petulans; parere* and *obedire; ater* and *niger; incipere* and *inchoare; mederi* and *sanare; vacuus* and *inanis; spernere* and *contemnere; tranquillus* and *quietus.* As long as the scholar has to contend with the elements of grammar, the teacher may leave him in the erroneous opinion, that these expressions have exactly the same meaning; but, when further advanced, he must be taught to distinguish them, partly in order to accustom him to that propriety of expression which is necessary in writing Latin; partly, without reference to composition, as a very useful mental exercise. In the third class I rank those words whose differences are not to be ascertained without trouble, and cannot be deduced with full evidence from the old authors, and which, probably, were but dimly discerned even by the ancients themselves; for instance, *lira* and *sulcus; remus* and *tonsa; pæne* and *prope; etiam* and *quoque, recordari* and *reminisci; lævus* and *sinister; velox* and *pernix; vesanus* and *vecors; fatigatus* and *fessus, collis* and *clivus.* Such distinctions are of little or no consequence in composition, except when it is necessary to use synonymous terms in express opposition to each other; for instance, *mare* and *amnis*, in opp. to *lacus* and *fluvius; metus* and *spes*, in opp. to *timor* and *fiducia:* when such occasions occur, the richness of a language in synonymes is available. A more scrupulous exactness in this respect would appear to me arrant pedantry, and necessarily obstruct the free movement of the mind in writing. As a teacher, I should wish that the synonymes of the first sort should be distinguished by boys in the elementary classes; those of the second, I would introduce into the higher classes, and teach the scholar, when about fourteen, to observe their differences in the choice of expressions in composition; I would also explain them in the interpretation of an author, but with moderation, as a spur to thinking, not as a clog in reading. Those of the third class I would never introduce, except in explaining such passages as render their introduction unavoidable; for instance, when an author combines *flumina et amnes*, I would explain their difference to defend him from the suspicion of tautology.

I have consulted convenience of reference in interweaving the alphabetical index with the context. By this means any one can find at once the word of which he is in search, which a separate index would render impossible.

These arrangements, combined with an almost studied precision of expression, have enabled me to reduce the six volumes of my larger work on Synonymes (which fills, including the Supplement, more than one hundred and forty-three sheets) to this Abridgment, of about fifteen. The etymological part of my researches I reserve for a separate volume, of about the same size as the present, which will make its appearance as an Etymological Hand-book of the Latin language.

May the present publication, and that which I announce, meet with the same favorable and indulgent reception that has fallen to the share of my larger work with all its defects.

*Erlangen, December*, **1839.**

# HANDBOOK

OF

# LATIN SYNONYMES.

---

## A.

Abdere, see *Celare*.

Abesse; Deesse; Deficere. 1. Abesse denotes absence as a local relation, 'to be away' from a place; but deesse denotes an absence by which a thing is rendered incomplete, and means 'to fail,' 'to be wanting,' in opp. to *esse* and *superesse*. Cic. Brut. 80. Calidio hoc unum, si nihil utilitatis habebat, *abfuit*, si opus erat, *defuit*. 2. Deesse denotes a *completed* (*i. e.* already existing), deficere a commencing state. Cic. Verr. i. 11. Vererer ne oratio *deesset*, ne vox viresque *deficerent*. (v. 339.)

Abnuere, see *Negare*.

Abolere (ἀπολέσαι) means 'to annul,' to 'annihilate,' and, as far as possible, to remove from the universe and cast into oblivion; but delere (διολέσαι, or δηλεῖν) 'to destroy,' to bring a thing to nought, and make it useless.

Abominari; Exsecrari; Detestari. Abominari means to recoil from, as of evil omen; and to avert a threatening evil by a ceremony, in opp. to *omen accipere*; exsecrari means to *curse*, when one would exclude a guilty person from human society as devoted to the infernal gods, in opp. to blessing; lastly, detestari (θέσσασθαι) means to curse, when one wishes to deprecate evil by an appeal to the gods against a dreaded person or thing, in opp. to praying in behalf of.

ABSCONDERE, see *Celare*.

ABSOLVERE, see *Finire*.

ABSTINENTIA, see *Modus*.

ABUNDARE; REDUNDARE. Abundare denotes plenteousness in a good sense, as the symbol of full measure and affluence, like περιεῖναι; redundare is used in a bad sense, as a symbol of over-abundance and luxury, like περισσεύειν: of that which is *abundans* there is an *ample supply* at hand; that which is *redundans* is superfluous and might be dispensed with.

ABUNDE, see *Satis*.

AC, see *Et*.

ACCENDERE; INCENDERE; INFLAMMARE; COMBURERE; CREMARE. Accendere, incendere, and inflammare, mean 'to set on fire:' accendere, from without, and at a single point, like ἀνάπτειν [hence to *light* a torch, etc.]; incendere, from within, like ἐνδαίειν [hence to *set fire* to *houses*, *villages*]; inflammare, 'to set on fire,' either from without or from within, but with bright flames, like ἀναφλογίζειν; comburere and cremare mean 'to burn up, or consume by fire;' comburere, with a glowing heat, as the causative of *ardere*, like κατακαίειν; cremare, with bright flames, as the causative of *flagrare* like πιμπράναι. Hence, mortui *cremantur* on a bright blazing funeral pile; vivi *comburuntur*, Cic. Fam. x. 32. Verr. i. 33 and 38, in order to make the torture of that mode of dying felt the more. (iv. 250.)

ACCEPTUS, see *Gratus*. ACCERSERE, see *Accessere*.

ACCIDERE; EVENIRE; CONTINGERE; OBVENIRE; OBTINGERE. Accidere and evenire denote both favorable and unfavorable occurrences; but the *acci dentia*, unexpected ones, overtaking us by surprise; the *evenientia* were expected, foreseen; contingere, obvenire, obtingere, are generally confined to *fortunate* occurrences. The *accidentia* are fortuitous, the *evenientia* result from foregoing acts or circumstances; the *contingentia* are the favors of Fortune; the *obtingentia* and *obvenientia* are the things that fall to one's *lot*. Cic. Fam. vi. 21. Timebam, ne *evenirent*, quæ *acciderunt:* the word *evenirent* has a *subjective* reference to his foresight, the word *acciderunt* is entirely *objective;* the point of view taken by it being that of those who *now* manifest *surprise.* See also Tac. H. iv. 19, and Sen. Ep. 119. Scies plura mala *contingere* nobis quam *accidere.* (v. 339.)

ACCIPERE, see *Sumere.*

ACCIRE, see *Arcessere.*

ACCUSARE, see *Arguere.*

ACER; VEHEMENS. Acer (ὠκύς) denotes eagerness in a good sense, as fire and energy, in opp. to *frigidus*, like ὀξύς: but vehemens (ἐχόμενος) in a bad sense, as heat and passion, in opp. to *lenis;* Cic. Or. ii. 49, 53, like σφοδρός. (iv. 450.)

ACERBUS; AMARUS. Acerbus (from κάρφω) means a biting bitterness, in opp. to *mitis*, like ὀξύς; amarus, a nauseous bitterness, in opp. to *dulcis*, like πικρός. Quintil. xi. 3. 169. Cic. Rep. iii. 8. Plin. H. N. xxvii. 9. Sen. Ir. i. 4. (vi. 4.)

ACERVUS; CONGERIES; STRUES; CUMULUS. 1 Acervus and congeries mean 'heaps' of homogeneous things collected and piled up in layers; acervus [from ἀγείρω], like σωρός, with arrangement, and mostly in a conical shape, but congeries, negligently, and altogether without regard to shape; strues denotes that something new is produced, and a determinate form given, serving a particular purpose; like θημών. Curt. viii. 7. 11. Passim *acervos struesque* accendebant; meaning by *acervos* '*heaps*' or '*piles*,' by *strues* '*stacks*' of wood. 2. Cumulus (from ἀκμή) means strictly, not the heap itself, but the top, by which the heap is completed as a whole, like the key-stone, by which any thing first reaches its proper and complete height, almost like κορυφή; and it has this meaning particularly in cumulare, which is like κορυφοῦν. Compare Liv. xxii. 59. Superstantes *cumulis* cæsorum corporum, with Cannenses campos *acervi* Romanorum corporum tegunt: and xxiii. 5. Molibus ex humanorum corporum *strue* faciendis. (ii. 118.)

Achivi; Achæi; Achaius; Achaicus; Troius; Troicus. 1. Achivi are the Homeric Greeks, or Ἀχαιοί; Achæi are either the inhabitants of Achaia, or, in the poets, the Greeks at large, as contemporaries of the Romans. Cic. Divin. i. 16. Cum *Achivi* cœpissent inter se strepere. Compare this with Cæcil. 20. Quod cum sibi *Achæi* patronum adoptarant. 2. Achaius is the adj. of Achivus. Hor. Od. i. 15. 37. Virg. Æn. ii. 462; but Achaicus is the adj. of Achæus. Cic. Att. i. 13. 3. Troius is the more *select* term, as adj. of the old heroic and Homeric Troja; Troicus, the usual adj. of the country Troas, without reference to the Trojan war. (v. 306.)

Acies; Acumen; Cacumen; Mucro; Cuspis. 1. Acies is the sharpness of a line adapted for cutting; acumen, of a tip or point adapted for sticking. Figuratively, the *acies mentis* is shown in the keen sifting of what is confused, in clear perception; the *acumen mentis* is the fathoming of that which is deeply hidden, in subtle discovery. 2. Acumen and cacumen mean a natural head or top; acumen, of a cone, beak, and so forth; cacumen, particularly that of a mountain: mucro and cuspis mean an artificial head, for the purpose of piercing and wounding; mucro, that of a sword, dagger, and so forth; cuspis, that of a spear, arrow, etc., like αἰχμή. (vi. 5.)

Acies, see *Pugna*.

Acta, see *Ripa*.

Actor; Comœdus; Ludio; Histrio. The generic term a c t o r, and the specific terms c o m œ d u s and t r a g œ d u s, denote the player, as a respectable artist; but l u d i o, l u d i u s, the *comedian*, the player, who makes acting his *trade*, with the accessory notion of commonness; lastly, h i s t r i o, sometimes the actor, sometimes the *comedian*, but mostly with the accessory notion of buffoonery and boasting. Cic. Sext. 54. Ipse ille maxime *ludius*, non solum spectator, sed *actor* et acroama. Rosc. Com: 10. Nemo ex pessimo *histrione* bonum *comœdum* fieri posse existimaret. Ep. ad Qu. Fr. i. a. E. Hortor ut tanquam poetæ boni et *actores* industrii solent, in extrema parte diligentissimus sis. Suet. Aug. 74, (v. 334.)

Acumen, see *Acies*.

Adamare, see *Amare*.

Adesse; Interesse; Præsentem esse. 1. A d e s s e means to be near a person or thing; but i n t e r e s s e, to assist in a transaction, to *take a part* in it. Cic. Verr. i. 40. Crimina ea, quæ notiora sunt his qui *adsunt*, quam nobis . . . . De illo nihil dixit, in quo *interfuit*. 2. A d e s s e denotes generally the presence in a circle to which we belong; p r æ s e n t e m e s s e, absolute, audible and visible presence. When an expected guest is within our walls, *adest;* he who is in the same room with us, *præsens est*. (v. 337.)

Adhuc; Hactenus; Hucusque. A d h u c refers to time, up to this moment; h a c t e n u s and h u c u s q u e have a local reference, up to this place, or this point.

Adigere, see *Cogere*. Adimere, see *Demere*.
Adipisci, see *Invenire*. Admirari, see *Vereri*.
Admodum, see *Perquam*. Adolere, see *Accendere*.
Adolescens, see *Puer*. Adorare, see *Vereri*.
Adscendere, see *Scandere*. Adsolere, see *Solere*.
Adspectus, Adspicere, see *Videre*.
Adulari, see *Assentiri*. Aduncus, see *Curvus*.
Advena, see *Externus*. Adventor, see *Hospes*.

ADVERSARIUS; HOSTIS; INIMICUS. 1. Adversarius is the generic term for every opposer, in the field, in politics, in a court of judicature, like ἀντιστάτης. Hostis (from ἔχθω) is 'the enemy' in the field, and war, opp. to *pacatus*. Cic. Rep. ii. 3. Sen. Q. N. vi. 7. like πολέμιος; inimicus, 'an enemy' in heart, opp. to *amicus*, like ἐχθρός. Cic. Man. 10. Pompeius sæpius cum *hoste* conflixit, quam quisquam cum *inimico* concertavit. Phil. xi. 1. Verr. i. 15. Curt. vii. 10. Liv. xxii. 39. Nescio an infestior hic *adversarius*, quam ille *hostis* maneat. 2. Hostilis and inimicus denote states of hatred become habitual qualities; infestus and infensus only as temporary states; infestus (ἀνασπαστός?) applies to a quiescent state of aversion, like disaffected, unkind, and thus it is applied to inanimate things that threaten hostility; infensus (from πένθος) denotes a passionate state of mind, like enraged, and is therefore applicable to persons only. Tac. Ann. xv. 28. Non *infensum*, nedum *hostili* odio Corbulonis nomen habebatur. Cic. Verr. iii. 24. Sall. Cat. 19. Sen. N. Q. iii. pr. Animus luxuriæ non *adversus* tantum, sed et *infestus*. Liv. ii. 20. Tarquinium *infesto* spiculo petit; Tarquinius *infenso* cessit *hosti*. (iv. 393.)

ADVOCATUS; CAUSIDICUS. Advocatus means in the writers of the silver age 'a counsel' in relation to his services and to his client, as his friend and assistant; causidicus, in relation to his station and profession, often with the contemptuous accessory notion of his being a hireling. (vi. 8.)

ÆDES, see *Templum*.

ÆDIFICIUM; DOMUS; ÆDES; FAMILIA. 1. Ædificium is the generic term for buildings of all sorts, like οἰκοδόμημα; domus, and ædes, ædium, mean 'a dwelling-house;' domus, as the residence and home of a family; ædes (αἴθω, αἴθουσα), as composed of several apartments, like δόμοι, δώματα. Virg. G. ii. 461. Ingentem foribus *domus* alta superbis mane salutantum totis vomit *ædibus* undam. (vi. 8.) 2. Domus denotes 'a family' in the patriarchal sense, as a separate society, of which the individuals are mutually connected; familia, in a political sense, as part of a gens, civitas, or populus. (v. 301.)

ÆGER; ÆGROTUS; MORBIDUS; MORBUS; VALETUDO; INVALETUDO. 1. Æger is the generic term for every sort of illness and uneasiness, whether mental or physical; ægrotus and morbidus indicate bodily illness: ægrotus is applied particularly to men; morbidus, to brutes: the *æger* feels himself ill; the *ægrotus* and *morbidus* actually are so. 2. Morbus and valetudo denote an actual illness; morbus, objectively, that which attacks men; valetudo, subjectively, the state of the sick, though this distinction was introduced by writers of the silver age; invaletudo means only an *indisposition.* (iv. 172.)

ÆGRE, see *Vix.* ÆGRITUDO, see *Cura.*
ÆGROTUS, see *Æger.* ÆMULATIO, see *Imitatio.*
ÆQUALIS, see *Æquus.* ÆQUOR, see *Mare.*

ÆQUUS; PAR; ÆQUALIS; PARILIS; COMPAR; IMPAR; DISPAR. 1. Æquum (from εἴκελος) is that of which *its own* component parts are alike, in opp. to *varius*, Cic. Verr. v. 49; par (from πείρω) is that which is like to some other person or thing, and stands *in the same rank* (on the *same level*) with it or him, in opp. to *superior* and *inferior.* Cic. Brut. 59, 215. Orat. ii. 52, 209. 39, 166. In *æquo marte* the battle between two parties is considered as a whole; in *pari marte* the fortune of one party is set against that of the other, and declared to be equal to it. 2. Par denotes similarity with respect to greatness, power, and value, or equality and proportion with regard to number, like ἴσος; æqualis refers to interior qualities, like ὅμοιος. The *par* is considered as in a state of activity, or, at least, as determined and prepared to measure himself with his match in contest; the *æqualis*, in a state of rest, and claiming merely comparison and equality as to rank. The *paria* are placed in opposition to each other, as *rivals* in the contest for pre-eminence; the *æqualia* are considered in a *friendly* relation to each other, in consequence of their common qualities and sympathies. Hence pariter means, in the same degree, ἴσα; æqualiter, in the same manner, ὁμοίως, ὁμῶς. Vell. Pat. ii. 124. 3. Par denotes *quite* like, parilis, *nearly* like, as a middle step between *par* and *similis*. 4. Par expresses equal to *another*, and hence may relate to only *one side*; compar, *mutually* equal, like *finitimi* and *confines*, ἐγγύς and σύνεγγύς. 5. Impar denotes inequality as to *quantity*, either arithmetical inequality with regard to number [= odd], or a *relative inferiority* as to strength; dispar refers to *quality*, without distinguishing on which side of the comparison the advantage lies. (iv. 77.)

ÆQUUS; PLANUS; CAMPUS. 1. Æquum (from εἴκελος) denotes that which is flat, a horizontal flatness, in opposition to that which rises or sinks, to *superior*, *inferior*, and *acclivis*. Cic. Fam. iii. 8. Orat. iii. 6. Tac. Agr. 35. Hist. iv. 23; planum (from πλάξ) denotes 'evenness,' in opp. to unevenness, to *montosus*, *saxosus*. Cic. Part. 10. Quintil. v. 10, 37. 21. Hence, figuratively, æquum denotes 'justice,' as injustice may be considered as beginning when one part is raised above another; in the same way planum denotes clearness and distinctness, where nothing rises to interrupt the view. 2. Æquor and planities denote a flat surface with regard to its form; campus, with regard to its position, as low-lands in opp. to high-lands. (iv. 71.)

ÆQUUS ANIMUS, see *Satis habere.*

AER, see *Anima.*

ÆRARIUM; FISCUS. Ærarium is 'the public treasury;' fiscus (from πίθος, πιθάκνη), 'the imperial treasury.' Tac. Ann. vi. 2. Bona Sejani ablata *ærario*, ut in *fiscum* cogerentur; tanquam referret! (vi. 10.)

ÆRUMNA, see *Labor*. ÆSTIMARE, see *Censere*.
ÆSTUARE, see *Calere*. ÆTERNUS, see *Continuus*.
AFFARI, see *Alloqui*. AFFATIM, see *Satis*.
AFFINIS, see *Necessarius*. AFFIRMARE, see *Dicere*.
AGER, see *Rus and Villa*.

AGERE; FACERE; GERERE; OPUS; FACTUM; AGE; I NUNC; DEGERE. 1. Agere (ἄγειν) has an effect that exists in time only, like to do; facere, an effect that exists in space also, as to make. The *acta* are past as soon as the *agens* ceases, and remain invisible in the memory; the *facta* cannot properly be said to exist till the *faciens* ceases. Quintil. ii. 18. The *agens* is supposed to be in a state of activity of some kind; the *faciens* in a state of *productive* activity. 2. Agere means 'to do' something for one's own interest; gerere (ἀγείρειν), for the interest of another, to execute a commission. Cic. Verr. i. 38. Quæ etiamsi voluntate Dolabellæ *fiebant*, per istum tamen omnia *gerebantur*. 3. Opus is the result of facere, as the work, ἔργον; factum is the result of agere, as the transaction; res gestæ are deeds [*e. g.* in war], πράξεις; acta are only political enactments. Cic. Att. xiv. 17. Multa de *facto* ac de *re gesta;* the former by the exertions of Amatius, the latter by his own wise and spirited animadversions through Dolabella. 4. Age, agedum, is an earnest exhortation, as 'On, on!' I nunc is an ironical exhortation, as 'Go to!' 5. Agere means to be active, and in the midst of business; degere, to live somewhere in a state of rest, in voluntary or involuntary inactivity. Tac. Ann. xv. 74. Deum honor principi non ante habetur, quam *agere* inter homines desierit, compared with iv. 54. Certus procul urbe *degere*. (v. 327.)

AGERE FERRE, see *Vastare*.

AGGER; VALLUM. Agger (from ἐσαγείρω) is a single line, like a dam; vallum or *mound* (ἀλκή) is a line which helps to enclose a space. Agger may serve in a warfare as the outwork of a *redoubt* [which is protected by a *single line* in front]; v a l l u m [*rampart*] always belongs to a fortress, camp, or entrenched place.

AGMEN, see *Caterva.*

AGRESTIS, see *Rus.*

AIO, see *Dicere.*

ALA; PENNA; PLUMA; PINNA. 1. A l a (from ἔχω, *vehere*) denotes 'the wing,' as a joint, like πτέρυξ; p e n n a (πέτεσθαι), with reference to its feathers, like πτερόν. Plaut. Pœn. iv. 2. 48. Meæ *alæ pennas* non habent. 2. P e n n a denotes the larger and harder feathers; p l u m a, the smaller and softer feathers, which serve as a clothing to the body of the bird, like πτίλον. Sen. Ep. 42. Meministi, cum quendam affirmares esse in tua potestate, dixisse me volaticum esse ac levem, et te non pedem ejus tenere, sed *pennam.* Mentitus sum; *pluma* tenebatur, quam remisit et fugit. Cic. N. D. ii. 47. 121. 3. P e n n a denotes the whole, consisting of quill and feathers; p i n n a, the feather only, in opposition to the quill. (v. 204.)

ALACER, see *Gaudere.* ALA, see *Armus.*

ALAPA; COLAPHUS. A l a p a (Goth. *lofa*, 'the flat hand,') denotes a blow with the flat hand on the face, as a gentle punishment, like a slap on the cheek, or box on the ear; c o l a p h u s (κόλαφος), a blow on the head with the clenched fist, betokening anger and rage, like a cuff, a thump. (vi. 14.)

ALBUS; CANDIDUS; ALBIDUS. 1. A l b u s (ἀλφός) denotes 'white,' as far as it is in general a negation of all color, as that which is colorless; c a n d i d u s (from ξανθός), as being itself a positive color, and, as such, the purest and brightest, near which all other colors have a shade of darkness and duskiness, as a fine brilliant white. A l b u s, opposed to *ater*, approaches, like λευκόν, to yellowish; c a n d i d u s, opposed to *niger*, approaches, like ἀργόν, to bluish. A l b a c u t i s is the skin of the sick and dropsical; c a n d i d a, that of the fair girl. Figuratively, a l b o r is the symbol of good fortune and joy; c a n d o r, of purity of mind and innocence. 2. A l b u s denotes 'white;' a l b i d u s, only 'whitish.' (iii. 193.)

Alere; Nutrire; Nutricare. A l e r e (from ἄλθω) denotes nourishment, as conducive to development and growth; n u t r i r e and n u t r i c a r e, only as it prolongs and secures existence. Or, a l i m e n t a adjuvant, n u t r i m e n t a sustentant. Cic. N. D. ii. 63. Neque *ali* neque sustentari. N u t r i r e involves a general notion; n u t r i c a r e is usually applied more particularly to brutes. (ii. 99.)

Algere, Algidus, see *Frigere*.

Alienigena, see *Externus*.

Alimenta; Penus; Cibus; Esca; Edulia; Cibare; Pascere. 1. A l i m e n t a and p e n u s are victuals in general, meat and drink; a l i m e n t a, mostly with reference to the wants of an individual; p e n u s, to the wants of a whole family. C i b u s and e s c a denote 'food,' in opposition to drink. Cic. Fin. i. 11, and ii. 28. C i b u s (from γεύω, to chew), natural food, as a means of nourishment; e s c a (from ἔδω), 'the food' that is artificially prepared as a dish. Hence c i b u s denotes the food of brutes also; but e s c a, only a bait, prepared as it were like a dish, and set before them. Cic. N. D. ii. 47. Animalia *cibum* partim dentibus capessunt: compare this with ii. 23. Dii nec *escis* nec potionibus vescuntur. 2. C i b a r i a are the most general and usual sorts of food; e d u l i a are savory and select sorts of food. Suet. Tib. 46. Comites nunquam salario, *cibariis* tantum sustentavit; compare with Cal. 40. Pro *eduliis* certum statumque exigebatur. 3. C i b a r e means to feed with one's hand, as nurses, etc.; p a s c e r e (from πάσασθαι), only to give out food, as a feeder or master. Suet. Tib. 72. Draconem manu sua *cibaturus;* compare with Vesp. 18. Sineret se plebeculam *pascere.* (v. 192.)

Aliquando, see *Nonnunquam*.

Alites, see *Volucres*.

ALLOQUI; APPELLARE; AFFARI. Alloqui denotes accosting, as addressing the first word, a salutation, and so forth, to a person with whom one is not unacquainted; appellare (from an old Gothic substantive, spellan), when one wishes to draw a person into conversation, and direct to him serious, or, at any rate, not insignificant words; affari denotes *addressing* from the impulse of a *feeling;* through peculiar friendliness or with solemnity. Cic. Cluent. 61. Quum nemo recipere tecto, nemo audire, nemo *alloqui*, nemo respicere vellet: compare with Phil. xiii. 2. Salutabunt benigne, comiter *appellabunt* unumquemque nostrum; and Brut. 3. Salutatio libri, quo me hic *affatus* quasi jacentem excitavit. (v. 107.)

ALSUS, see *Frigere.*

ALTERCATIO, see *Disceptatio.*

ALTUS; EDITUS; PROCERUS; ARDUUS; CELSUS; EXCELSUS; SUBLIMIS. 1. Altus denotes, as a general expression, height or depth, as mathematical dimensions, in opp. to length and breadth, and, consequently, height, in opp. to *humilis;* Cic. Tusc. v. 13. 24. Orat 57. N. D. ii. 47, like ὑψηλός; editus denotes height, in opp. to *planus*, Tac. Ann. xv. 38: lastly, procerus denotes height or length in reference to growth. The *altum* has no measure and no limits; the *editum* has the bulk of a hill; the *procerum* has the bulk of a tree, the full stature of the human figure, and so forth. 2. Altus, editus, and procerus, denote height merely in relation to space; arduus means height, which is at the same time steep and inaccessible; thence, figuratively, 'difficult, impossible;' celsus, height, that thrusts itself out, and stretches upwards; thence, figuratively, 'proud;' excelsus and præcelsus, what overtops something that is itself high, hence 'pre-eminent;' sublimis, what is on high without touching the ground, soaring in the air, like μετέωρος; thence, figuratively, 'grand,' of an elevated nature. (ii. 99.)

Amans, Amator, see *Amicus*.

Amare, see *Diligere*. Amarus, see *Acerbus*.

Ambiguus, see *Dubius*.

Ambire; Circumire. Circumire denotes motion in any circular form, but on the boundaries of a space, so as to go round it; ambire denotes going hither and thither in zigzag, or going about. Plin. Ep. ii. 9. *Ambio* domos, stationesque *circumeo*: and Cic. Att. xiv. 21. Antonium *circumire* veteranos, ut acta Cæsaris sancirent; that is, He made in his canvassing the round, from first to last;—stronger than *ambire*, which would only express his canvassing, and addressing the veterans in general.

Ambo, see *Uterque*.

Ambulare; Spatiari; Deambulare; Inambulare; Obambulare. 1. Ambulare (from *ambire*) denotes taking a walk as a leisurely motion, like going up and down, in opp. both to *stare* and *cubare*, and also to *currere* and *salire;* Plaut. Bacch. iv. 8. 56. Plin. Ep. ix. 36. Cic. Fat. 5. Fin. v. 17. Sen. Ep. 113. Gell. ii. 9. Sen. Ir. ii. 35. Plin. H. N. x. 38: spatiari denotes motion in open space, as to walk out, in opp. to the confinement which a room imposes. 2. Deambulare denotes going up and down till one is tired; inambulare, within a bounded space; obambulare, with reference to a fixed object, *along which* one walks, or to a person walking with us. (iii. 48.)

Amens; Demens; Insanus; Vesanus; Excors; Vecors; Furor; Delirium; Rabies; Cerritus; Lymphatus. 1. Amentia shows itself negatively and passively; dementia, positively and energetically. The *amens* is without reason, and either acts not at all, or acts without reason, like the idiot, ἄφρων; the *demens*, while he fancies that he is doing right, acts in direct opposition to reason, like the madman, παράφρων. Hence, *amens* metu, terrore; *demens* scelere, discordia, etc. 2. Insanus has a *privative;* vesanus, a *depravative* meaning. The *insanus* in his passion oversteps the measure and bounds of right, and gives one the impression of a guilty person; the *vesanus*, in his delusion, wanders from the right path, follows a false object, and gives one the impression of an unfortunate person. 3. E x c o r s means of weak understanding in general, without the ability of reflecting and examining, in opp. to *cordatus;* v e c o r s means, of a perverted understanding, without the ability of reflecting calmly, from the mind being taken up with one fixed idea. 4. F u r o r (fervere) denotes mental irritation, ecstasy, as raging, *μανικός*; d e l i r i u m (ληρεῖν), a physical and childish remission of the mental faculties; r a b i e s (*ῥαβάσσειν, ἄραβος*), a half-moral condition of a passionate insanity, as frantic, *λύσσα*. The *furibundus* forgets the bounds of sense, the *delirus* babbles nonsense, the *rabidus* will bite and injure when he can. 5. C e r r i t u s and l y m p h a t u s betoken frenzy, as a demoniacal state, as possessed, c e r r i t u s or c e r i t u s, by Ceres, l y m p h a t u s, by the nymphs; they may also be considered as derived from *κόρυζα*, mucus narium, and from λέμφος, mucus, as symbols of stupidity. (v. 89.)

AMICTUS, AMICULUM, see *Vestis*.

AMICUS; AMANS; AMATOR. A m i c u s involves the notion of reciprocity, but means only a sincere and calm affection, like *φίλος*; a m a n s and a m a t o r denote a more glowing affection, but do not imply reciprocity; a m a n s denotes this affection as a temporary state; a m a t o r as an habitual feeling, like *ἐραστής*. Cic. Verr. v. 63. Alba tunc antiquissimus non solum *amicus*, verum etiam *amator*. Tusc. iv. 12. Inter ebriositatem et ebrietatem interest, aliudque est *amatorem* esse, aliud *amantem*. (iv. 102.)

AMICUS, see *Socius*.

AMITTERE; PERDERE; JACTURA. 1. A m i t t e r e means to lose something, so that it ceases to be in our possession, like *ἀποβαλεῖν*, opp. to *retinere*, Cic. Rep. v. i. Sext. 47. Suet. Tib. 15. Ter. Phorm. iii. 2,

22; perdere means, to lose something, so that it is destroyed, and rendered useless, like διολέσαι, opp. to *servare*. Plaut. Rud. iv. 4, 120. Ter. Ad. ii. 2, 32. Sen. Contr. iii. 21.—Tac. Ann. ii. 25. *Perdita* classe, *amissis* armis. 2. Amissio is an involuntary, jactura, a voluntary, loss, which a person undergoes, a sacrifice that is made to avoid a greater loss, as in the case of the master of a ship, who throws the freight overboard, to save his ship and his life. Plin. Ep. i. 12. *Jacturam* gravissimam feci, si *jactura* dicenda est tanti viri *amissio*. (iii. 289.)

AMITTERE, see *Mittere*.

AMNIS, see *Fluvius*.

AMOR, see *Diligere*.

AMPLECTI; COMPLECTI. Amplecti denotes embracing, often with one arm only, as a sign of calm affection and protection; complecti, clasping and surrounding with both arms, as a sign of passionate love, or familiar confidence. Amplecti means, figuratively, to lay hold of something, in opp. to slighting and disdaining; complecti, to take fully in one's grasp, in opp. to a half and superficial possession. (v. 281.)

AMPLUS, see *Magnus*.

ANCILLA, see *Servus*.

ANCEPS, see *Dubius*.

ANGUIS, see *Repere*.

ANGOR, see *Cura*.

ANGUSTUS; ARCTUS; DENSUS; SPISSUS. 1. Angustus and arctus relate to space itself, and to the proximity of its enclosing limits; densus and spissus, to things existing in space, and to their proximity to one another. The *angustum* (ἐγγυστός) is bounded only by lines, and forms mostly an oblong, *narrow*, opp. to *latus*, Cic. Att. iv. 29, like στενός; the *arctum* (from *arcere*, εἴργω) is fenced in by lists, walls, or mounds, and forms mostly a square or circle, and so forth, *close*, in opp. to *laxus*, Cic. Orat. 25, like στενωπός. The clavus angustus can therefore never be arctus. Mel. iii. 2, 8. Rhenus ad dextram primo *angustus*, ıt sui similis, post ingens lacus Flevo dicitur . . .

fitque iterum *arctior*, iterumque fluvius emittitur; in which passage the banks of the Rhine are considered only as lines, or as walls. 3. D e n s u s (from ἀδινός? or ϑαμά?) denotes objects only as pressed near *to* one another, and without any observable gaps, in opp. to *rarus*, like δασύς and ϑαμειός: s p i s s u s, as pressed close *into* one another, and without any intervals between, in opp. to *solutus*, loose, like πυκνός and συχνός. In d e n s u s the principal notion is, the rich abundance of objects, which have no need to keep far apart, if they are to fill a wide space; in s p i s s u s, the want of empty space, from all the spaces between objects being filled up, owing to their being crowded together. (iv. 431.)

Anima; Aer; Aura; Spiritus; Sublime. A n i m a and a ë r denote 'air' as an element, like ἀήρ, and a n i m a (ἄνεμος), in opp. to *terra*, *mare*, *ignis;* but a ë r, a learned term (ἀήρ, from ἀείρω?) in opp. to *æther;* a u r a and s p i r i t u s denote 'air' when put in motion; a u r a (αὔρα, from ἀέσαι, or from ἀεῖραι), the gently waving and *fanning* air; s p i r i t u s, the *streaming* and breath-like air, like πνεῦμα; lastly, s u b l i m e (from sublevare?), the air that hovers over us, simply in a local relation, in opp. to *humus*, like μετάρσιον, μετέωρον. (v. 92.)

Anima; Animus; Mens. 1. A n i m a denotes 'the soul,' physiologically, as the principle of animal life, in men and brutes, that ceases with the breath, like ψυχή: a n i m u s (ἄνεμος), psychologically and ethically, as the principle of moral personality, that ceases with the will, like ϑυμός. The souls of the departed also are called, in a mythological point of view, a n i m æ, as shades; but, in a metaphysical point of view, a n i m i, as spirits. A n i m a is a part of bodily existence; a n i mus, in direct opposition to the body. Sen. Ep. 4. Difficile est *animum* perducere ad contemtionem *animæ:* and 58. Juven. xv. 148. Principio indulsit communis conditor illis tantum *animas*, nobis *animum* quoque. 2.

Animus denotes also the human soul, as including all its faculties, and is distinguished from mens (μένος, μανθάνω), the thinking faculty, as a whole from one of its parts. Cic. Rep. ii. 40. Ea quæ latet in *animis* hominum, quæque pars *animi mens* vocatur. Lucr. iii. 615. iv. 758. Catull. 65, 3. Plaut. Cist. iii. 1, 6. As in practical life the energy of the soul is displayed in the faculty of volition, so animus itself stands for a part of the soul, namely, feeling and energy of will in co-ordinate relation to mens, the intellect or understanding. Tac. H. i. 84. Quem nobis *animum*, quas *mentes* imprecentur. Ter. Andr. i. 1. 137. Mala *mens*, malus *animus*. And, lastly, so far as thought precedes the will, and the will itself, or determination, stands as mediator between thought and action, in the same way as the body is the servant of the will, so mens is related to animus, as a whole to its part. Cic. Tusc. iii. 5. *Mens*, cui regnum totius *animi* a natura tributum est. Liv. xxxvii. 45. (v. 94.)

Animadvertere; Notare. Animadvertere means, to observe mentally, and take notice of; but notare, to make distinguishable by a mark. (vi. 20.)

Animal; Animans; Bellua; Bestia; Pecus; Fera. 1. Animal and animans are the animal as a living being, including man; animal, with reference to his nature, according to which he belongs to the class of living animals, in opp. to *inanimus*, like ζῶον; animans, with reference to his state, as still living and breathing,[1] in opp. to *exanimus;* bellua, bestia, and pecus, as irrational beings, in opp. to man, and bellua and pecus, with intellectual reference, as devoid of reason, in peculiar opp. to *homo*, Cic. N. D. ii. 11; bestia and fera, with moral reference, as wild, and hostile to man. 2. Bellua (from βλάξ) denotes, particularly, a great unwieldy animal, as the elephant, whale, principally sea-monsters; pecus, a domestic

[1] Hence *animalium cadavera*, not *animantium*.

animal, particularly of the more stupid kinds, as a bullock, sheep, in opp. to the wild; b e s t i a, a destructive animal, particularly those that are ravenous, as the tiger, wolf, etc., in opp. to birds, Justin. ii. 14, like θηρίον; f e r a (φῆρες), a wild animal of the wood, as the stag, wolf, tiger, in opp. to domestic animals. Curt. ix. 10. Indi maritimi *ferarum* pellibus tecti piscibus sole duratis, et majorum quoque *belluarum*, quos fluctus ejecit, carne vescuntur. And Tac. G. 17. (iv. 291.)

Annales; Historiæ. A n n a l e s means a comprehensive historical work, principally and especially a history of former ages, composed from documents, like Livy and Tacitus; h i s t o r i æ, particularly a work on the history of the times in which the author himself has lived, as Sallust and Tacitus.

Antiquus; Priscus: Vetus; Vetustus; Veternus; Pristinus. 1. A n t i q u u m and p r i s c u m denote the age that formerly existed, and is now no more, in opp. to *novum*, like παλαιός; v e t u s and v e t u s t u m (from ἔτος), what has existed for a long time, and has no longer any share in the disadvantages or advantages of youth, in opp. to *recens*, like γέρων, γεραιός, γερούσιος. Hence a n t i q u u s h o m o is a man who existed in ancient times; v e t u s, an old man. A n t i q u i s c r i p t o r e s means the classics, inasmuch as the age in which they flourished has long been past; v e t e r e s, inasmuch as they have lived and influenced manhood for 2000 years. Cic. Verr. i. 21. Vereor ne hæc nimis *antiqua* et jam obsoleta videantur: compare with Orat. i. 37. Ut illi *vetus* atque usitata exceptio daretur. 2. V e t u s refers only to length of time, and denotes age, sometimes as a subject of praise, sometimes as a reproach; v e t u s t u s refers to the superiority of age, inasmuch as that which is of long standing is at the same time stronger, more worthy of honor, more approved of, than that which is new, in opp. to *novicius;* lastly, v e t e r n u s refers to the disadvantages of age, inasmuch as, after many years' use, a thing becomes worn out, or, through long existence, weak and spiritless. Moreover, v e t e r n u s, in the writers of the golden age, is only admitted as a substantive, v e t e r n u m, as lethargy; v e t u s regularly supplies its place, and denotes more frequently the weakness than the strength of age. Tac. Ann. xi. 14 and 15. *Veterrimis* Græcorum, and *vetustissima* Italiæ disciplina. 3. A n t i q u u s denotes age only in relation to time, as a former age in opp. to the present; p r i s c u s (from πάρος), as a solemn word, with the qualifying accessory notion of a former age worthy of honor, and a sacred primitive age, like ἀρχαῖος, in opp. to the fashion of the day. 4. A n t i q u u s and p r i s c u s denote a time long past; p r i s t i n u s, generally, denotes only a time that is past, like πρότερος. (iv. 83.)

ANTRUM, see *Specus*.

ANUS; VETULA. A n u s (as the fem. to *senex*) denotes an old lady, with respect, and also as a term of reproach; an old woman, with reference to her weakness, credulity, loquacity, and so forth: v e t u l a, an old woman, with reference to her ugliness and disagreeableness. (iv. 92.)

APERIRE; PATEFACERE; APERTE; PALAM; MANIFESTO; PROPALAM. 1. A p e r i r e (from πεπαρεῖν) means 'to open' a space that is covered at top, and therefore in a horizontal direction, as, for instance, pits and springs, and thereby to make them visible; p a t e f a c e r e, 'to open' a space whose sides are closed; hence, to open in a perpendicular direction, as, for instance, gates, roads, and fields, and thereby to make them accessible. 2. R e t u r a r e (from στέφω, German stopfen) means, to make accessible an opening that has been stopped up; r e c l u d e r e, an opening that has been shut up; r e s e r a r e, an opening that has been barred up. 3. A p e r t e means 'openly,' and without concealment, so that everybody can perceive and know, in opp. to *occulte*, like φανερῶς; p a l a m (from planus), 'openly,' and without hiding anything, so that everybody can see and hear, in opp. to *clam*, like ἀναφανδόν; m a n i f e s t o, palpably, so that one is spared all inquiry, all conjecture, all exertion of the senses and of the mind, like δῆλον. 4. P a l a m denotes that openness which does not shun observation; p r o p a l a m, that which courts observation. Cic. Orat. i. 35. Neque proposito argento neque tabulis et signis *propalam* collocatis; that is, to everybody's admiration: compare with Pis. 36. Mensis *palam* propositis; that is, without fear and constraint. (v. 291.)

APPARET; EMINET. A p p a r e t means what is visible to him who observes; e m i n e t, what forces itself upon observation, and attracts the eye. Sen. Ir. i. 1. *Apparent* alii affectus, hic (scil. iræ) *eminet*. (vi. 23.)

APPARET, see *Constat*.

APPELLARE, see *Alloqui* and *Nominare*.

APTUS, see *Idoneus*.

AQUA; UNDA; FLUCTUS; FLUENTUM. 1. A q u a (from ὠκεανός) denotes water materially as an element, in opp. to *terra;* u n d a (from νέδη, wet), as a flowing, continually moving element, in opp., as it were, to *solum;* l y m p h a (λέμφος) is merely a poetical synonyme of *aqua*, with the accessory notion of clearness and brightness, to which the similar sound of the adjective *limpidus*, though not derived from it, gave occasion. 2. U n d a stands in the middle, between *aqua* and *fluctus*, as *aura* does between *aër* and *ventus*. For u n d a denotes, like wave, that which apparently moves *itself*, whereas f l u c t u s and f l u e n t a, like billows, the water moved by something external, as storms and so forth; f l u c t u s, the billows more in connection with the whole, the billowy sea, whereas f l u e n t u m denotes a single billow. It is only the stormy sea, the boisterous stream, that urges on its billows, but every piece of water, that is not entirely stagnant, has its waves. Hence there is a great distinction between these two images in Cicero, Mil. 2, 5. Tempestates et procellas in illis duntaxat *fluctibus* concionum semper putavi Miloni esse subeundas; that is, in the tumultuously agitated assemblies: and Planc. 6, 15. Si campus atque illæ *undæ* comitiorum, ut mare profundum et immensum, sic effervescunt quodam quasi æstu; that is, the lightly moving assemblies. Sen. N. Q. iii. 10. Quid si ullam *undam* superesse miieris, quæ superveniat tot *fluctibus* fractis. And iv. 2. Nec mergit cadens *unda*, sed planis *aquis* tradit. (ii. 10.)

Aquosus, see *Udus*.

Arbitrari, see *Censere*.

Arcana; Secreta; Mysteria. Arcana denotes secrets, in a good sense, such as are so of themselves, and from their own nature, and should be spoken of with awe; thus arcana, as a popular term, denotes secrets of all sorts; on the other hand, mysteria, as a learned term, denotes religious secrets, like the Eleusinian mysteries; lastly, secreta denotes secrets, in the most ordinary sense, such as are made so by men, and which seek concealment from some particular fear. Tac. Ann. i. 6. Sallustius Crispus particeps *secretorum* . . . monuit Liviam, ne *arcana* domus vulgarentur. (iv. 429.)

Arcere; Prohibere. Arcere (ἀρκεῖν, from ἐρύκειν) means to keep off and bar the entry, in opp. to *admittere*, Plin. H. N. xii. 1; on the other hand, prohibere means to keep at a distance, and prevent the approach, in opp. to *adhibere*. The *arcens* makes defensive opposition, like the *resistens*, and protects the threatened; but the *prohibens* acts on the offensive, like the *propulsans*, and retaliates hostility on the assailant. (iv. 430.)

Arcessere; Accire; Evocare; Accersere. 1. Arcessere and accersere denote, in the most general sense, merely, to send for; accire supposes a co-ordinate relation in those that are sent for, as, tc invite; evocare, a subordinate relation, as, to summon. The *arcessens* asks, the *acciens* entreats, the *evocans* commands, a person to make his appearance. Cic. Att. v. 1. Tu invita mulieres, ego *accivero* pueros: compare with Dejot. 5. Venit vel rogatus ut amicus, vel *arcessitus* ut socius, vel *evocatus* ut qui senatui parere didicisset. Or, Liv. x. 19. Collegæ auxilium, quod *acciendum* ultro fuerit, with xliv. 31. *Evocati* literis imperatoris. And xxix. 11. Æbutia *accita* ad Sulpiciam venit; and 12. Ut Hispalam libertinam *arcesseret* ad sese. 2. A r c e s s e r e (from cedere) means, originally, to order to approach; on the other hand, a c c e r s e r e (from σκαίρω), to come quickly, or, to make haste; but both words have been confounded with each other, from similarity of sound. (iii. 283.)

ARCTUS, see *Angustus*.

ARDERE; FLAGRARE. A r d e r e (from ἐρεύθειν) means to be in a visible glowing heat, like αἴθειν; on the other hand, f l a g r a r e, to be in bright flames, like φλέγεσθαι. Hence, metaphorically, a r d e r e is applied to a secret passion; f l a g r a r e, to a passion that bursts forth. Cic. Or. iii. 2, 8. Non vidit Crassus *flagrantem* bello Italiam, non *ardentem* invidia senatum. (iv. 21.)

ARDUUS; DIFFICILIS. A r d u u s (from ὀρθός) means difficult to ascend, in opp. to *pronus;* on the other hand, d i f f i c i l i s means difficult to execute, in opp. to *facilis*. A r d u u s involves a stronger notion of difficulty, and denotes the difficult when it borders on the impossible. Plin. Ep. iv. 17. Est enim res *difficilis ardua*. Tac. Hist. ii. 76. Æstimare debent, an quod inchoatur, reipublicæ utile, ipsis gloriosum, aut promptum effectu, aut certe non *arduum* sit. Cic. Verr. i. 51. Cum sibi omnes ad illum allegationes *difficiles*, omnes aditos *arduos*, ac pæne interclusos, viderent. (ii. 105.)

ARDUUS, see *Altus*.

ARENA, see *Sabulo*.

ARGUERE; INCUSARE; CULPARE; CRIMINARI; INSIMULARE; DEFERRE; ACCUSARE. A r g u e r e (from ἀργός) is the most general expression for any imputation of supposed or actual guilt, whether in a court of justice or not, as to tax or charge with; incusare, and the less frequent term culpare, denote only a complaint made out of a court of justice; criminari, an accusation with hostile or evil intention, in a calumnious spirit; insimulare, in an undeserved or slanderous manner, through suspicion; deferre, to impeach before a judge; accusare, to impeach in a criminal court. Cic. Lig. 4, 10. *Arguis* fatentem. Non est satis. *Accusas* eum. (ii. 163.)

Aridus; Torridus; Siccus. Aridus and torridus denote an internal want of moisture; but things that are *arida* (from areo) have lost their moisture from a heat acting within, like αὖος, in opp. to *humidus*. Plin. Pan. 30, 4; on the other hand, *torrida* (from τέρσω), from a heat penetrating from without, in opp. to *uvidus*, like σκληρός;—siccus denotes dryness that is only external, confined to the surface, in opp. to *madidus*, like ξηρός. Plin. H. N. xii. 12. Ne sint fragilia et *arida* potius quam *sicca* folia. And xv. 29. Cato docuit vinum fieri ex nigra myrta *siccata* usque in *ariditatem* in umbra. Colum. vii. 4. (vi. 244.)

Arista, see *Culmus*.

Armentum, see *Pecus*.

Armus; Humerus; Ala; Axilla. Armus (ramus?) is the highest part of the upper arm in men; the fore-leg in beasts; the shoulder-blade, as part of the whole body, distinguished from *scapula*, as part of the skeleton, like ὦμος; humerus, the flat surface, which in the human body is over the upper arm, the shoulder, like ἐπωμίς; ala and axilla, the cavity which is under the upper arm, the arm-pit, like μασχάλη. Ovid, Met. xii. 396. Ex *humeris* medios coma dependebat in *armos*. And x. 599. xiv. 304. Plin. H. N. xi 43. (iv. 27.)

Arrogantia, see *Superbia*. Artes, see *Literæ*.

Artifex, see *Faber*. Artus, see *Membrum*.

ARUNDO, see *Culmus*. ARVUM, see *Villa*.

ASCIA; SECURIS. Ascia is the carpenter's axe, to split wood; securis, the butcher's cleaver, to cut meat.

ASPER, see *Horridus*.

ASPERNARI, see *Spernere*.

ASSENTIRI; ASSENTARI; BLANDIRI; ADULARI. 1. Assentiri means to assent from conviction, in opp. to *dissentire;* but assentari, to express assent, whether from conviction or from hypocrisy, in opp. to *adversari*. Vell. P. ii. 48. Cic. Rosc. Am. 16, 99. Plaut. Most. i. 3, 100. Amph. ii. 2, 70. 2. Assentari denotes the flattery which shuns contradicting a person, like θωπεύειν; blandiri (μέλδειν), that which says what is agreeable to another, like ἀρεσκεύειν; adulari (from δοῦλος), that which would please at the expense of self-degradation, like κολακεύειν. The *assentans*, as a flatterer, would, by surrendering his right to an independent opinion; the *blandiens*, by complaisance and visible signs of affection; the *adulans*, by self-degradation, and signs of an unworthy subserviency, gain the favor of another. Assentatio, or the art of the assenter, has its origin in cowardice or weakness; blanditiæ, or fair-speaking, in the endeavor to be amiable, and, at worst, in self-interest; adulatio, or flattery, and servility, κολακεία, in a degrading, slavish, spaniel-like spirit. Sen. Ir. iii. 8. Magis adhuc proderunt submissi et humani et dulces, non tamen usque in *adulationem;* nam iracundos nimia *assentatio* offendit. Erit certe amicus . . . . cui non magis tutum erat *blandiri* quam maledicere. And ii. 28. Sæpe *adulatio*, dum *blanditur*, offendit. (ii. 174.)

ASSEVERARE, see *Dicere*. ASSES, see *Axes*.

ASSIDUITAS, see *Opera*.

ASTRUM, see *Sidus*. ASSEQUI, see *Invenire*.

ASTUTUS; CALLIDUS; VAFER; VERSUTUS. Astutus or in old Latin astus (from ἀκή, acuere), and callidus, denote cunning, more in an intellectual sense, as a mark of cleverness; astutus, indeed, acuteness in the invention and execution of a secret project, synonymous with *solers;* but callidus (from κάλλος), sharp-sightedness in judging of a complicated question of conduct, or worldly wisdom, as the consequence of a knowledge of mankind, and of intercourse with the world, synonymous with *rerum peritus*, as judicious, and, in its degenerate signification, crafty, like κερδαλέος; on the other hand, vafer and versutus denote cunning in a moral sense, as a mark of dishonesty, and, indeed, vafer (ὑφή), adroitness in introducing tricks, particularly in judicial affairs, as the tricks of a lawyer, like πανοῦργος; versutus (ἀρτυτός), versatility in dissimulation, and in the art of getting out of a scrape by some means or other; in opp. to *simplex*, Cic. Fin. iv. 25, like στροφαῖος. Plin. Ep. vii. 6. Juvenis ingeniosus, sed parum *callidus*. Cic. Brut. 48. *Callidus*, et in capiendo adversario *versutus*. (iii. 220.)

Ater; Niger; Pullus. 1. Ater (αἴθός) denotes black, as a negation of color, in opp. to *albus;* whereas niger (πνιγόεις) denotes black, as being itself a color, and indeed the darkest, in opp. to *candidus*. The *atrum* makes only a dismal and dark impression; but the *nigrum*, a positive, and imposing and beautiful impression, as Hor. Carm. i. 32, 11. Lycum *nigris* oculis, *nigroque* crine decorum. Tac. G. 43. *Nigra* scuta, tincta corpora; *atras* ad prœlia noctes legunt. (iii. 194.) 2. Ater and niger denote a deep dark black; whereas pullus only swarthy, with reference to the affinity of the dark color to dirt. (iii. 207.)

Atque, see *Et*.

Atrox; Trux; Truculentus; Dirus; Sævus; Torvus. 1. Atrox, trux, and truculentus, (from τρηχύς, ταράξαι), denote that which has an exterior exciting fear; that which makes an impression of terror on the fancy, and eye, and ear; atrox, indeed, as a property of things, but trux and truculentus as properties of persons; whereas d i r u s and s æ v u s mean that which is really an object of fear, and threatens danger; d i r u s, indeed (from δέος), according to its own nature, as a property of things, means dreadful, δεινός; but s æ v u s (from αἶ, heu!) according to the character of the person, as a property of living beings, means blood-thirsty, cruel, αἰνός. Plin. Pan. 53. *Atrocissima* effigies *sævissimi* domini. Mela ii. 7. Ionium pelagus . . . *atrox*, *sævum*; that is, looking dangerous, and often enough also bringing misfortune. 2. T r u x denotes dreadfulness of look, of the voice, and so forth, in the tragic or heroic sense, as a mark of a wild disposition or of a cruel purpose; but t r u c u l e n t u s, in the ordinary and comic sense, as a mark of ill-humor or trivial passion; the slave in Plautus is *truculentus;* the wrathful Achilles is *trux*. Sometimes, however, *truculentior* and *truculentissimus* serve as the comparative and superlative of *trux*. 3. T r u x and t r u c u l e n t u s v u l t u s is a terrific, angry look, like τραχύς; t o r v u s, merely a stern, sharp, and wild look, as τορόν, or ταυρηδὸν βλέπειν. Plin. H. N. xi. 54. Contuitu quoque multiformes; *truces*, *torvi*, flagrantes. Quintil. vi. 1. 43. (i. 40.)

Attonitus; Stupens. A t t o n i t u s, thunder-struck, denotes a momentary, s t u p e n s (ταφεῖν) a petrified, a lasting condition. Curt. viii. 2, 3. *Attoniti*, et *stupentibus* similes. Flor. ii. 12. (vi. 31.)

Audere; Conari; Moliri. A u d e r e denotes an enterprise with reference to its danger, and the courage of him who undertakes it, whereas c o n a r i (from incohare), with reference to the importance of the enterprise, and the energy of him who undertakes it; lastly, m o l i r i, with reference to the difficulty of the enterprise, and the exertion required of him who undertakes it. (iii. 295.)

Audentia, Audacia, see *Fides*.

Audire; Auscultare. A u d i r e (from *ausis*, *auris*, οὖας) means to hear, ἀκούειν, as a mere passive sensation, like *olfacere;* on the other hand, auscultare (from auricula), to hearken, *ἀκροᾶσθαι*, that is, to wish to hear, and to hear attentively, whether secretly or openly, by an act of the will, like *odorari.* Ter. And. iv. 5, 45. Æsch. Pater, obsecro, *ausculta.* Mic. Æschine, *audivi* omnia. Cato ap. Gell. i. 15. Pacuv. ap. Cic. Div. i. 57. (iii. 293.)

AUFERRE, see *Demere.*

AUGURIA; AUSPICIA; PRODIGIA; OSTENTA; PORTENTA; MONSTRA; OMINA. Auguria and auspicia are appearances in the ordinary course of nature, which for the most part possess a meaning for those only who are skilful in the interpretation of signs; auguria (from augur, *αὐγάζειν*) for the members of the college of augurs, who are skilled in such things; auspicia, for the magistrates, who have the right to take auspices: whereas prodigia, ostenta, portenta, monstra, are appearances out of the ordinary course of nature, which strike the common people, and only receive a more exact interpretation from the soothsayer: lastly, omina (*ὄθματα, ὄσσαι*) are signs which any person, to whom they occur, can interpret for himself, without assistance. The primary notion in prodigium is, that the appearance is replete with meaning, and pregnant with consequences; in ostentum, that it excites wonder, and is great in its nature; in portentum, that it excites terror, and threatens danger; in monstrum, that it is unnatural and ugly. (v. 173.)

AURA, see *Anima.*

AUSCULTARE, see *Audire.*

AUSPICIA, see *Auguria.*

AUSTERUS; SEVERUS; DIFFICILIS; MOROSUS; TETRICUS. 1. Austerus (*αὐστηρός*, from *αὔω*) denotes gravity as an intellectual, severus (*αὐηρός*) as a moral quality. The *austerus* in opp. to *jucundus*, Plin. H. N. xxxiv. 8. xxxv. 11, is an enemy to jocularity and frivolity, and seeks in science, learning, and social intercourse, always that which is serious and real, at the risk of passing for dull; the *severus*, in opp. to *luxuriosus*, Quintil. xi. 3, 74, is rigid, hates all dissoluteness and laxity of principle, and exacts from himself and others self-control and energy of character, at the risk of passing for harsh. The stoic, as a philosopher, is *austerus*, as a man, *severus*. 2. Austerus and severus involve no blame; whereas difficilis, morosus, and tetricus, denote an excess or degeneracy of rigor. The *difficilis* understands not the art of easy and agreeable converse, from hypochondria and temperament; the *morosus* (from mos) is scrupulous, and wishes everything to be done according to rule, from scrupulosity and want of tolerance; the *tetricus* (redupl. of trux, τραχύς) is stiff and constrained, from pedantry and want of temper. (iii. 232.)

Autumare, see *Censere*.

Auxilium; Opem ferre; Opitulari; Juvare; Adjuvare. 1. Auxilium, opem ferre, and opitulari, suppose a person in a strait, whom one would rescue from necessity and danger, in opp. to *deserere, destituere*, and so forth; the *auxilium ferens* is to be considered as an ally, who makes himself subservient to the personal safety, or to the interest of him who is in a strait; the *opem ferens*, as a benefactor, who employs his power and strength for the benefit of the weak; whereas juvare and adjuvare (ἰᾶσθαι) suppose only a person striving to do something, which he may be enabled to do better and quicker by help, in opp. to *impedire*, Cic. Verr. i. 6. Ter. Heaut. v. 2, 39. Matres solent esse filiis in peccato *adjutrices*, *auxilio* in paterna injuria. When in Liv. ii. 6, Tarquin entreats the Veientes, *ferrent opem*, *adjuvarent*, he is first considered as exulans, then as regnum repetiturus. 2. Opem and auxilium ferre derive their emphasis from the noun, to bring help, and nothing else; whereas opitulari, and the poetical word, auxiliari, derive their emphasis from their verbal form, and mean to bring help, and not to refuse. (v. 70.)

Ave; Salve; Vale. A v e (from εὖ) is a salutation used at meeting and at parting, like χαῖρε; whereas s a l v e is used at meeting only, v a l e at parting, like ἔῤῥωσο. Suet. Galb. 4. Ut liberti mane *salvere*, vespere *valere* sibi singuli dicerent. (i. 28.)

Aves, see *Volucres*.

Avidus, see *Velle*.

Axes; Plancæ; Tabulæ. A x e s or a s s e s, and p l a n c æ, are unwrought boards, as they come from the saw, and a s s e s as a usual term, p l a n c æ as a technical term; whereas t a b u l æ are boards that have been made smooth by the plane, to serve the purposes of luxury. (vi. 34.)

Axilla, see *Armus*.

## B.

Balbus; Blæsus. B a l b u s (from balare) denotes stammering as an habitual quality, whereas B l æ s u s, as a temporary condition. (iii. 79.)

Baculus, see *Fustis*. Bajulare, see *Ferre*.

Bardus, see *Stupidus*. Basium, see *Osculum*.

Baubari, see *Latrare*. Beatus, see *Felix*.

Bellua, see *Animal*. Bene moratus, see *Bonus*.

Benevolentia, see *Studium*.

Benignus, see Largus.

Bestia, see *Animal*.

Bibere; Potare. B i b e r e (reduplic. of bua) means to drink like a human being, πίνειν; whereas p o t a r e (from ποτός) to drink like a beast, and, metaphorically, to tipple, σπᾶν. Sen. Ep. 122. Inter nudos *bibunt*, imo *potant*. Plaut. Curc. i. 1, 88. Agite, *bibite*, festivæ fores, *potate*, fite mihi volentes propitiæ. (1. 149.)

Bifariam, see *Duplex*. Bilis, see *Fel*.

Blæsus, see *Balbus*. Blandiri, see *Assentiri*.

Blatire, Blaterare, see *Garrire*.

Boni consulere, see *Satis habere*.

Bonus; Bene moratus; Probus; Frugi; Honestus; Sanctus. 1. Bonus, bene moratus, probus, and frugi, denote a low degree of morality, in which a man keeps himself free from blame and punishment, hatred and contempt:—bonus (anciently duonus, δύναμαι), in the popular sense, in which benevolence and goodness of heart constitute the principal part of morality, in opp. to *malus*, like ἀγαθός; bene moratus, in a more philosophical sense, as an acquired character, in which, before all things, self-control, conscientiousness, and freedom from common selfishness are cultivated, like εὔτροπος; probus (πραΰς), so far as a man injures no one, nor does what is unjust, as a worthy, upright, just man; frugi, so far as a man, by discretion, conscientiousness, and diligence, qualifies himself to be useful in practical life, in opp. to *nequam*, like χρηστός. Quintil. vi. 4, 11. Non est altercandi ars . . . res animi jacentis et mollis supra modum frontis, fallitque plerumque quod *probitas* vocatur, quæ est imbecillitas. Dic. Dejot. 10. *Frugi* hominem dici non multum laudis habet in rege. Quintil. i. 6, 29. 2. Whereas honestus and sanctus denote a higher degree of morality, which, from higher motives, rises above the standard of ordinary men, and what is called social morality; honestus, as an honorable and chivalrous spirit and demeanor, derived from a principle of honor and distinction, in opp. to *turpis;* sanctus, as a saintly and holy spirit, derived from a principle of piety. (v. 347.)

Brachium, see *Ulna*.

Brevis; Curtus. Brevis (βραχύς) means short by nature; whereas curtus (καρτός, from κείρω), means shortened.

Brutus, see *Stupidus*.

## C.

CABALLUS, see *Equus*.

CACHINNARI, see *Ridere*.

CACUMEN, see *Acies*.

CADAVER; CORPUS. Cadaver denotes the dead body as a mere material substance, like *carcass*; but corpus as the remains of personality, like *corpse*, and is always used when the dead body is spoken of with feeling. (vi. 45.)

CADERE, see *Labi*. CÆDERE, see *Verberare*.

CÆRIMONIA, see *Consuetudo*. CÆSAR, see *Primus*.

CÆSARIES, see *Crinis*.

CÆTERI; RELIQUI. Cæteri (comparat. from ἐκεῖ) denotes others, as in direct opposition to those first mentioned, like *οἱ ἄλλοι*; whereas reliqui, the rest, as merely the remainder that complete the whole, like *οἱ λοιποί*. Cic. Brut. 2, 6. Si viveret Hortensius, *cætera* fortasse desideraret una cum *reliquis* bonis civibus; hunc aut præter *cæteros*, aut cum paucis sustineret dolorem. (i. 183.)

CALAMITAS, see *Infortunium*.

CALAMUS, see *Culmus*.

CALCULUS, see *Saxum*.

CALERE; FERVERE; ÆSTUARE; CALEFACERE; FOVERE. 1. Calere and fervere denote, objectively, warmth by itself, and, indeed, calidus (κηλέῳ πυρί), in opp. to *frigidus*, a moderate degree of warmth, but fervidus, in opp. to *gelidus*, a degree of warmth on the point of boiling, heat; whereas æstuare (from αἴθω), subjectively, the feeling of heat, in opp. to *algere*. (iii. 89.) 2. Calefacere means to make warm, in a purely physical sense, without any accessory notion; whereas fovere (from ἀφαύω), with reference to the genial sensation, or salutary effect of the warmth. (vi. 48.)

CALIGO, see *Obscurum*.

CALIX, see *Poculum.*

CALLIDUS, see *Astutus* and *Sapiens.*

CALLIS, see *Iter.*

CAMPUS, see *Æquum* and *Villa.*

CANDELA; LUCERNA. Candela is a candle, which can be carried about like a torch, as λαμπάς, whereas lucerna can only be considered as a burning light on a table, like λύχνος. (vi. 50.)

CANDIDUS, see *Albus.*

CANERE; CANTARE; PSALLERE; CANTICUM; CANTILENA; CARMEN; POEMA; POETA; VATES. 1. Camere (from καναχεῖν) means, in the most general sense, to make music, voce, tibiis, fidibus, like μέλπειν; cantare, with vocal music, like ἀείδειν; psallere, with instrumental music, and indeed with string-instruments, like ψάλλειν. 2. Cantica and cantilenæ are only songs adapted for singing, in which, as in popular ballads, the words and melodies are inseparable, and serve to excite mirth and pleasure, in opp. to speech, and that which is spoken; and, indeed, canticum means a favorite piece, still in vogue; cantilena, a piece which, being generally known, has lost the charm of novelty, and is classed with old songs; whereas carmina and poemata are poems which may be sung, but the words of which claim value as a work of art, and serve religion or music as an art, in opp. to prose and real truth; carmina, indeed, were originally religious hymns, ἐπῳδαί, and, in a wider sense, poems of another sort, mostly, however, minor poems, and of a lyrical sort, like ᾠδαι; but poemata are the products of cultivated art, and extensive poems, mostly of the epic or tragic sort, like ποιήματα. The *carmen* (κάρω, κράζω) is the fruit of natural, but the *poema* of calm and self-conscious inspiration. 3. Poeta is a technical expression, and denotes a poet only as an artist; vates (ἠχέτης) is an old Latin and religious expression, and denotes a poet as a sacred person. Tac. Dial. 9. (v. 99.)

CANNA, see *Culmus*. CANTARE, see *Canere*.

CANTERIUS, see *Equus*.

CANTICUM, CANTILENA, see *Canere*.

CAPER; HIRCUS; HŒDUS. Caper (κάπρος) is the general name for a he-goat, and that which is used in natural history, τράγος; hircus (from χήρ) is an old full-grown he-goat, χίμαρος? whereas hædus, hœdus (χοῖρος), a kid, ἔριφος. (v. 336.)

CAPERE, see *Sumere*.

CAPILLUS, see *Crinis*.

CARCER, see *Custodia*.

CARERE; EGERE; INDIGERE. 1. Carere (from κείρειν) relates to a desirable possession, in opp. to *habere*, Cic. Tusc. i. 36; whereas egere and indigere, to a necessary and indispensable possession, in opp. to *abundare*, Lucil. Fr. Sat. viii. Senec. Vit. B. 7. Voluptate virtus sæpe *caret*, nunquam *indiget*. Epist. 9. Sapiens *eget* nulla re; *egere* enim necessitatis est. Cic. Ep. ad. Qu. Fr. i. 3, 2. Nunc commisi, ut me vivo *careres*, vivo me aliis *indigeres*. 2. Egere (from χάω, χαίνω ἀχήν) denotes, objectively, the state of need, in opp. to *uti*, Cato ap. Gell. xiii. 23; indigere, subjectively, the galling sense of need, and eager longing to satisfy it. (iii. 113.)

CARITAS, see *Diligere*.

CARMEN, see *Canere*.

CARO; PULPA; VISCERA; EXTA; INTESTINA; ILIA. 1. Caro means flesh in its general sense, as a material substance, in opp. to fat, nerves, muscles, and so forth; pulpa, especially, eatable and savory flesh, in opp. to bones; viscera, all flesh, and every fleshy substance between the skin and the bones. 2. Viscera, in a narrower sense, means generally, the inner parts of the body; whereas exta means the inner parts of the upper part of the body, as the heart, lungs, and so forth; intestina, interanea, and ilia, the inner parts of the lower part of the body, namely, the entrails; and indeed intestina, and, in the age after

Augustus, i n t e r a n e a, meant the guts as digestive organs; i l i a, all that is contained in the lower part of the body, and particularly those parts that are serviceable. (v. 145.)

CASSIS; GALEA; CUDO. C a s s i s, c a s s i d a (from κόττα), is a helmet of metal; g a l e a (γαλέη), a helmet of skin, and properly of the skin of a weasel; c u d o (κεύθων), a helmet of an indefinite shape. Tac. G. 6. Paucis loricæ; vix uni alterive *cassis* aut *galea.*

CASSIS, see *Rete.*

CASTIGATIO, see *Vindicta.*

CASTUS; PUDICUS; PUDENS; PUDIBUNDUS. 1. C a s t u s (from καθαρός) denotes chastity as a natural quality of the soul, as pure and innocent; whereas p u d i c u s, as a moral sentiment, as bashful and modest. 2. P u d i c u s, p u d i c i t i a, denote natural shame, aversion to be exposed to the gaze of others, and its fruit, chaste sentiment, merely in its sexual relation, like bashfulness; whereas p u d e n s, p u d o r, denote shame in a general sense, or an aversion to be exposed to the observation of others, and to their contempt, as a sense of honor. Cic. Catil. ii. 11, 25. Ex hac parte *pudor* pugnat, illinc petulantia; hinc *pudicitia,* illinc stuprum. 3. P u d i c u s and p u d e n s denote shame as an habitual feeling; p u d i b u n d u s as a temporary state of the sense of shame, when excited. (iii. 199.)

CASU; FORTE; FORTUITO; FORTASSE; FORSITAN; HAUD SCIO AN. C a s u, f o r t e, and f o r t u i t o, denote a casualty, and indeed, c a s u, in opp. to *consulto,* συμβεβηκότως; f o r t e, without particular stress on the casualty, τυχόν; f o r t u i t o, f o r t u i t u, emphatically, by mere chance, in opp. to *causa,* ἀπὸ τύχης; whereas f o r t a s s e, f o r s i t a n, and h a u d s c i o a n, denote possibility, and indeed f o r t a s s e, f o r t a s s i s, with an emphatic perception and affirmation of the possibility, as approaching to probability, and are in construction with the indicative, ἴσως; f o r s i t a n, f o r s a n, with merely an occasional perception of the possibility, and are in construction with a conjunctive, τάχ' ἄν; h a u d s c i o a n, with a modest denial of one's own certainty; consequently, h a u d s c i o a n is an euphemistic limitation of the assertion. F o r t a s s e v e r u m e s t, and f o r s i t a n v e r u m s i t, mean, perhaps it is true, perhaps not; but h a u d s c i o a n v e r u m s i t means, I think it true, but I will not affirm it as certain. (v. 294.)

CASUS; FORS; FORTUNA; FORS FORTUNA; FATUM. 1. C a s u s denotes chance as an inanimate natural agent, which is not the consequence of human calculation, or of known causes, like συμφορά; whereas f o r s denotes the same chance as a sort of mythological being, which, without aim or butt, to sport as it were with mortals, and baffle their calculations, influences human affairs, like τύχη. 2. F o r s, as a mythological being, is this chance considered as blind fortune; whereas F o r t u n a is fortune, not considered as blind, and without aim, but as taking a part in the course of human affairs from personal favor or disaffection; lastly, f o r s f o r t u n a means a lucky chance, ἀγαθὴ τύχη. 3. All these beings form an opposition against the D i i and F a t u m, which do not bring about or prevent events from caprice or arbitrary will, but according to higher laws; and the gods, indeed, according to the intelligible laws of morality, according to merit and worth, right and equity; f a t u m, according to the mysterious laws by which the universe is eternally governed, like εἱμαρμένη, μοῖρα. Tac. Hist. iv. 26. Quod in pace *fors* seu natura, tunc *fatum* et ira deorum vocabatur. (295.)

CATENÆ, see *Vincula*.

CATERVA; COHORS; AGMEN; GREX; GLOBUS; TURBA. C a t e r v a, c o h o r s, and a g m e n, denote an assembled multitude in regular order, and c a t e r v a, as a limited whole, according to a sort of military arrangement; c o h o r s, as respecting and observing the leadership of a commanding officer; a g m e n, as a solemn procession; whereas t u r b a, g r e x, and g l ob u s, denote a multitude assembled in no regular order; g r e x, without form or order; t u r b a, with positive disorder and confusion; g l o b u s, a thronging mass of people, which, from each person pressing towards the centre, assumes a circular form. (v. 361.)

CATUS, see *Sapiens.*

CAUPONA, see *Deversorium.*

CAUSIDICUS, see *Advocatus.*

CAUTES, see *Saxum.*

CAVERNA, see *Specus.* CAVILLATOR, see *Lepidus.*

CELARE; OCCULERE; OCCULTARE; CLAM; ABDERE; CONDERE; ABSCONDERE; RECONDERE. 1. C e l a r e has an abstract or intellectual reference to its object, like *κεύθειν*, in opp. to *fateri*, and so forth; synonymously with r e t i c e r e, Liv. xxiv. 5. Curt. vi. 9; whereas o c c u l e r e, o c c u l t a r e, have a concrete and material reference to their object, like *κρύπτειν*, in opp. to *aperire*, synonymously with o b t e g e r e; Cic. Acad. iv. 19. N. D. ii. 20. Fin. i. 9, 30. Att. v. 15: the *celanda* remain secret, unless they happen to be discovered; but the *occultanda* would be exposed to sight, unless particular circumspection and precaution were used. 2. In the same manner c l a m and c l a n c u l u m denote secretly, in opp. to *palam*, Cic. Rosc. Am. 8; whereas o c c u l t e, in opp. to *aperte*, Cic. Rull. i. 1. 3. O c c u l e r e denotes any concealment; o c c u l t a r e, a careful or very anxious concealment, and on this account finds no place in negative propositions, or as seldom, for example, as *redolere*. 4. O c c u l t a r e means to prevent anything being seen, by keeping it covered; whereas a b d e r e, c o n d e r e, and a b s c o n d e r e, by removing the thing itself; a b d e r e (*ἀποθεῖναι*) by laying it aside, and putting it away, like *ἀποκρύπτειν*; c o n d e r e (*καταθεῖναι*), by depositing it in a proper place of safety, like *κατακρύπτειν*; r e c o n d e r e, by hiding it carefully and thoroughly; a b s c o n d e r e, by putting it away, and preserving it. (iv. 45.)

Celeber; Inclytus; Clarus; Illustris; Nobilis. Celeber (from κλέος) and inclytus (from κλυτός) denote celebrity, as general expressions, chiefly as belonging to things, and seldom as belonging to persons, except in poetry; clarus, illustris, and nobilis, with an especial political reference; clarus (γαληρός) means renowned for eminent services to one's country; illustris (from ἀναλεύσσω) renowned for rank and virtue; nobilis (from novisse) belonging to a family whose members have already been invested with the honors of the state.

Celebrare, see *Sæpe*. Celer, see *Citus*.

Celer, see *Navigium*. Celsus, see *Altus*.

Censere; Judicare; Arbitrari; Æstimare; Opinari; Putare; Reri; Autumare; Existimare; Credere. 1. Censere, judicare, arbitrari, æstimare, denote passing judgment with competent authority, derived from a call to the office of judge; censere, as possessing the authority of a censor, or of a senator giving his vote; judicare, as possessing that of a judge passing sentence; arbitrari, as possessing that of an arbitrator; æstimare (αἰσθέσθαι), as that of a taxer, making a valuation; whereas, opinari, putare, reri, and autumare, denote passing judgment under the form of a private opinion, with a purely subjective signification; opinari (ὀπίς) as a mere sentiment and conjecture, in opp. to a clear conviction and knowledge. Cic. Orat. i. 23. Mur. 30. Tusc iv. 7. Rosc. Am. 10; putare, as one who casts up an account; reri as a poetical, and autumare as an antiquated term. 2. Æstimare denotes passing judgment under the form of the political function of an actual taxer, to estimate anything exactly, or according to its real value, or price in money; but existimare, as a moral function, to estimate anything according to its worth or truth; hence Cicero contrasts *existimatio*, not *æstimatio*, as a private opinion, with competent judgment, *judicio;* Cluent. 29. Verr. v. 68. 3. Cens e r e denotes judgment and belief, as grounded upon one's own reflection and conviction; c r e d e r e, as grounded on the credit which is given to the testimony of others. 4. O p i n o r, parenthetically, implies modesty, like οἶμαι; whereas c r e d o implies irony, like ὡς ἔοικεν, sometimes in propositions that are self-evident, whereby the irony reaches the ears of those to whom the truth could not be plainly spoken or repeated, or who might be inclined to doubt it; sometimes, in absurd propositions which a man thinks fit to put in the mouth of another; sometimes, in propositions so evident as scarcely to admit of controversy. (v. 300.)

CERNERE, see *Videre*. CERRITUS, see *Amens*.

CERTARE, see *Imitatio*.

CESSARE, see *Vacare* and *Cunctari*.

CHORDA; FIDES. C h o r d a (χορδή) is a single string; f i d e s (σφιδή) in the sing. and plur. means a complete collection of strings, or a string-instrument.

CIBARE, CIBUS, see *Alimenta*.

CICATRIX, see *Vulnus*.

CICUR; MANSUETUS. C i c u r (redupl. of κορίζομαι) denotes tameness, merely in a physical sense, and as a term in natural history, in opp. to *ferus;* whereas m a n s u e t u s, in a moral sense also, as implying a mild disposition, in opp. to *sævus*. (iv. 257.)

CINCINNUS, see *Crinis*. CIRCULUS, see *Orbis*.

CIRCUMIRE, see *Ambire*. CIRCUMVENIRE, see *Fallere*

CIRRUS, see *Crinis*.

CITUS: CELER; VELOX; PERNIX; PROPERUS; FESTINUS. 1. C i t u s and c e l e r denote swiftness merely as quick motion, in opp. to *tardus*, Cic. Or. iii 57. Sall. Cat. 15. Cic. Fin. v. 11. N. D. ii. 20. Rosc Com. 11. Top. 44; v e l o x and p e r n i x, nimbleness, as bodily strength and activity, in opp. to *lentus*; p r o p e r u s and f e s t i n u s, haste, as the will to reach a certain point in the shortest time, in opp. to *segnis* Gell. x. 11. 2. C i t u s denotes a swift and lively motion, approaching to *vegetus;* c e l e r, an eager and impetuous motion, approaching to *rapidus*. 3. Pernicitas is, in general, dexterity and activity in all bodily movements, in hopping, climbing, and vaulting; but velocitas, especially in running, flying, and swimming, and so forth. Plaut. Mil. iii. 1, 36. Clare oculis video, *pernix* sum manibus, pedibus mobilis. Virg. Æn. iv. 180. Curt. vii. 7, 53. Equorum *velocitati* par est hominum *pernicitas*. 4. Properus, properare, denote the haste which, from energy, sets out rapidly to reach a certain point, in opp. to *cessare;* whereas festinus, festinare, denote the haste which springs from impatience, and borders upon precipitation. (ii. 144.)

CIVILITAS, see *Humanitas*. CIVITAS, see *Gens*.
CLAM, see *Celare*. CLARITAS, see *Gloria*.
CLARUS, see *Celeber*. CLAUSTRUM, see *Sera*.
CLEMENTIA, see *Mansuetudo*.
CLIVUS, see *Collis*. CLYPEUS, see *Scutum*.
CODICILLI, see *Literæ*.

CLANGERE; CLAMARE; VOCIFERARI. Clangere is the cry of animals and the clang of instruments, like *κλάγγειν*; clamare and vociferari, the cry of men; clamare, an utterance of the will, but vociferari, of passion, in anger, pain, in intoxication. Rhet. ad. Her. iii. 12. Acuta exclamatio habet quiddam illiberale et ad muliebrem potius *vociferationem*, quam ad virilem dignitatem in dicendo accommodatum. Senec. Ep. 15. Virg. Æn. ii. 310. Exoritur *clamor*que virum *clangor*que tubarum. (v. 103.)

CŒNUM, see *Lutum*.

CŒPISSE, see *Incipere*.

COERCERE; COMPESCERE. Coercere denotes restriction, as an act of power and superior strength; whereas compescere (from pedica, *πεδᾶν*) as an act of sovereign authority and wisdom. (iv. 427.)

CŒTUS, see *Concilium*.

COGERE; ADIGERE. Cogere (from co-igere) means by force and power to compel to something; ad-i g e r e, by reflection and the suggestion of motives to persuade to something. Tac. Ann. vi. 27. Se ea necessitate ad preces *cogi*, per quas consularium aliqui capessere provincias *adigerentur*. (vi. 70.)

COGITARE; MEDITARI; COMMENTARI. 1. C o g i t a r e (from the Goth. hugjan) denotes the usual activity of the mind, which cannot exist without thinking, or employing itself about something; m e d i t a r i (from μέδεσθαι), the continued and intense activity of the mind, which aims at a definite result. Ter. Heaut. iii. 3, 46. Quid nunc facere *cogitas?* Compare this with Adelph. v. 6, 8. *Meditor* esse affabilis. Cic. Cat. i. 9, 22. In Tusc. iii. 6, c o g i t a t i o means little more than consciousness; whereas m e d i t a t i o means speculative reflection. 2. M e d i t a r i has an intensive meaning, with earnestness, exertion, and vivacity; c o m m e n t a r i (only in Cicero) means to reflect leisurely, quietly, and profoundly. (v. 198.)

COGNATUS, see *Necessarius*.

COGNITIO; NOTITIA; SCIENTIA; IGNARUS; INSCIUS; NESCIUS. 1. C o g n i t i o is an act of the mind by which knowledge is acquired, whereas n o t i t i a and s c i e n t i a denote a state of the mind; n o t i t i a, together with n o s s e, denotes a state of the merely receptive faculties of the mind, which brings an external appearance to consciousness, and retains it there; whereas s c i e n t i a, together with s c i r e, involves spontaneous activity, and a perception of truth; n o t i t i a may be the result of casual perception; s c i e n t i a implies a thorough knowledge of its object, the result of mental activity. Cic. Sen. 4, 12. Quanta *notitia* antiquitatis! quanta *scientia* juris Romani! 2. The *ignarus* is without *notitia*, the *inscius* without *scientia*. Tac. H. i. 11. Ægyptum provinciam *insciam* legum, *ignaram* magistratuum; for legislation is a science, and must be studied; government an art, and may be learnt by practice. 3. I n s c i u s denotes a person who has not learnt something, with blame; n e s c i u s, who has accidentally not heard of, or experienced something, indifferently. Cic. Brut. 83. *Inscium* omnium rerum et rudem. Compare this with Plin. Ep. viii. 23, Absens et impendentis mali *nescius*. (v. 266.)

COGNOSCERE, see *Intelligere*. COHORS, see *Caterva*.

COLAPHUS, see *Alapa*. COLERE, see *Vereri*.

COLLIS; CLIVUS; TUMULUS; GRUMUS; Collis and clivus denote a greater hill or little mountain; collis (from *celsus*) like κολωνός, as an eminence, in opp. to the plain beneath, and therefore somewhat steep; clivus, like κλιτύς, as a sloping plain, in opp. to an horizontal plain, and therefore only gradually ascending; whereas tumulus and grumus mean only a hillock, or great mound; tumulus, like ὄχθος, means either a natural or artificial elevation; grumus, only an artificial elevation, like χῶμα. Colum. Arbor. a. f. *Collem* autem et *clivum*, modum jugeri continentem repastinabis operis sexaginta. Liv. xxi. 32. Erigentibus in primos agmen *clivos*, apparuerunt imminentes *tumulos* insidentes montani. Hirt. B. Hisp. 24. Ex *grumo* excelsum *tumulum* capiebat. (ii. 121.)

COLLOQUIUM, see *Sermo*. COLONUS, see *Incolere*.

COLUBER, see *Anguis*. COMA, see *Crinis*.

COMBURERE, see *Accendere*.

COMERE; DECORARE; ORNARE. 1. Comere and decorare denote ornament, merely as an object of sense, as pleasing the eye; ornare, in a practical sense, as at the same time combining utility. 2. Comere (κοσμεῖν) denotes ornament as something little and effeminate, often with blame, like *nitere*, in opp. to nature, noble simplicity, or graceful negligence, like κομμοῦν, whereas decorare and ornare, always with praise, like *splendere*, as denoting affluence and riches; decorare (from δίκη) in opp. to that which is ordinary and unseemly, like κοσμεῖν; ornare (from ὀρίνω?) in opp. to that which is paltry and incomplete, like ἀσκεῖν. 3. Comere implies only a change in form, which by arranging and polishing gives to the whole a smart appearance, as in combing and braiding the hair; but decorare and ornare effect a material change, inasmuch as by external addition new beauty is conferred, as by a diadem, and so forth. Quintil. xii. 10, 47. *Comere* caput in gradus et annulos; compare with Tibull. iii. 2, 6. Sertis *decorare* comas; and Virg. Ecl. vi. 69. Apio crines *ornatus* amaro. (iii. 261.)

COMMISSATIO, see *Epulæ*.

COMITARI; DEDUCERE; PROSEQUI. Comitari means to accompany for one's own interest, ἀκολουθεῖν; deducere, from friendship, with officiousness; prosequi, from esteem, with respect, προπέμπειν. (vi. 73.)

COMITAS, see *Humanitas*. COMITIA, see *Concilium*.

COMMENTARI, see *Cogitare*. COMMITTERE, see *Fidere*.

COMMODARE; MUTUUM DARE. Commodare means to lend without formality and stipulation, on the supposition of receiving the thing lent again when it is done with. Mutuum dare is to grant a loan on the supposition of receiving an equivalent when the time of the loan expires. Commodatio is an act of kindness; mutuum datio is a matter of business. (iv. 137.)

COMMUNICARE, see *Impertire*.

COMŒDUS, see *Actor*. COMPAR, see *Æquus*.

COMPEDES, see *Vincula*. COMPENDIUM, see *Lucrum*.

COMPESCERE, see *Coercere*. COMPLECTI, see *Amplecti*.

COMPLEMENTUM; SUPPLEMENTUM. Complementum serves, like a keystone, to make anything complete, to crown the whole, whereas supplementum serves to fill up chasms, to supply omissions.

CONARI, see *Audere*.

CONCEDERE; PERMITTERE; CONNIVERE. Concedere and permittere mean, to grant something which a man has full right to dispose of; concedere, in consequence of a request or demand, in opp. to refusing, like συγχωρῆσαι; permittere, from confidence in a person, and liberality, in opp. to forbidding, like ἐφεῖναι; whereas indulgere and connivere mean to grant something, which may properly be forbidden; indulgere (ἐνδελεχεῖν?), from evident forbearance; connivere (καταν εύειν), from seeming oversight.

CONCESSUM EST; LICET: FAS EST. Concessum est means, what is generally allowed, like ἔξεστι, and has a kindred signification with licet, licitum est, which mean what is allowed by human laws, whether positive, or sanctioned by custom and usage, like θέμις ἐστί; fas est means what is allowed by divine laws, whether the precepts of religion, or the clear dictates of the moral sense, like ὅσιόν ἐστι. (v. 167.)

CONCILIUM; CONCIO; COMITIA; CŒTUS; CONVENTUS. 1. Concilium, concio, and comitia are meetings summoned for fixed purposes; concilium (ξυγκαλεῖν), an assembly of noblemen and persons of distinction, of a committee, of the senate, the individual members of which are summoned to deliberate, like συνέδριον; whereas concio and comitia mean a meeting of the community, appointed by public proclamation, for passing resolutions or hearing them proposed; concio (ciere, κιών) means any orderly meeting of the community, whether of the people or of the soldiery, in any state or camp, like σύλλογος; comitia (from coire) is an historical term, confined to a Roman meeting of the people, as ἐκκλησία to an Athenian, and ἁλία to a Spartan. 2. Cœtus and conventus are voluntary assemblies; cœtus (from coire) for any purpose, for merely social purposes, for a conspiracy, and so forth, like σύνοδος; whereas conventus, for a serious purpose, such as the celebration of a festival, the hearing of a discourse, and so forth, like ὁμήγυρις, πανήγυρις. (v. 108.)

CONCLAVE, CUBICULUM. Conclave is the most general term for any closed room, and especially a room of state; cubiculum is a particular expression for a dwelling-room. (vi. 75.)

CONCORDIA, see *Otium*. CONCUBINA, see *Pellex*.

CONDERE, see *Celare* and *Sepelire*.

CONDITIO; STATUS. Conditio (ξύνθεσις, συνθεσία) is a state regulated by the will; status is a state arising from connection. Cic. Fam. xii. 23. Omnem *conditionem* imperii tui, *statumque* provinciæ demonstravit mihi Tratorius. (vi. 76.)

CONFESTIM, see *Repente*. CONFIDENTIA, see *Fides*.

CONFIDERE, see *Fidere*. CONFINIS, see *Vicinus*.

CONFISUS; FRETUS. Confisus means, subjectively, like *securus*, depending on something, and making one's self easy, πεποιθώς; whereas fretus (φρακτός, ferox) means, objectively, like *tutus*, protected by something, ἐῤῥωμένος. (i. 20.)

CONFITERI, see *Fateri*. CONFLIGERE, see *Pugnare*.

CONFUTARE, see *Refutare*.

CONGERIES, see *Acervus*. CONJUX, see *Femina*.

CONNIVERE, see *Concedere*.

CONSANGUINEUS, see *Necessarius*.

CONSCENDERE, see *Scandere*.

CONSECRARE, see *Sacrare*. CONSEQUI, see *Invenire*.

CONJUGIUM; MATRIMONIUM; CONTUBERNIUM; NUPTIÆ. Conjugium and matrimonium denote the lasting connection between man and wife, for the purpose of living together and bringing up their offspring; conjugium is a very general term for a mere natural regulation, which also takes place among animals; contubernium means the marriage connection between slaves; matrimonium, the legal marriage between freemen and citizens, as a respectable and a political regulation; whereas nuptiæ means only the commencement of *matrimonium*, the wedding, or marriage-festival.

CONSIDERARE; CONTEMPLARI. Considerare (from κατειδεῖν) denotes consideration as an act of the understanding, endeavoring to form a judgment; contemplari (from καταθαμβεῖν) an act of feeling, which is absorbed in its object, and surrenders itself entirely to the pleasant or unpleasant feeling which its object excites. (v. 130.)

CONSORS, see *Socius*.

CONSPECTUS, CONSPICERE, see *Videre*.

CONSTAT; APPARET; ELUCET; LIQUET. Constat means a truth made out and fixed, in opp. to a wavering and unsteady fancy or rumor; whereas apparet elucet, and liquet denote what is clear and evident; apparet, under the image of something stepping out of the back-ground into sight; elucet, under the image of a light shining out of darkness; liquet, under the image of frozen water melted. (vi. 78.)

CONSTITUERE, see *Destinare*.

CONSUETUDO; MOS; RITUS; CÆRIMONIA. Consuetudo denotes the uniform observance of anything as a custom, arising from itself, and having its foundation in the inclination or convenience of an individual or people, *ἔθος*; whereas mos (modus) is the habitual observance of anything, as a product of reason, and of the self-conscious will, and has its foundation in moral views, or the clear dictates of right, virtue, and decorum, *ἦθος*; lastly, ritus denotes the hallowed observance of anything, either implanted by nature as an instinct, or introduced by the gods as a ceremony, or which, at any rate, cannot be traced to any human origin. Consuetudines are merely factitious, and have no moral worth; mores are morally sanctioned by silent consent, as jura and leges by formal decree; ritus (from *ἀριθμός, ῥυθμός*), are natural, and are hallowed by their primæval origin, and are peculiar to the animal. (v. 75.) 2. Ritus is a hallowed observance, as directed and taught by the gods or by nature; whereas cærimonia (*κηδεμονία*) is that which is employed in the worship of the gods.

CONSUEVISSE, see *Solere*. CONSUMMARE, see *Finire*.

CONTAGIUM, see *Lues*.

CONTAMINARE; INQUINARE; POLLUERE. Contamnare (from contingo, contagio) means defilement in its pernicious effect, as the corruption of what is sound and useful; inquinare (from cunire, or from πίνος), in its loathsome effect, as marring what is beautiful, like μορύσσειν; polluere (from pullus, πελλός), in its moral effect, as the desecration of what is holy and pure, like μιαίνειν. Cic. Cæcil. 21, 70. Judiciis corruptis et *contaminatis;* compare with Cœl. 6. Libidinibus *inquinari;* and Rosc. Am. 26, 71. Noluerunt in mare deferri, ne ipsum *pollueret,* quo cætera quæ violata sunt, expiari putantur. (ii. 56.)

CONTEMNERE, see *Spernere.*

CONTEMPLARI, see *Considerare.*

CONTENDERE, see *Dicere.*

CONTENTIO, see *Disceptatio.*

CONTENTUM ESSE, see *Satis habere.*

CONTINENTIA, see *Modus.* CONTINGERE, see *Accidere.*

CONTINUO, see *Repente.*

CONTINUUS; PERPETUUS; SEMPITERNUS; ÆTERNUS. 1. Continuum means that which hangs together without break or chasm; perpetuum, that which arrives at an end, without breaking off before. Suet Cæs. 76. *Continuos* consulatus, *perpetuam* dictaturam. 2. Perpetuus, sempiternus, and æternus, denote continued duration; but perpetuus, relatively, with reference to a definite end, that of life for example; sempiternus and æternus, absolutely, with reference to the end of time in general; sempiternus means, like ἀΐδιος, the everlasting, what lasts as long as time itself, and keeps pace with time; æternum (from ætas) like αἰώνιον, the eternal, that which outlasts all time, and will be measured by ages, for Tempus est pars quædam *æternitatis.* The sublime thought of that which is without beginning and end, lies only in æternus, not in sempiternus, for the latter word rather suggests the long duration between beginning and end, without noting that eternity *has* neither beginning nor end. Sempiternus involves the mathematical, æternus the metaphysical notion of eternity. Cic. Orat. ii. 40, 169. Barbarorum est in diem vivere; nostra consilia *sempiternum* tempus spectare debent; compare with Fin. i. 6, 17. Motum atomorum nullo a principio, sed *æterno* tempore intelligi convenire. (i. 1.)

CONTRARIUS, see *Varius.*

CONTROVERSIA, see *Disceptatio.*

CONTUBERNIUM, see *Conjugium.*

CONTUMACIA, see *Pervicacia.*

CONTUMELIA; INJURIA; OFFENSIO. I. Contumelia (from contemnere) denotes a wrong done to the honor of another; injuria, a violation of another's right. A blow is an *injuria,* so far as it is the infliction of bodily harm; and a *contumelia,* so far as it brings on the person who receives it, the imputation of a cowardly or servile spirit. Senec. Clem. i. 10. *Contumelias,* quæ acerbiores principibus solent esse quam *injuriæ.* Pacuv. Non. Patior facile *injuriam,* si vacua est *contumelia.* Phædr. Fab. v. 3, 5. Cic. Quint. 30, 96. Verr. iii. 44. 2. Contumelia and injuria are actions, whereas offensio denotes a state, namely, the mortified feeling of the offended person, resentment, in opp. to *gratia.* Plin. H. N. xix. 1. Quintil. iv. 2. Plin. Pan. 18. (iv. 194.)

CONVENTUS, see *Concilium.*

CONVERTERE, see *Vertere.*

CONVIVIUM, see *Epulæ.*

CONVICIUM, see *Maledictum.*

COPIA, see *Occasio.* COPIÆ, see *Exercitus.*

COPIOSUS, see *Divitiæ.* CORDATUS, see *Sapiens.*

CORPULENTUS, see *Pinguis.*

CORPUS, see *Cadaver.*

CORRIGERE; EMENDARE. Corrigere means to amend, after the manner of a rigid schoolmaster or disciplinarian, who would make the crooked straight, and set the wrong right; whereas emendare, after the manner of an experienced teacher, and sympathizing friend, who would make what is defective complete.

Plin. Pan. 6, 2. Corrupta est disciplina castrorum, ut tu *corrector emendator*que contingeres; the former by strictness, the latter by wisdom. Cic. Mur. 29. Verissime dixerim, nulla in re te (Catonem) esse hujusmodi ut *corrigendus* potius quam leviter inflectendus viderere; comp. with Plin. Ep. i. 10. Non castigat errantes, sed *emendat*. (v. 319.)

CORRUMPERE, see *Depravare*.

CORUSCARE, see *Lucere*.

COXA; LATUS; FEMUR. Coxa and coxendix (κοχώνη) mean the hip; latus, the part between the hip and shoulder; femur and femen, the part under the hip, the thigh. (vi. 84.)

CRAPULA, see *Ebrietas*. CRATER, see *Poculum*.

CREARE; GIGNERE; PARERE; GENERARE. 1. Creare (from κύρω) means, by one's own will and creative power to call something out of nothing; gignere (γίγνεσθαι, γενέσθαι) by procreation or parturition; gignere is allied to generare only by procreation, and to parere (πεπαρεῖν, πεῖρειν), only by parturition. 2. Gignere is a usual expression, which represents procreation as a physical and purely animal act, and supposes copulation, conception, and parturition; whereas generare is a select expression, which represents procreation as a sublime godlike act, and supposes only creative power; hence, for the most part, homines et belluæ *gignunt*, natura et dii *generant*. And, Corpora *gignuntur*, poemata *generantur*. Cic. N. D. iii. 16. Herculem Jupiter *genuit*, is a mythological notice; but Legg. i. 9. Deus hominem *generavit*, is a metaphysical axiom. (v. 201.)

CREBRO, see *Sæpe*.

CREDERE, see *Censere* and *Fidere*.

CREMARE, see *Accendere*. CREPITUS, see *Fragor*.

CREPUSCULUM, see *Mane*. CRIMINARI, see *Arguere*.

CRINIS; CAPILLUS; COMA; CÆSARIES; PILUS; CIRRUS; CINCINNUS. 1. Crinis and capillus denote the natural hair merely in a physical sense, like θρίξ; crinis (from κάρηνον), any growth of hair, in opposition to the parts on which hair does not grow; capillus (from caput), only the hair of the head, in opp. to the beard, etc. Liv. vi. 16. Suet. Aug. 23. Cels. vi. 2. Cic. Tusc. v. 20. Rull. ii. 5; whereas in coma and cæsaries the accessory notion of beauty, as an object of sense, is involved, inasmuch as hair is a natural ornament of the body, or itself the object of ornament; coma (κόμη) is especially applicable to the hair of females; cæsaries, to that of males, like ἔθειρα. Hence crinitus means nothing more than covered with hair; capillatus is used in opp. to bald-headed, Petron. 26, and the Galli are styled *comati*, as wearing long hair, like καρεκομόωντες. 2. Crinis, capillus, coma, cæsaries, denote the hair in a collective sense, the whole growth of hair; whereas pilus means a single hair, and especially the short and bristly hair of animals. Hence pilosus is in opp. to the beautiful smoothness of the skin, as Cic. Pis. 1; whereas crinitus and capillatus are in opp. to ugly nakedness and baldness. (iii. 14.) 3. Cirrus and cincinnus denote curled hair; cirrus (κόῤῥη) is a natural, cincinnus (κίκιννος) an artificial curl. (iii. 23.)

CRUCIATUS; TORMENTUM. Cruciatus, crucimenta (κρόκα, κρέκω), denote in general any pangs, natural and artificial; tormenta (from torquere), especially pangs caused by an instrument of torture, like the rack. Cic. Phil. xi. 4. Nec vero graviora sunt carnificum *tormenta* quam interdum *cruciamenta* morborum. (vi. 87.)

CRUDELITAS, see *Sævitia.*

CRUENTUS, CRUOR, see *Sanguis.*

CUBARE; JACERE; SITUM ESSE. Cubare (from κεῖω) denotes the lying down of living beings; situm esse (ἑτόν, εἷσαι) of lifeless things; jacere, of both. Cubare and jacere are neuter; situm esse, always passive. Further, cubare gives the image of one who is tired, who wishes to recruit his strength, in opp. to standing, as requiring exertion, whereas j a c e r e gives the image of one who is weak, without any accessory notion, in opp. to standing, as a sign of strength. (i. 138.)

CUBICULUM, see *Conclave*.

CUBILE; LECTUS. C u b i l e is a natural couch for men and animals, a place of rest, like *κοίτη*, *εὐνή*; l e c t u s, an artificial couch, merely for men, a bed, like *λέκτρον*. (v. 279.)

CUBITUS, see *Ulna*. CUDERE, see *Verberare*.

CUDO, see *Cassis*.

CULCITA; PULVINUS; PULVINAR. C u l c i t a (from calcare?) is a hard-stuffed pillow; p u l v i n u s and p u l v i n a r, a soft elastic pillow; p u l v i n u s, such as is used on ordinary civil occasions; p u l v i n a r, such as is used on solemn religious occasions. (vi. 89.)

CULMEN; FASTIGIUM. C u l m e n means the top, the uppermost line of the roof; f a s t i g i u m, the summit, the highest point of this top, where the spars of the roof by sloping and meeting form an angle; therefore f a s t i g i u m is a part of c u l m e n. Virg. Æn. ii. 458. Evado ad summi *fastigia culminis*. Liv. xl. 2. Vitruv. iv. 2. Arnob. ii. 12. And figuratively c u l m e n denotes the top only, with a local reference, as the uppermost and highest point, something like *κολοφών*; but f a s t i g i u m with reference to rank, as the principal and most imposing point of position, something like *κορυφή*; therefore c u l m e n t e c t i is only that which closes the building, but f a s t i g i u m that which crowns it; and f a s t i g i u m also denotes a throne, whence *culmina montium* is a much more usual term than *fastigia*. (ii. 111.)

CULMUS; CALAMUS; STIPULA; SPICA; ARISTA; ARUNDO; CANNA. 1. C u l m u s means the stalk, with reference to its slender height, especially of corn; c a l a m u s (*κάλαμος*) with reference to its hollowness, especially of reeds. 2. C u l m u s means the stalk of corn, as bearing the ear, as the body the head, as an integral part of the whole; stipula, as being compared with the ear, a worthless and useless part of the whole, as stubble. 3. Spica is the full ear, the fruit of the corn-stalk, without respect to its shape, arista, the prickly ear, the tip or uppermost part of the stalk, without respect to its substance, sometimes merely the prickles. Quintil. i. 3, 5. Imitatæ *spicas* herbulæ inanibus *aristis* ante messem flavescunt. 4. Calamus, as a reed, is the general term; arundo (from ῥοδανός) is a longer and stronger reed; canna (from κανών?) a smaller and thinner reed. Colum. iv. 32. Ea est *arundineti* senectus; cum ita densatum est, ut gracilis et *cannæ* similis *arundo* prodeat. (v. 219.)

Culpa; Noxia; Noxius; Nocens; Sons. 1. Culpa (κολάψαι) denotes guilt as the state of one who has to answer for an injury, peccatum, delictum, maleficium, scelus, flagitium, or nefas; hence a responsibility, and, consequently, a rational being is supposed, in opp. to *casus*, Cic. Att. xi. 9. Vell. P. ii. 118, or to *necessitas*, Suet. Cl. 15; whereas noxia, as the state of one who has caused an injury, and can therefore be applied to any that is capable of producing an effect, in opp. to *innocentia*. Liv. iii. 42, 2. Illa modo in ducibus *culpa*, quod ut odio essent civibus fecerant; alia omnis penes milites *noxia* erat. Cic. Marc. 13. Etsi aliqua *culpa* tenemur erroris humani, a scelere certe liberati sumus; and Ovid, Trist. iv. 1, 23. Et *culpam* in facto, non scelus esse meo, coll. 4, 37; hence culpa is used as a general expression for every kind of fault, and especially for a fault of the lighter sort, as delictum. 2. Culpa and noxia suppose an injurious action; but vitium (from αὐάτη, ἄτη) merely an action or quality deserving censure, and also an undeserved natural defect. 3. Nocens, innocens, denote guilt, or absence of guilt, in a specified case, with regard to a single action; but noxius, innoxius, together with the poetical words nocuus, innocuus, relate to the nature and character in general. Plaut. Capt. iii. 5, 7. Decet *innocentem* servum atque *innoxium* confidentem esse; that is, a servant who knows himself guiltless of some particular action, and who, in general, does nothing wrong. 4. Noxius denotes a guilty person only physically, as the author and cause of an injury, like *βλαβερός*; but sons (*ὀνοτός*) morally and juridically, as one condemned, or worthy of condemnation, like *θῶος*. (ii. 152.)

Culpare, see *Arguere*. Cultus, see *Vestis*.

Cumulus, see *Acervus*.

Cunæ; Cunabula. Cunæ (*κοῖται*) is the cradle itself; incunabula, the bed, etc., that are in the cradle. Plaut. Truc. v. 13. Fasciis opus est, pulvinis, *cunis, incunabulis*. (vi. 69.)

Cunctari; Hæsitare; Cessare. Cunctari (from *ξυνέκειν*, or *κατέχειν*), means to delay from consideration, like *μέλλειν*; hæsitare, from want of resolution; cessare (*καθίζειν*?) from want of strength and energy, like *ὀκνεῖν*. The *cunctans* delays to begin an action; the *cessans*, to go on with an action already begun. (iii. 300.)

Cuncti, see *Quisque*. Cupere, see *Velle*.

Cupido; Cupiditas; Libido; Voluptas. 1. Cupido is the desire after something, considered actively, and as in action, in opp. to aversion; whereas cupiditas is the passion of desire, considered neutrally, as a state of mind, in opp. to tranquillity of mind. Cupido must necessarily, cupiditas may be, in construction with a genitive, expressed or understood; in this case, cupido relates especially to possession and money, cupiditas, to goods of every kind. Vell. P. ii. 33. Pecuniæ *cupidine*: and further on, Interminatam imperii *cupiditatem*. 2. Cupido and cupiditas stand in opp. to temperate wishes; libido (from *λίψ*) the intemperate desire and capricious longing after something, in opp. to rational will, *ratio*, Suet. Aug. 69, or *voluntas*, Cic. Fam. ix. 16. Libidines are lusts, with reference to the want of self-government; voluptates, pleasures, in opp. to serious employments, or to pains. Tac. H. ii. 31. Minus Vitellii ignavæ *voluptates* quam Othonis flagrantissimæ *libidines* timebantur. (v. 60.)

CUR; QUARE. Cur (from quare? or κῶς;) serves both for actual questions, and for interrogative forms of speech; whereas quare serves for those questions only, to which we expect an answer. (vi. 93.)

CURA; SOLLICITUDO; ANGOR; DOLOR; ÆGRITUDO. Cura, sollicitudo, and angor, mean the disturbance of the mind with reference to a future evil and danger; cura (from the antiquated word *coera*, from κοίρανος) as thoughtfulness, uneasiness, apprehension, in opp. to *incuria*, like φροντίς; sollicitudo, as sensitiveness, discomposure, anxiety, in opp. to *securitas*, Tac. H. iv. 58, like μέριμνα; angor (from ἄγχω) as a passion, anguish, fear, in opp. to *solutus animus;* whereas dolor and ægritudo relate to a present evil; dolor (from θλᾶν?) as a hardship or pain, in opp. to *gaudium*, ἄλγος; ægritudo, as a sickness of the soul, like ἀνία, in opp. to *alacritas*. Cic. Tusc. v. 16. Cic. Fin. i. 22. Nec præterea res ulla est, quæ sua natura aut *sollicitare* possit aut *angere*. Accius apud Non. Ubi *cura* est, ibi *anxitudo*. Plin. Ep. ii. 11. Cæsar mihi tantum studium, tantam etiam *curam* — nimium est enim dicere *sollicitudinem* — præstitit, ut, etc. Quintil. viii. pr. 20. *Curam* ego verborum, rerum volo esse *sollicitudinem*. (iv. 419.)

CURVUS; UNCUS; PANDUS; INCURVUS; RECURVUS; REDUNCUS; REPANDUS; ADUNCUS. 1. Curvus, or in prose mostly curvatus, denotes, as a general expression, all crookedness, from a slight degree of crookedness to a complete circle; uncus supposes a great degree of crookedness, approaching to a semi-circle, like the form of a hook; pandus, a slight crookedness, deviating but a little from a straight line, like that which slopes. 2. The curva form a continued crooked line; the incurva suppose a straight line ending in a curve, like ἐπικαμπής, the augur's staff, for example, or the form of a man who stoops, etc. 3. Recurvus, reduncus, and repandus, denote that which is bent outwards; aduncus, that which is bent inwards. Plin. H. N. xi. 37. Cornua aliis *adunca*, aliis *redunca*. (v. 184.)

CUSPIS, see *Acies*.

CUSTODIA; CARCER; ERGASTULUM. Custodia (from κεύθω) is the place where prisoners are confined, or the prison; carcer (κάρκαρον, redupl. of καρίς, circus), that part of the prison that is meant for citizens; ergastulum (from ἐργάζομαι, or εἴργω), the house of correction for slaves.

CUTIS, see *Tergus*. CYATHUS, see *Poculum*.

CYMBA, see *Navigium*.

## D.

DAMNUM; DETRIMENTUM; JACTURA. Damnum (δαπάνη) is a loss incurred by one's self, in opp. to *lucrum*. Plaut. Cist. i. 1, 52. Capt. ii. 2, 77. Ter. Heaut. iv. 4, 25. Cic. Fin. v. 30. Sen. Ben. iv. 1. Tranq. 15; whereas detrimentum (from detrivisse) means a loss endured, in opp. to *emolumentum*. Cic. Fin. i. 16. iii. 29; lastly, jactura is a voluntary loss, by means of which one hopes to escape a greater loss or evil, a sacrifice. Hence damnum is used for a fine; and in the form, Videant Coss., ne quid resp. *detrimenti* capiat, the word *damnum* could never be substituted for *detrimentum*. (v. 251.)

DAPES, see *Epulæ*. DEAMARE, see *Diligere*.

DEAMBULARE, see *Ambulare*.

DEBERE, see *Necesse est*. DECERNERE, see *Destinare*.

DECIPERE, see *Fallere*. DECLARARE, see *Ostendere*.

DECORARE, see *Comere*. DEDECUS, see *Ignominia*.

DEDICARE, see *Sacrare*. DEDUCERE, see *Comitari*.

DEESSE, see *Abesse*. DEFENDERE, see *Tueri*.

DEFERRE, see *Arguere*.

DEFICERE, see *Abesse* and *Turbæ*.
DEFLERE, see *Lacrimare*. DEFORMIS, see *Tæter*.
DEGERE, see *Agere*. DE INTEGRO, see *Iterum*.
DELECTATIO, see *Oblectatio*.
DELERE, see *Abolere*.

DELIBUTUS; UNCTUS; OBLITUS. Delibutus (from λείβειν, λιβάζειν), besmeared with something greasy, is the general expression; unctus (from ὑγρός? or νήχειν?) means anointed with a pleasant ointment; and oblitus from oblino), besmeared with something impure. (vi. 98.)

DELICTUM; PECCATUM; MALEFACTUM; MALEFICIUM; FACINUS; FLAGITIUM; SCELUS; NEFAS; IMPIETAS. 1. Delictum and peccatum denote the lighter sort of offences; delictum, more the transgression of positive laws, from levity; peccatum (from παχύς), rather of the laws of nature and reason, from indiscretion. 2. A synonyme and as it were a circumlocution of the above words is malefactum; whereas maleficium and facinus involve a direct moral reference; maleficium is any misdeed which, as springing from evil intention, deserves punishment; but facinus, a crime which, in addition to the evil intention, excites astonishment and alarm from the extraordinary degree of daring requisite thereto. 3. There are as many sorts of evil deeds, as there are of duties, against oneself, against others, against the gods; flagitium (from βλαγίς) is an offence against oneself, against one's own honor, by gluttony, licentiousness, cowardice; in short, by actions which are not the consequence of unbridled strength, but of moral weakness, as evincing *ignavia*, and incurring shame; whereas scelus (σκληρόν) is an offence against others, against the right of individuals, or the peace of society, by robbery, murder, and particularly by sedition, by the display, in short, of malice; nefas (ἄφατον) is an offence against the gods, or against nature, by blasphemy, sacrilege, murder of kindred, betrayal of one's country; in short, by the display of *impietas*, an impious outrage. Tac. G. 12. (ii. 139.)

DELIGERE; ELIGERE. Deligere means to choose, in the sense of not remaining undecided in one's choice; eligere, to choose, in the sense of not taking the first thing that comes. (v. 98.)

DELIRIUM, see *Amens*. DELUBRUM, see *Templum*.

DEMENS, see *Amens*.

DEMERE; ADIMERE; EXIMERE; AUFERRE; ERIPERE; SURRIPERE; FURARI. 1. Demere, adimere, and eximere, denote a taking away without force or fraud; demere (from de-imere) means to take away a part from a whole, which thereby becomes less, in opp. to *addere*, or *adjicere*. Cic. Orat. ii. 25. Fam. i. 7. Acad. iv. 16. Cels. i. 3. Liv. ii. 60; adimere, to take away a possession from its possessor, who thereby becomes *poorer*, in opp. to *dare* and *reddere*. Cic. Verr. i. 52. Fam. viii. 10. Phil. xi. 8. Suet. Aug. 48. Tac. Ann. xiii. 56; eximere, to remove an evil from a person oppressed by it, whereby he feels himself lightened. 2. Auferre, eripere, surripere, and furari, involve the notion of an illegal and unjust taking away; auferre, as a general expression for taking away anything; eripere, by force to snatch away; surripere and furari, secretly and by cunning; but surripere may be used for taking away privily, even when just and prudent self-defence may be pleaded as the motive; whereas furari (φωρᾶν, φέρω) is only applicable to the mean handicraft of the thief. Sen. Prov. 5. Quid opus fuit *auferre?* accipere potuistis; sed ne nunc quidem *auferetis*, quia nihil *eripitu* nisi retinenti. Cic. Verr. i. 4, 60. Si quis clam *surripiat* aut *eripiat* palam atque *auferat:* and ii. 1, 3. Non *furem* sed *ereptorem*. (iv. 123.)

DEMOLIRI, see *Destruere*. DEMORI, see *Mors*.

DENEGARE, see *Negare*. DENSUS, see *Angustus*.

DENUO, see *Iterum*.

DEPLORARE, see *Lacrimare*.

DEPRAVARE; CORRUMPERE. Depravare denotes to make anything relatively worse, provided it is still susceptible of amendment, as being merely perverted from its proper use; whereas corrumpere denotes to make anything absolutely bad and useless, so that it is not susceptible of amendment, as being completely spoilt. (v. 321.)

DERIDERE, see *Ridere*. DESCISCERE, see *Turbæ*.

DESERERE, see *Relinquere*. DESERTUM, see *Solitudo*.

DESIDERARE, see *Requirere*. DESIDIA, see *Ignavia*.

DESINERE; DESISTERE. Desinere denotes only a condition in reference to persons, things, and actions, as, to cease; whereas desistere, an act of the will, of which persons only are capable, as to desist. (iii. 101.)

DESOLATUS, see *Relinquere*.

DESPERANS, see *Exspes*. DESPICERE, see *Spernere*.

DESTINARE; OBSTINARE; DECERNERE; STATUERE; CONSTITUERE. 1. Destinare and obstinare denote forming a resolution as a psychological, whereas decernere and statuere as a political, act. 2. Destinare means to form a decided resolution, by which a thing is set at rest; obstinare, to form an unalterable resolution, whereby a man perseveres with obstinacy and doggedness. 3. Decernere denotes the final result of a formal consultation, or, at least, of a deliberation approaching the nature and seriousness of a collegial discussion; statuere, to settle the termination of an uncertain state, and constituere is the word employed, if the subject or object of the transaction is a multitude. Cic. Fr. Tull. Hoc judicium sic expectatur, ut non unæ rei *statui*, sed omnibus *constitui* putetur. (iv. 178.)

DESTINATIO, see *Pervicacia*.

DESTITUERE, see *Relinquere*.

DESTRUERE; DEMOLIRI. Destruere means to pull down an artificially constructed, demoliri, a solid, building. (vi. 2.)

DETERIOR; PEJOR. D e t e r i o r (a double comparative from de) means, like χείρων, that which has degenerated from a good state, that which has become less worthy; whereas p e j o r (from πεζός), like κακίων, that which has fallen from bad to worse, that which is more evil than it was. Hence Sallust. Or. Phil. 3. Æmilius omnium flagitiorum postremus, qui *pejor* an ignavior sit deliberari non potest:—in this passage *deterior* would form no antithesis to *ignavior*. The *deterrimi* are the objects of contempt, the *pessimi* of abhorrence; Catullus employs the expression *pessimas puellas*, 'the worst of girls,' in a jocular sense, in a passage where this expression has a peculiar force; whereas *deterrimus* could, under no circumstances, be employed as a jocular expression, any more than the words *wretched, depraved.* (i. 53.)

DETESTARI, see *Abominari*. DETINERE, see *Manere*.

DETRECTATIO, see *Invidia*.

DETRIMENTUM, see *Damnum*. DEUS, see *Numen*.

DEVERSORIUM; HOSPITIUM; CAUPONA; TABERNA; POPINA; GANEUM. D e v e r s o r i u m is any house of reception on a journey, whether one's own property, or that of one's friends, or of inn-keepers; h o s p i t i u m, an inn for the reception of strangers; c a u p o n a (from καρποῦσθαι?) a tavern kept by a publican. These establishments afford lodging as well as food; whereas t a b e r n æ, p o p i n æ, g a n e a, only food, like restaurateurs; t a b e r n æ (from trabes?), for the common people, as eating-houses; p o p i n æ (from popa, πέψαι), for gentlefolks and gourmands, like ordinaries; g a n e a (from ἀγανός?), for voluptuaries. (vi. 101.)

DEVINCIRE, see *Ligare*. DICARE, see *Sacrare*.

DICERE; AIO; INQUAM; ASSEVERARE; AFFIRMARE; CONTENDERE; FARI; FABULARI. 1. D i c e r e denotes to say, as conveying information, in reference to the hearer, in opp. to *tacere*, like the neutral word *loqui.* Cic. Rull. ii. 1. Ver. ii. 1, 71, 86. Plin. Ep. iv. 20.

vii. 6, like λέγειν; but a i o expresses an affirmation, with reference to the speaker, in opp. to *nego*. Cic. Off. iii. 23. Plaut. Rud. ii. 4, 14. Terent Eun. ii. 2, 21, like φάναι. 2. A i t is in construction with an indirect form of speech, and therefore generally governs an infinitive; whereas i n q u i t is in construction with a direct form of speech, and therefore admits an indicative, imperative, or conjunctive. 3. A i o denotes the simple affirmation of a proposition by merely expressing it, whereas a s s e v e r a r e, a f f i r m a r e, c o n t e n d e r e, denote an emphatic affirmation; a s s e v e r a r e is to affirm in earnest, in opp. to a jocular, or even light affirmation, *jocari*. Cic. Brut. 85; a f f i r m a r e, to affirm as certain, in opp. to doubts and rumors, *dubitare*, Divin. ii. 3, 8; c o n t e n d e r e, to affirm against contradiction, and to maintain one's opinion, in opp. to yielding it up, or renouncing it. 4. D i c e r e (δεῖξαι) denotes to say, without any accessory notion, whereas l o q u i (λακεῖν), as a transitive verb, with the contemptuous accessory notion that that which is said is mere idle talk. Cic. Att. xiv. 4. Horribile est quæ *loquantur*, quæ minitentur. 5. L o q u i denotes speaking in general; f a b u l a r i, a good-humored, or, at least, pleasant mode of speaking, to pass away the time, in which no heed is taken of the substance and import of what is said, like λαλεῖν; lastly, d i c e r e, as a neuter verb, denotes a speech prepared according to the rules of art, a studied speech, particularly from the rostrum, like λέγειν. Liv. xlv. 39. Tu, centurio, miles, quid de imperatore Paulo senatus decreverit potius quam quid Sergio Galba *fabuletur* audi, et hoc *dicere* me potius quam illum audi; ille nihil præterquam *loqui*, et id ipsum maledice et maligne *didicit*. Cic. Brut. 58. Scipio sane mihi bene et *loqui* videtur et *dicere*. Orat. iii. 10. Neque enim conamur docere eum *dicere* qui *loqui* nesciat. Orat. 32. Muren. 34, 71. Suet. Cl. 4. Qui tam ἀσαφῶς *loquatur*, qui possit quum declamat σαφῶς *dicere* quæ *dicenda* sunt non video

6. Fari (φάναι) denotes speaking, as the mechanical use of the organs of speech to articulate sounds and words, nearly in opp. to *infantem esse;* whereas loqui (λακεῖν), as the means of giving utterance to one's thoughts, in opp. to *tacere.* And as fari may be sometimes limited to the utterance of single words, it easily combines with the image of an unusual, imposing, oracular brevity, as in the decrees of fate, *fati;* whereas loqui, as a usual mode of speaking, is applicable to excess in speaking, *loquacitas.* (iv. 1.)

DICTERIUM, see *Verbum.*

DICTO AUDIENTEM ESSE, see *Parere.*

DIES; TEMPUS; TEMPESTAS; DIE; INTERDIU. 1. Dies (from ἔνδιος) denotes time in its pure abstract nature, as mere extension and progression; whereas tempus and tempestas, with a qualifying and physical reference, as the weather and different states of time; tempus denotes rather a mere point of time, an instant, an epoch; tempestas, an entire space of time, a period. Hence dies docebit refers to a long space of time, after the lapse of which information will come, like χρόνος; whereas tempus docebit refers to a particular point of time which shall bring information, like καιρός. (iv. 267.) 2. Die means by the day, in opp. to by the hour or the year; whereas interdiu and diu, by day, in opp to *noctu;* but interdiu stands in any connection; diu only in direct connection with *noctu.* (iv. 288.)

DIES FESTI, see *Solemnia.*

DIFFERRE; PROFERRE; PROCRASTINARE; PROROGARE. 1. Differre denotes delay in a negative sense, whereby a thing is not done at present, but laid aside; whereas proferre and procrastinare, delay in a positive sense, as that which is to take place at a future time; proferre refers to some other time in general; procrastinare, to the very next opportunity. 2. Differre denotes an action, the beginning of which is put off; prorogare, a condition or state, the ending of which is put off, as to protract. (vi. 102.)

Difficilis, see *Arduus* and *Austerus*.

Digladiari, see *Pugnare*.

Dignum esse, see *Merere*. Diligentia, see *Opera*.

Diligere; Amare; Deamare; Adamare; Caritas; Amor; Pietas. 1. Diligere (from ἀλέγειν) is love arising from esteem, and, as such, a result of reflection on the worth of the beloved object, like φιλεῖν; whereas amare is love arising from inclination, which has its ground in feeling, and is involuntary, or quite irresistible, like ἐρᾶν, ἔρασθαι; diligere denotes a purer love, which, free from sensuality and selfishness, is also more calm; amare, a warmer love, which, whether sensual or platonic, is allied to passion. Cic. Att. xiv. 17. Tantum accessit ut mihi nunc denique *amare* videar, ante *dilexisse*. Fam. xiii. 47. Brut. i. 1. Plin. Ep. iii. 9. 2. Amare means to love in general; deamare, as an intensive, to love desperately, like *amore deperire;* and adamare, as an inchoative, to fall in love. 3. Caritas, in an objective sense, means to be dear to some one; amor, to hold some one dear: hence the phrases, *Caritas* apud aliquem; *amor* erga aliquem. 4. Caritas, in a subjective sense, denotes any tender affection, especially that of parents towards their children, without any mixture of sensuality, and refers merely to persons, like ἀγάπη or στοργή; whereas amor denotes ardent passionate love to persons or things, like ἔρως; lastly, pietas (from ψήχω, ψίης), the instinctive love to persons and things, which we are bound to love by the holy ties of nature, the gods, those related to us by blood, one's native country, and benefactors. Caritas rejoices in the beloved object and its possession, and shows itself in friendship and voluntary sacrifices; amor wishes evermore to get the beloved object in its power, and loves with a restless unsatisfied feeling; pietas follows a natural impulse and religious feeling. (iv. 97.)

DILUCULUM, see *Mane*.

DIMETARI, DIMETIRI, see *Metiri*.

DIMICARE, see *Pugnare*. DIMITTERE, see *Mittere*.

DIRIMERE, see *Dividere*. DIRIPERE, see *Vastare*.

DIRUS, see *Atrox*.

DISCEPTATIO; LITIGATIO; CONTROVERSIA; CONTENTIO; ALTERCATIO; JURGIUM; RIXA. 1. Disceptatio, litigatio, and controversia, are dissensions, the settling of which is attempted quietly, and in an orderly way; contentio, altercatio, and jurgium, such as are conducted with passion and vehemence, but which are still confined to words; rixæ (ὀρέκτης), such as, like frays and broils come to blows, or at least threaten to come to blows, and are mid-way between *jurgium* and *pugna*. Liv. xxxv. 17. Ex *disceptatione altercationem* fecerunt. Tac. Hist. i. 64. *Jurgia* primum, mox *rixa* inter Batavos et legionarios. Dial. 26. Cassius Severus non pugnat, sed *rixatur*. 2. Controversia takes place between two parties the moment they place themselves in array on opposite sides; disceptatio, when they commence disputing with each other, in order to arrive at the path of truth, or to discover what is right, but without a hostile feeling; litigatio, when a hostile feeling and a personal interest are at the bottom of the dispute. 3. Contentio would maintain the right against all opponents, and effect its purpose, whatever it may be, by the strenuous exertion of all its faculties; altercatio would not be in debt to its opponent a single word, but have the last word itself; jurgium (from ὀργή) will, without hearkening to another, give vent to its ill-humor by harsh words. Contentio presents the serious image of strenuous exertion; altercatio, the comic image of excessive heat, as in women's quarrels; jurgium, the hateful image of rude anger. (v. 274.)

DISCERNERE; DISTINGUERE. Discernere (διακρίνειν) means to distinguish by discrimination and judgment; distinguere (διαστίξαι, or διατέγγειν), by signs and marks. (vi. 103.)

DISCIPLINÆ, see *Literæ*. DISCRIMEN, see *Tentare*.

DISERTUS; FACUNDUS; ELOQUENS. Disertus and facundus denote a natural gift or talent for speaking, whereas eloquens, an acquired and cultivated art. Disertus is he who speaks with clearness and precision; facundus, he who speaks with elegance and beauty; eloquens, he who combines clearness and precision with elegance and beauty. The *disertus* makes a good teacher, who may nevertheless be confined to a one-sided formation of intellect; the *facundus* is a good companion, whose excellence may nevertheless be confined to a superficial adroitness in speaking, without acuteness or depth, whereas the *eloquens*, whether he speaks as a statesman or as an author, must, by talent and discipline in all that relates to his art, possess a complete mastery over language, and the resources of eloquence. Cic. Orat. 5, 19. Antonius . . . . *disertos* ait se vidisse multos, *eloquentem* omnino neminem. Quintil. viii. pr. 13. *Diserto* satis dicere quæ oporteat; ornate autem dicere proprium est *eloquentissimi*. Suet. Cat. 53. *Eloquentiæ* quam plurimum adtendit, quantumvis *facundus* et promptus. (iv. 14.)

DISPAR, see *Æquus*. DISPERTIRE, see *Dividere*.

DISPUTARE, see *Disserere*.

DISSERERE; DISPUTARE. Disserere (διερεῖν) means to express an opinion in a didactic form, and at the same time to explain the grounds of that opinion; but disputare (διαπυθέσθαι) in a polemical form, and to take into consideration the arguments against it, and with one's opponent, whether an imaginary person or actually present, to weigh argument against argument, and ascertain on which side the balance of truth lies. The *disserens* takes only a subjective view of the question; but the *disputans* would come at a result of objective validity. Disserere, moreover, denotes a freer, disputare a more methodical discussion of the subject. Cic. Rep. iii. 16. i. 24. Fin. i. 9, 31. Orat. ii. 3, 13. (iv. 19.)

DISTINGUERE, see *Discernere*.

DISTRIBUERE, see *Dividere*.

DIU, DIUTIUS, DIUTINUS, see *Pridem*.

DIVELLERE, see *Frangere*. DIVERSUS, see *Varius*.

DIVIDERE; PARTIRI; DIRIMERE; DISPERTIRE; DISTRIBUERE. 1. Dividere and dirimere mean to divide something, merely in order to break the unity of the whole, and separate it into parts, whereas partiri means to divide, in order to get the parts of the whole, and to be able to dispose of them. Hence the phrases *divide et impera*, and *dividere sententias*, but *partiri prædam*. 2. Divisio denotes, theoretically, the separation of a genus into its species, whereas partitio, the separation of the whole into its parts. Quintil. v. 10, 63. Cic. Top. 5. 3. Dividere refers to a whole, of which the parts are merely locally and mechanically joined, and therefore severs only an exterior connection; but dirimere refers to a whole, of which the parts organically cohere, and destroys an interior connection. Liv. xxii. 15. Casilinum urbs . . . Volturno flumine *dirempta* Falernum ac Campanum agrum *dividit:* for the separation of a city into two halves by a river, is an interior separation, whereas the separation of two neighboring districts by a city, is an exterior separation. 4. Dividere means also to separate into parts, without any accessory notion, whereas dispertire, with reference to future possessors, and distribuere, with reference to the right owners, or to proper and suitable places. (iv. 156.)

DIVINARE; PRÆSAGIRE; PRÆSENTIRE; PRÆVIDERE; VATICINARI; PRÆDICERE. 1. Divinare denotes foreseeing by divine inspiration and supernatural aid, like μαντεύεσθαι; præsagire (præ and ἡγεῖσθαι), in a natural way, by means of a peculiar organization of mind bordering on the supernatural; præsentire and prævidere, by an unusual measure of natural talent; præsentire, by immediate presentiment; prævidere, by foresight, by an acute and happy combination. 2. Divinare, etc., are merely acts of perception, whereas vaticinatio and prædictio, the open expression of what is foreseen; vaticinatio, that of the *divinans* and *præsagiens*, like προφητεία, prophecy; but prædictio, that of the *præsentiens* and *prævidens*, prediction. (vi. 105.)

Divitiæ; Opes; Gazæ; Locuples; Opulentus; Copiosus. 1. Divitiæ and gazæ denote riches quite generally, as possessions and the means of satisfying one's wishes of any sort, whereas opes, as the means of attaining higher ends, of aggrandizing one's self, and of acquiring and maintaining influence. Divitiæ (from δεύειν) denotes the riches of a private person, like πλοῦτος; opes (opulentus, πολύς), the instrument of the statesman, or of the ambitious in political life; gazæ, the treasure of a king or prince, like θησαυροί. 2. Dives means rich in opp. to poor, Quintil. v. 10, 26, like πλούσιος; locuples (loculos πλήθων), well-off, in opp. to *egens*, *egenus*, Cic. Planc. 35. Ros. Com. 8, like ἀφνειός; opulentus and copiosus, opulent, in opp. to *inops*, Cic. Parad. 6. Tac. H. iii. 6, like εὔπορος. (v. 81.)

Divortium, see *Repudium*. Divus, see *Numen*.

Doctor, Præceptor; Magister. Doctor means the teacher, as far as he imparts theory, with reference to the student, in opp. to the mere hearer; præceptor, as far as he leads to practice, in reference to the pupil, in opp. to the mere scholar; magister, in a general sense, with reference to his superiority and ascendency in knowledge, in opp. to the laity. Cic. Orat. iii. 15. Vetus illa doctrina eadem videtur et recte faciendi et bene dicendi magistra, neque disjuncti *doctores*, sed iidem erant vivendi *præceptores* atque dicendi. And. Mur. 31. (vi. 105).

Doctrina; Eruditio. Doctrina denotes learning as a particular species of intellectual cultivation, whereas eruditio the learned result, as the crown of intellectual cultivation. Doctrina evinces a superiority in particular branches of knowledge, and stands as a co-ordinate notion with exercitatio, which is distinguished from it by involving a superiority in the ready use of learning, and can therefore, even as a mere theory, be of more evident service in practice than that which is indirectly important; eruditio stands in still closer relation to practice, and involves the co-operation of the different branches of knowledge and different studies to the ennobling of the human race; it denotes genuine zeal for the welfare of mankind in an intellectual, as *humanitas* does in a moral, point of view. (v. 268.)

DOCTRINA, see *Literæ*.

DOLOR; TRISTITIA; MŒSTITIA; LUCTUS. 1. Dolor (from θλᾶν, ἄθλιος?) denotes an inward feeling of grief, opp. to *gaudium*, Cic. Phil. xiii. 20. Suet. Cæs. 22, like ἄλγος; whereas tristitia, mœror, luctus, denote an utterance or external manifestation of this inward feeling. Tristitia and mœstitia are the natural and involuntary manifestation of it in the gestures of the body and in the countenance; luctus (ἀλυκτός), its artificial manifestation, designedly, and through the conventional signs of mourning, as cutting off the hair, mourning clothes, etc., at an appointed time, like πένθος. Mœror also serves for a *heightened* expression of *dolor*, and luctus of *mœror* and *tristitia*, as far as the manifestation *is added* to distinguish the feeling from it. Cic. Att. xii. 28. *Mœrorem* minui; *dolorem* nec potui, nec si possem vellem. Phil. xi. 1. Magno in *dolore* sum, vel in *mœrore* potius, quem ex miserabili morte C. Trebonii accepimus. Plin. Ep. v. 9. Illud non *triste* solum, verum etiam *luctuosum*, quod Julius avitus decessit. Tac. Agr. 43. Finis vitæ ejus nobis *luctuosus*, amicis *tristis*; for relations only put on mourning. Tac. Ann. ii. 82. Quanquam nec insignibus lugentium abstinebant, altius animis *mœrebant*. Cic. Sext. 29, 39. *Luctum* nos hausimus majorem *dolorem* ille animi non minorem. 2. T r i s t i t i a (from ταρακτός ?) denotes the expression of grief in a bad sense, as gloom, fretfulness, and ill-humor, opp. to *hilaratus*, Cic. Att. xii. 40. Fin. v. 30. Cæcil. ap. Gell. xv. 9. Quintil. xi. 3, 67, 72, 79, 151; whereas m œ s t i t i a (from μύρω) denotes grief, as deserving of commiseration, as affliction, when a most just grief gives a tone of sadness, in opp. to *lætus*, Sall. Cat. f. Tac. Ann. i. 28. T r i s t i t i a is more an affair of reflection; m œ s t i t i a, of feeling. The *tristis*, like the *truculentus*, is known by his forbidding look, his wrinkled forehead, the contraction of his eyebrows; the *mœstus*, like the *afflictus*, by his lack-lustre eyes and dejected look. Tac. Hist. i. 82. Rarus per vias populus *mœsta* plebs; dejecti in terram militum vultus, ac plus *tristitæ* quam pœnitentiæ. Cic. Mur. 24, 49. *Tristem* ipsum, *mœstos* amicos: and Orat. 22, 74. (iii. 234.)

DOLOR, see *Cura*. DOMUS, see *Aedificium*.

DONUM; MUNUS; LARGITIO; DONARIUM; DONATIVUM; LIBERALITAS. 1. D o n u m (δωτίνη) means a present, as a gratuitous gift, by which the giver wishes to confer pleasure, like δῶρον; whereas m u n u s, as a reward for services, whereby the giver shows his love or favor, like γέρας; lastly, l a r g i t i o, as a gift from self interested motives, which under the show of beneficence would win over and bribe, generally for political ends. Suet. Cæs. 28. Aliis captivorum millia *dono* afferens; that is, not merely as a loan: compare with Ner. 46. Auspicanti Sporus annulum *muneri* obtulit; that is, as a handsome return. Tac. H. ii. 30. Id comitatem bonitatemque faventes vocabant, quod sine modo (Vitellius) *donaret* sua *largiretur* aliena. 2. D o n a r i u m denotes particularly a gift to a temple; d o n a t i v u m, a military gift, or earnest-money, which the new emperor at his accession to the throne distributes among the soldiers; l i b e r a l i t a s, a gift which the emperor bestowed, generally on a poor nobleman, for his support. (iv. 142.)

DORSUM; TERGUM. D o r s u m (from δέρας) denotes

the back, in an horizontal direction, consequently the back of an animal, in opp. to the belly, like νῶτον; t e r g u m (from τράχηλος), the back, in a perpendicular direction, consequently the part between the shoulders in a man, in opp. to the breast, like μετάφρενον. Hence d o r s u m m o n t i s denotes the uppermost surface; t e r g u m m o n t i s, the hinder part of a mountain. (v. 15.)

DUBIUS; AMBIGUUS; ANCEPS. D u b i u s (δοιός) and a m b i g u u s (ἀμφὶς ἔχων) denote doubt, with reference to success or failure, fortune or misfortune; a n c e p s, with reference to existence itself, to the being or not being. Vell. Pat. ii. 79. Ea patrando bello mora fuit, quod postea *dubia* et interdum *ancipiti* fortuna gestum est. Tac. Ann. iv. 73. (v. 282.)

DUDUM, see *Pridem*. DULCIS, see *Suavis*.

DUMI; SENTES; VEPRES. D u m i denotes bushes growing thickly together, which present the appearance of a wilderness; s e n t e s, prickly and wounding bushes, thorn-bushes; v e p r e s combines both meanings; thorn-bushes w ich make the ground a wilderness. (vi. 108.)

DUPLEX; DUPLUM; GEMINUS; DUPLICITER; BIFARIAM. 1. D u p l e x (δίπλαξ) denotes double, as distinct magnitudes to be counted: d u p l u m (διπλοῦν) as continuous magnitudes to be weighed or measured. D u p l e x is used as an adjective, d u p l u m as a substantive. Quintil. viii. 6, 42. In quo et numerus est *duplex* et *duplum* virium. 2. In d u p l e x (as in διπλοῦς), *doubleness* is the *primary*, *similarity* and *equality* the *secondary* notion; in g e m i n u s (as in δίδυμος), the notion of *similarity* and *equality* is the *primary*, that of *doubleness* the *secondary* one. In Cic. Part. 6. Verba *geminata* et *duplicata* vel etiam sæpius iterata; the word *geminata* refers to the repetition of the same notion by synonymes; *duplicata* to the repetition of the same word. 3. D u p l i c i t e r is always modal; in two different manners, with double purpose; b i f a r i a m is local, in two places, or two parts. Cic.

Fam. ix. 20. *Dupliciter* delectatus sum literis tuis; compare with Tusc. iii. 11. *Bifariam* quatuor perturbationes æqualiter distributæ sunt. (v. 281.)

## E.

EBRIUS; VINOLENTUS; TREMULENTUS; CRAPULA; EBRIOSUS. 1. Ebrietas places the consequences of the immoderate use of wine in its most favorable point of view, as the exaltation and elevation of the animal spirits, and in its connection with inspiration, like μέθη; whereas vinolentia, and the old word temulentia, in its disgusting point of view, as brutal excess, and in its connection with the loss of recollection, like οἴνωσις; lastly, crapula, the objective cause of this condition, like κραιπάλη. 2. Ebrius, and the word of rare occurrence, madusa, denote a person who is drunk, with reference to the condition; ebriosus, a drunkard, with reference to the habit. (v. 330.)

ECCE, see *En*.
EDULIA, see *Alimenta*.
EGESTAS, see *Paupertas*.
ELABORARE, see *Labor*.
E LONGINQUO, see *Procul*.
EDITUS, see *Altus*.
EGERE, see *Carere*.
EJULARE, see *Lacrimare*.
ELIGERE, see *Diligere*.
ELOQUENS, see *Disertus*.

ELOQUI; ENUNCIARE; PROLOQUI; PRONUNCIARE; RECITARE. 1. Eloqui and enunciare denote an act of the intellect, in conformity to which one utters a thought that was resting in the mind; but the *eloquens* regards therein both substance and form, and would express his thought in the most perfect language; whereas the *enuncians* regards merely the substance, and would only make his thought *publici juris*, or communicate it; hence elocutio belongs to rhetoric, enuntiatio to logic. 2. On the other hand, proloqui denotes a moral act, in conformity to which one resolves to give utterance to a secret thought, in opp. to *reticere*, like *profiteri;* lastly, pronuntiare, a physical act, by which one utters any thing, whether thought of, or written mechanically by the organs of speech, and makes it heard, like *recitare*. Pronuntiare, however, is a simple act of the organs of speech, and aims merely at being fully heard; recitare is an act of refined art, and aims by just modulation, according to the laws of declamation, to make a pleasing impression. Pronuntiatio relates only to single letters, syllables, and words, as the elements and body of speech, whereas recitatio relates both to the words and to their import, as the spirit of speech. (iv. 4.)

ELUCET, see *Constat*. EMENDARE, see *Corrigere*.

EMERE; MERCARI; REDIMERE. 1. Emere means to buy, where furnishing one's self with the article is the main point, the price the next point, like *πρίασθαι*; whereas mercari (from *ἀμέργειν*) means to buy, as a more formal transaction, generally as the mercantile conclusion of a bargain, like *ἐμπολᾶν*. 2. Emere refers to the proper objects of trade; redimere to things which, according to the laws of justice and morality, do not constitute articles of trade, and which the buyer might either claim as his due, or ought to receive freely and gratuitously, such as peace, justice, love, and so forth. Cic. Sext. 30, 36. Quis autem rex qui illo anno non aut *emendum* sibi quod non habebat, aut *redimendum* quod habebat, arbitrabatur? (iv. 116.)

EMINENS; EXCELLENS; PRÆCLARUS; PRÆSTANS; INSIGNIS; SINGULARIS; UNICUS. 1. Eminens, excellens, præclarus, and præstans, involve a quiet acknowledgment of superiority; whereas egregius, with an expression of enthusiasm, like glorious; eximius, with an expression of admiration, like excellent. 2. Eximius, &c. relate altogether to good qualities, like superior, and can be connected with vices and faults only in irony; whereas insignis, singularis, and unicus, are indifferent, and serve as well to heighten blame as praise, like distinguished, matchless. (vi. 111.)

EMINET, see *Apparet*. EMINUS, see *Procul*.

EMISSARIUS, see *Explorator*.

EMOLUMENTUM, see *Lucrum*. EMORI, see *Mors*.

EN; ECCE. E n (ἠνί) means, see here what was before hidden from thee! like ἤν, ἠνί, ἠνίδε; whereas e c c e (ἔχε? or the reduplication of the imperative of Eco, to see, oculus?) means, see there what thou hast not before observed! like ἰδού. (vi. 112.)

ENSIS, see *Gladius*. ENUNCIARE, see *Eloqui*.

EPISTOLA, see *Literæ*.

EPULÆ; CONVIVIUM; DAPES; EPULUM; COMMISSATIO. E p u l æ is the general expression, the meal, whether frugal or sumptuous, whether en famille or with guests, at home or in public; c o n v i v i u m is a social meal, a convivial meal; d a p e s (from δάψαι, δεῖπνον), a religious meal, a meal of offerings; e p u l u m, a solemn meal, mostly political, a meal in honor of something, a festival; c o m i s s a t i o (from κομάζειν), a gormandizing meal, a feast. (v. 195.)

EQUUS; CABALLUS; MANNUS; CANTERIUS. E q u u s (from the antiquated word, ehu) denotes a horse, as a general expression, a term in natural history; c a b a l l u s (from καφάζω), a horse for ordinary services; m a n n u s, a smaller kind of horse, like palfrey, for luxury; c a n t e r i u s, a castrated horse, a gelding. Sen. Ep. 85. Cato censorius *canterio* vehebatur et hippoperis quidem impositis. Oh quantum decus sæculi! Catonem uno *caballo* esse contentum, et ne toto quidem! Ita non omnibus obesis *mannis* et asturconibus et tolutariis præferres unum illum *equum* ab ipso Catone defrictum. (iv. 287.)

ERGASTULUM, see *Custodia*. ERIPERE, see *Demere*.

ERRARE; VAGARI; PALARI. E r r a r e (ἔῤῥειν) is to go astray, πλανᾶσθαι, an involuntary wandering about, when one knows not the right way; v a g a r i and p a l a r i, on the other hand, mean a voluntary wandering; v a g a r i, like ἀλᾶσθαι, when one disdains a settled residence, or straight path, and wanders about unsteadily; palari (from pandere?) when one separates from one's company, and wanders about alone. Erramus *ignari*, vagamur *soluti*, palamur *dispersi*. Tac. H. i. 68. Undique populatio et cædes; ipsi in medio vagi; abjectis armis magna pars, saucii aut *palantes* in montem Vocetiam perfugiunt. (i. 89.)

ERUDIRE; FORMARE; INSTITUERE. Erudire and formare denote education as an ideal good, and as a part of human improvement; erudire, generally, and as far as it frees from ignorance; formare, specially, and as far as it prepares one in a particular sphere, and for a particular purpose, and gives the mind a bent thereto; whereas instituere denotes education as a real good, in order to qualify for a particular employment. (vi. 113.)

ERUDITIO, see *Literæ*.

ESCA, see *Alimenta*.

ESCENDERE, see *Scandere*.

ESURIES, see *Fames*.

ET; QUE; AC; ATQUE. Et (ἔτι) is the most general copulative particle; que and et—et connect opposites; que (καί), simply because they are opposites, as *terra marique;* but et—et, in order to point them out emphatically as opposites [and closely connected notions of *the same kind*], as *et terra et mari;* whereas ac and atque connect synonymes, *atque* before vowels and gutturals; ac before the other consonants; as, for example, vir fortis *ac* strenuus. (vi. 114.)

EVENIRE, *Accidere*.

EVERTERE, see *Perdere*.

EVESTIGIO, see *Repente*.

EVOCARE, see *Arcessere*.

EXCELLENS, see *Eminens*.

EXCELSUS, see *Altus*.

EXCIPERE, see *Sumere*.

EXCORS, see *Amens*.

EXCUBIÆ; STATIONES; VIGILIÆ. Excubiæ are the sentinels before the palace, as guards of honor and safeguards; stationes, guards stationed at the gate as an outpost; vigiliæ, guards in the streets during the night as a patrol.

EXCUSATIO, see *Purgatio*.

EXEMPLUM; EXEMPLAR. Exemplum means an example out of many, chosen on account of its relative aptness for a certain end; whereas exemplar means an example before others, chosen on account of its absolute aptness to represent the idea of a whole species, a model. Cic. Mur. 31. Vell. P. ii. 100. Antonius singulare *exemplum* clementiæ Cæsaris; compare with Tac. Ann. xii. 37. Si incolumem servaveris, æternum *exemplar* clementiæ ero; not merely tuæ *clementiæ*, but of clemency in general. (v. 359.)

EXERCITUS; COPIÆ. Exercitus is an army that consists of several legions; but copiæ mean troops, which consist of several cohorts.

EXHIBERE, see *Præbere*. EXIGERE, see *Petere*.

EXIGUUS, see *Parvus*.

EXILIS; MACER; GRACILIS; TENUIS. Exilis and macer denote leanness, with reference to the interior substance and with absolute blame, as a consequence of want of sap, and of shrivelling; exilis (from egere, exiguus,) generally as applicable to any material body, and as poverty and weakness, in opp. to *uber*, Cic. Or. i. 12; macer (*μακρός*, meagre,) especially to animal bodies, as dryness, in opp. to *pinguis*, Virg. Ecl. iii. 100; whereas gracilis and tenuis, with reference to the exterior form, indifferently or with praise; tenuis (*ταvύς*, *thin*), as approaching to the notion of *delicate*, and as a *general* term, applicable to all bodies, in opp. to *crassus*, Cic. Fat. 4. Vitruv. iv. 4; but gracilis as approaching to the notion of *tall*, *procerus*, and especially as applicable to animal bodies, like slender, in opp. to *opimus*, Cic. Brut. 91; *obesus*, Cels. i. 3, 30. ii. 1. Suet. Dom. 18. (v. 25.)

EXIMERE, see *Demere*. EXISTIMARE, see *Censere*.

EXITIUM, EXITUS, see *Lues*.

EXPERIRI, see *Tentare*. EXPETERE, see *Velle*.

EXPILARE, see *Vastare*.

EXPLORATOR; SPECULATOR; EMISSARIUS. Exploratores are scouts, publicly ordered to explore the state of the country or the enemy; speculatores, spies, secretly sent out to observe the condition and plans of the enemy; emissarii, secret agents, commissioned with reference to eventual measures and negotiations. (vi. 117.)

EXPROBRARE, see *Objicere*.

EXSECRARI, see *Abominare*.

EXSEQUIÆ, see *Funus*. EXSOMNIS, see *Vigil*.

EXSPECTARE, see *Manere*.

EXSPES; DESPERANS. Exspes denotes hopelessness, as a state; but desperans, despondency, as the painful feeling of hopelessness.

EXSTRUCTUS, see *Prœditus*. EXSUL, see *Perfuga*.

EXSULTARE, see *Gaudere*. EXTA, see *Caro*.

EXTEMPLO, see *Repente*.

EXTERUS; EXTERNUS; PEREGRINUS; ALIENIGENA. EXTRARIUS; EXTRANEUS; ADVENA; HOSPES. 1. Exterus and externus denote a foreigner, as one dwelling in a foreign country; whereas peregrinus, alienigena, advena, and hospes, as one who sojourns for a time in a country not his own. 2. Externus denotes a merely local relation, and is applicable to things as well as to persons; but exterus, an intrinsic relation, and is an epithet for persons only. *Externœ nationes* is a merely geographical expression for nations that are situated without; *exterœ nationes*, a political expression for foreign nations. 3. Extraneus means, that which is without us, in opp. to relatives, family, native country; whereas extrarius, in opp. to one's self. Cic. ap. Colum. xii. Comparata est opera mulieris ad domesticam diligentiam; viri autem ad exercitationem forensem et *extraneam:* comp. with Juv. ii. 56. Utilitas aut in corpore posita est aut in *extrariis* rebus: or Quintil. vii. 2, 9, with vii. 4, 9. 4. Peregrinus is one who does not possess the right of citizenship, in opp. to *civis*, Sen. Helv. 6; alienigena, one born in another country, in opp. to *patrius* and *indigena;* advena, the emigrant, in opp. to *indigena*, Liv. xxi. 30; hospes, the foreigner, in opp. to *popularis*. 5. Peregrinus is the political name of a foreigner, as far as he is without the rights of a citizen and native inhabitant, with disrespect; h o s p e s, the name given to him from a feeling of kindness, as possessing the rights of hospitality. Cic. Rull. ii. 34. Nos autem hinc Romæ, qui veneramus, jam non *hospites* sed *peregrini* atque *advenœ* nominabamur. (iv. 386.)

Extorris, see *Perfuga.*

Extraneus, Extrarius, see *Exterus.*

Extremus; Ultimus; Postremus; Novissimus. E x t r e m u s and u l t i m u s denote the last in a continuous magnitude, in a space; e x t r e m u s, the outermost part of a space, or of a surface, in opp. to *intimus* and *medius*, Cic. N. D. ii. 27, 54. Cluent. 65, like ἔσχατος; u l t i m u s (superl. from ollus), the outermost point of a line, in opp. to *citimus* and *proximus.* Cic. Somn. 3. Prov. cons. 18. Liv. v. 38, 41, like λοῖσθος. Whereas p o s t r e m u s and n o v i s s i m u s denote the last in a discrete quantity, or magnitude consisting of separate parts, in a row of progressive numbers; p o s t r e m u s, the last in a row that is completed, in which it occupies the last place, in opp. to those that precede it, *primus*, *princeps*, *tertius*, like ὕστατος; whereas n o v i s s i m u s denotes the last in a row that is not complete, in which, as the last comer, it occupies the last place, in opp. to that which has none to follow it, but is last of all, like νέατος.

Exuviæ, see *Prœda.*

## F.

Faber; Opifex; Artifex. F a b r i (from favere, fovere,) are such workmen as labor with exertion of bodily strength, carpenters and smiths, χειρώνακτες; o p i f i c e s such as need mechanical skill and industry, βάναυσοι; a r t i f i c e s such as employ mind and invention in their mechanical functions, τεχνῖται. (v. 329.)

Fabulari, see *Loqui*, *Garrire*, and *Dicere.*

FACERE, see *Agere*. FACETIÆ, see *Lepidus*.

FACIES; OS; VULTUS; OCULI. Facies (from species) and oculi (from ὄκκος) denote the face and eyes only in a physical point of view, as the natural physiognomy and the organs of sight; but os and vultus with a moral reference, as making known the temporary, and even the habitual state of the mind by the looks and eyes; os (from ὄσσομαι), by the glance of the eye, and the corresponding expression of the mouth; vultus (from ἑλικτός), by the motion of the eye, and the simultaneous expression of the parts nearest to it, the serene and the darkened brow. Tac. Agr. 44. Nihil metus in *vultu;* gratia *oris* supererat. (iv. 318.)

FACILITAS, see *Humanitas*. FACINUS, see *Delictum*.

FACULTAS, see *Occasio*. FACTUM, see *Agere*.

FACUNDUS, see *Disertus*. FACTIO, see *Partes*.

FALLACITER, see *Perperam*.

FALLERE; FRUSTRARI; DECIPERE; CIRCUMVENIRE; FRAUDARE; IMPONERE. Fallere, frustrari, and imponere, mean to deceive, and effect an exchange of truth for falsehood, σφάλλειν; the *fallens* (σφάλλων) deceives by erroneous views; the *frustrans* (from ψύθος), by false hopes; the *imponens*, by practising on the credulity of another. Decipere and circumvenire mean to outwit, and obtain an unfair advantage, ἀπατᾶν; the *decipiens*, by a suddenly executed; the *circumveniens*, by an artfully laid plot. *Fraudare* (ψεύδειν) means to cheat, or injure and rob anybody by an abuse of his confidence. (v. 357.)

FALSE, FALSO, see *Perperam*. FAMA, see *Rumor*.

FAMES; ESURIES; INEDIA. Fames is hunger from want of food, like λιμός, in opp. to *satietas*; whereas esuries is hunger from an empty and craving stomach, in opp. to *sitis;* lastly, inedia is not eating, in a general sense, without reference to the cause, though for the most part from a voluntary resolution, like ἀσιτία. Hence *fame* and *esurie perire* mean to die of hunger, whereas *inedia perire* means to starve one's self to death. (iii. 119.)

FAMILIA, see *Ædificium*. FAMILIARIS, see *Socius*.
FAMULUS, see *Servus*. FANUM, see *Templum*.
FAS EST, see *Concessum est*.
FASTIDIUM, see *Spernere*. FASTIGIUM, see *Culmen*.
FASTUS, see *Superbia*. FANUM, see *Dicere*.

FATERI; PROFITERI; CONFITERI. F a t e r i means to disclose, without any accessory notion, in opp. to *celare*, Liv. xxiv. 5. Curt. vi. 9; p r o f i t e r i means to avow, freely and openly, without fear and reserve, whether questioned or not; c o n f i t e r i, to confess in consequence of questions, menaces, compulsion. The *professio* has its origin in a noble consciousness, when a man disdains concealment, and is not ashamed of that which he has kept secret; the *confessio*, in an ignoble consciousness, when a man gives up his secret out of weakness, and is ashamed of that which he confesses. Cic. Cæc. 9, 24. Ita libenter *confitetur*, ut non solum *fateri*, sed etiam *profiteri* videatur. Planc. 25, 62. Rabir. perd. 5. (iv. 30.)

FATIGATUS; FESSUS; LASSUS. F a t i g a t u s and f e s s u s express the condition in which a man after exertion longs for rest, from subjective weariness; whereas l a s s u s and l a s s a t u s, the condition in which a man after active employment has need of rest, from objective weakness. Cels. i. 2, 15. Exercitationis finis esse debet sudor aut certe *lassitudo*, quæ citra *fatigationem* sit. Sall. Jug. 57. Opere castrorum et prœliorum *fessi lassique* erant. (i. 105.)

FATUM, see *Casus*. FATUUS, see *Stupidus*.
FAUSTUS, see *Felix*.

FAUX; GLUTUS; INGLUVIES; GUTTUR; GURGULIO; GULA. F a u x, g l u t u s, and i n g l u v i e s, denote the space within the throat; g l u t u s (γλῶττα), in men; i n g l u v i e s, in animals; f a u x (φάρυγξ), the upper part, the entrance into the throat; whereas g u t t u r, g u r g u l i o, and g u l a, denote that part of the body which encloses the space within the throat; gurgulio (redupl. of gula), in animals; gula, in men; guttur, in either. (v. 149.)

FAX; TÆDA; FUNALE. Fax is the general expression for any sort of torch; tæda is a natural pine torch; funale, an artificial wax-torch.

FEL; BILIS. Fel (from φλέγω, φλέγμα,) is the gall of animals, and, figuratively, the symbol of bitterness to the taste; whereas bilis is the gall of human beings, and, figuratively, the symbol of exasperation of mind. (v. 120.)

FELIX; PROSPER; FAUSTUS; FORTUNATUS; BEATUS. Felix, fœlix, (φῦλον ἔχων) is the most general expression for happiness, and has a transitive and intransitive meaning, making happy and being happy; prosper and faustus have only a transitive sense, making happy, or announcing happiness; prosperum (πρόσφορος) as far as men's hopes and wishes are fulfilled; faustum (from ἀφαύω, φαυστήριος,) as an effect of divine favor, conferring blessings; whereas fortunatus and beatus have only an intransitive or passive meaning, being happy; fortunatus, as a favorite of fortune, like εὐτυχής; beatus (ψίης) as conscious of happiness, and contented, resembling the θεοὶ ῥεῖα ζώοντες, like μακάριος. (vi. 125.)

FEMINA; MULIER; UXOR; CONJUX; MARITA. 1. Femina (φυομένη) denotes woman with regard to her physical nature and sex, as bringing forth, in opp. to *mas;* whereas mulier (from mollis), woman, in a physical point of view, as the weaker and more tender sex, in opp. to *vir;* whence femina only can be used for the female of an animal. 2. Mulier denotes also the married woman, in opp. to *virgo*, Cic. Verr. ii. 1; whereas uxor and conjux, the wife, in opp. to the husband; uxor, merely in relation to the man who has married her, in opp. to *maritus*, Tac. G. 18; conjux (from conjungere), in mutual relation to the husband, as half of a pair, and in opp. to *liberi*, Cic. Att. viii. 2.

Catil. iii. 1. Liv. v. 39, 40. Tac. Ann. iv. 62. H. iii. 18. 67. Suet. Cal. 17. Accordingly, uxor belongs to the man; conjux is on a par with the man; uxor refers to an every-day marriage, like wife; conjux, to a marriage between people of rank, like consort. Vell. Pat. ii. 100. Claudius, Gracchus, Scipio, quasi cujuslibet *uxore* violata pœnas perpendere, quum Cæsaris filiam et Nerones violassent *conjugem*. 3. Uxor is the ordinary, marita a poetical, expression for a wife. (iv. 327.)

FEMUR, see *Coxa*.
FERA, see *Animal*.
FERAX, see *Fœcundus*.
FERE, see *Pæne*.
FERIÆ, see *Solemnia*.
FERIARI, see *Vacare*.
FERIRE, see *Verberare*.
FERME, see *Pæne*.

FEROCIA; FEROCITAS; VIRTUS; FORTITUDO. Ferocia and ferocitas (from φράξαι) denote natural and wild courage, of which even the barbarian and wild beast are capable; ferocia, as a feeling, ferocitas, as it shows itself in action; whereas virtus and fortitudo denote a moral courage, of which men only of a higher mould are capable; virtus, that which shows itself in energetic action, and acts on the offensive; fortitudo (from the old word forctitudo, from farcire,) that which shows itself in energetic resistance, and acts on the defensive, like *constantia*. Pacuv. Nisi insita *ferocitate* atque *ferocia*. Tac. Ann. xi. 19. Nos *virtutem* auximus, barbari *ferociam* infregere: and ii. 25. (i. 44.)

FERRE; PORTARE; BAJULARE; GERERE. 1. Ferre means, like φέρειν, to carry any thing portable from one place to another; portare and bajulare, like βαστάζειν, to carry a load; portare (from πορίζειν), for one's self, or for others; bajulare, as a porter. In Cæs. B. G. i. 16. Ædui frumentum . . . . *conferri*, *comportari*, adesse dicere; conferre refers to the delivery and the contribution from several subjects to the authorities of the place; comportare, the delivery of these contributions by the authorities of the place to

Cæsar. 2. Ferre, portare, and bajulare, express only an exterior relation, that of the carrier to his load, whereas gerere (ἀγείρειν) gestare, like φόρειν, an interior relation, that of the possessor to his property. As, then, bellum ferre means only either *inferre bellum* or *tolerare*, so bellum gerere has a synonymous meaning with *habere*, and is applicable only to the whole people, or to their sovereign, who resolved upon the war, and is in a state of war; but not to the army fighting, nor to the commander who is commissioned to conduct the war. *Bellum geret* populus Romanus, administrat consul, capessit miles. (i. 150.)

FERRE; TOLERARE; PERFERRE; PERPETI; SUSTINERE; SINERE; SUSTENTARE. 1. Ferre (φέρειν) represents the bearing, only with reference to the burden which is borne, altogether objectively, like φέρειν; whereas tolerare, perferre, and pati, perpeti, with subjective reference to the state of mind of the person bearing; the *tolerans* and *perferens* bear their burden without sinking under it, with strength and self-control, synonymously with *sustinens*, sustaining, like τολμῶν; the *patiens* and *perpetiens* (παθεῖν) without striving to get rid of it, with willingness or resignation, enduring it, synonymously with *sinens*. Ferre and tolerare have only a noun for their object, but pati also an infinitive. 2. Perferre is of higher import than *tolerare*, as perpeti is of higher import than *pati*, to endure heroically and patiently. Poet. ap. Cic. Tusc. iv. 29. Nec est malum, quod non natura humana patiendo *ferat:* compare with Tac. Ann. i. 74. Sen. Thyest. 307. Leve est miserias *ferre; perferre* est grave. Plin. H. N. xxvi. 21. Qui *perpeti* medicinam non *toleraverant*. Tac. Ann. iii. 3. Magnitudinem mali *perferre* visu non *toleravit*. 3. Tolerare (from τλῆναι) means to keep up under a burden, and not sink down; but sustinere means to keep up the burden, and not let it sink. 4. Pati denotes an intellectual permission, no opposition being made, like to let happen; whereas s i n e r e (ἀνεῖναι) denotes a material permission, not to hold any thing fast nor otherwise hinder, to leave free. P a t i has, in construction, the action itself for its object, and governs an infinitive; s i n e r e, the person acting, and is in construction with *ut*. (iv. 259.) 5. S u s t i n e r e means to hold up, in a general sense, whereas s u s t e n t a r e, to hold up with trouble and difficulty. Curt. viii. 4, 15. Forte Macedo gregarius miles seque et arma *sustentans* tandem in castra venit; compare with v. 1, 11. Tandem Laconum acies languescere, lubrica arma sudore vix *sustinens*. Also, Liv. xxiii. 45. Senec. Prov. 4. a. f. (iii. 293.)

FERTILIS, see *Fœcundus*.
FERVERE, see *Calere*.
FESTA, see *Solemnia*.
FESTIVUS, see *Lepidus*.
FIDELITAS, see *Fides*.
FERULA, see *Fustis*.
FESSUS, see *Fatigatus*.
FESTINUS, see *Citus*.
FIDELIS, see *Fidus*.

FIDERE; CONFIDERE; FIDEM HABERE; CREDERE; COMMITTERE; PERMITTERE. 1. F i d e r e (πείθειν) means to trust; c o n f i d e r e, to trust firmly, both with reference to strength and assistance; whereas f i d e m h a b e r e, to give credit, and c r e d e r e, to place belief, namely, with reference to the good intentions of another. Liv. ii. 45. Consules magis non *confidere* quam non *credere* suis militibus: the former with reference to their valor, the latter with reference to their fidelity. 2. F i d e r e, etc., denote trust as a feeling; c o m m i t t e r e, p e r m i t t e r e, as an action; the *committens* acts in good trust in the power and will of another, whereby he imposes upon him a moral responsibility; to intrust; the *permittens* acts to get rid of the business himself, whereby he imposes at most only a political or legal responsibility, as to leave (or, give up) to. Cic. Font. 14. Ita ut *commissus* sit fidei, *permissus* potestati. Verr. i. 32. v. 14. (v. 259.)

FIDES; FIDELITAS; FIDUCIA; CONFIDENTIA; AU

DACIA; AUDENTIA. 1. Fides and fidelitas mean the fidelity which a man himself observes towards others; fides, in a more general sense, like πίστις, the keeping of one's word and assurance from conscientiousness, together with the reliance of others upon us as springing from this quality, the credit we possess; fidelitas denotes, in a more special sense, like πιστότης, the faithful adherence to persons to whom we have once devoted ourselves; whereas fiducia and confidentia denote the trust we place in others; fiducia, the laudable trust in things, in which we actually can trust, which is allied to the courage of trusting in ourselves, in opp. to *timor;* Cic. Div. ii. 31. Plin. Ep. v. 17, like θάρσος; but confidentia denotes a blamable blind trust, particularly in one's own strength, in opp. to foresight and discretion, and which converts spirit into presumption, like θράσος. 5. Fiducia and confidentia have their foundation in trusting to the prosperous issue of anything; audacia and audentia, in the contempt of danger; audacia sometimes means a laudable boldness, as a word of higher import than *fiducia;* sometimes a blamable boldness, as a civil term for *temeritas*, like τόλμα; but audentia is always a laudable spirit of enterprise. Juven. xiii. 108. Quum magna malæ superest *audacia* causæ, creditur a multis *fiducia.* Sen. Ep. 87. Quæ bona sunt, *fiduciam* faciunt, divitiæ *audaciam.* (v. 256.)

FIDES, see *Religio*. FIDES, see *Chorda*.

FIDUCIA, see *Fides*.

FIDUS; FIDELIS; INFIDUS; INFIDELIS; PERFIDUS; PERFIDIOSUS. 1. Fidus denotes a natural quality, like trustworthy, with relative praise; whereas fidelis denotes a moral characteristic, as faithful, with absolute praise. Liv. xxii. 22. Eo vinculo Hispaniam vir unus solerti magis quam *fideli* consilio exsolvit. Abellex erat Sagunti, nobilis Hispanus, *fidus* ante Pœnis. 2. Infidus means unworthy of trust; infidelis, unfaithful; perfidus, treacherous, in particular ac tions; perfidiosus, full of treachery, with reference to the whole character. (v. 255.)

FIGURA; FORMA; SPECIES. Figura (from fingere, φέγγειν,) denotes shape altogether indifferently, in its mathematical relation, as far as it possesses a definite outline, like σχῆμα; whereas forma (φόριμος, φόρημα,) denotes it in an *æsthetical* relation, as far as it is a visible stamp and copy of an interior substance, to which it corresponds, like μορφή; lastly, species, in its physical relation, as far as it stands opposed to the inner invisible substance, which it covers as a mere outside, like εἶδος. Hence figurare means to shape, that is, to give a definite outline to a formless mass; whereas formare means to form, that is, to give the right shape to an unwrought mass; and lastly, speciem addere means to bedeck any thing, in the old sense of the word, that is, to give to a mass already formed an exterior that shall attract the eye. According to this explanation figura refers exclusively to the outline or lineaments, whilst forma, or at least species, involves color, size, and the like. (iii. 25.)

FIMUS, see *Lutum*.

FINDERE; SCINDERE. Findere means to separate a body according to its natural joints, consequently to divide it, as it were, into its component parts, to cleave; but scindere (σκεδάσαι) to divide it by force, without regard to its joints, and so separate it into fragments, to chop or tear to pieces. Hence findere lignum means to cleave a log of wood, with the assistance of nature herself, lengthways; scindere, to chop it by mere force breadthways. The *findens æquor nave* considers the sea as a conflux of its component waters; the *scindens*, merely as a whole. (iv. 154.)

FINIRE; TERMINARE; CONSUMMARE; ABSOLVERE; PERFICERE. Finire and terminare denote the mere ending of anything, without regard to how far the object of the undertaking is advanced; finire (φθίνειν ?) to end, in opp. to *incipere*, Cic. Orat. iii.

59; but terminare, to make an end, in opp. tc *continuare;* whereas consummare, absolvere, and perficere denote the completion of a work; consummare, as the most general term in opp. to doing a thing by halves; absolvere refers to a duty fulfilled, and a difficult work which is now done, and leaves the workman free, in opp. to *inchoare*; perficere refers to an end attained, and a self-chosen task, which is now done, and may be called complete, in opp. to *conari.* Cic. Orat. 29, 30. Verr. i. 27. Absolutus also has an extensive signification, and refers to the completeness of the work, like ἐντελής; perfectus, an intensive signification, and refers to the excellence of the work, like τέλειος. (iv. 366.)

Finis; Terminus; Limes. Finis (from φθίνω) denotes a boundary, as a mathematical line, like τέλος; terminus and limes, a mark, as the material sign of a boundary; terminus (τειρόμενος, τέρμα,) a stone set up, as the sign of a bounding point, like τέρμα; limes, a ridge, as the sign of a bounding line, like ὅρος. Cic. Læl. 16. Constituendi sunt qui sint in amicitia *fines* et quasi *termini* diligendi. Hor. Carm. ii. 18, 24. Revellis agri *terminos* et ultra *limites* clientium salis avarus. (iv. 359.)

Finitimus, see *Vicinus.* Firmus, see *Validus.*
Fiscus, see *Ærarium.* Flagitare, see *Petere.*
Flagitium, see *Delictum.* Flagrare, see *Ardere.*
Flavus, see *Luteus.* Flere, see *Lacrimare.*
Fluctus, see *Aqua.* Fluentum, see *Aqua.*

Fluere; Manare; Liquere. Fluere (φλύω) denotes flowing, with reference to the motion of the fluid; manare (from μανός, or *madere*,) with reference to the imparting of the fluid; and liquere, with reference to the nature of the fluid. The cause of the *fluendi* is, that the fluid has no dam, and according to the law of gravity flows on; whereas the cause of the *manandi* is the over-fulness of the spring; lastly, liquere, to be fluid, is the negative state of *fluere* and *manare*. Hence fluere, with its synonyme labi, is more opposed to *hærere* and *stare*; and moreover labari, with its synonyme effundi, more opposed to *contineri*, *claudi*; lastly, liquere, with its synonyme dissolvi, more opposed to *concrevisse*, *rigere*. Gell. xvii. 11. Plato potum dixit *defluere* ad pulmonem, eoque satis humectato, demanare per eum, quia sit rimosior, et *confluere* inde in vesicam. (ii. 1.)

Fluvius; Flumen; Amnis. Fluvius, flumen, (from φλύω) denote, like ῥόος, ῥεῦμα, an ordinary stream, in opp. to a pond and lake; whereas amnis (ἀμένας, *manare*,) like ποταμός, a great and mighty river, in opp. to the sea. Cic. Div. i. 50. and Divin. i. 35, 78. Ut *flumina* in contrarias partes fluxerint, atque in *amnes* mare influxerit. Tac. Ann. xv. 58. Senec. N. Q. iii. 19. Habet ergo non tantum venas aquarum terra, ex quibus corrivatis *flumina* effici possunt, sed et *amnes* magnitudinis vastæ. Then: Hanc magnis *amnibus* æternam esse materiam, cujus non tangantur extrema sicut *fluminum* et fontium. Tac. Hist. v. 23. Quo Mosæ *fluminis* os *amnem* Rhenum oceano affundit. Curt. ix. 4, 5. (ii. 7.)

Fœcundus; Fertilis; Ferax; Uber; Frugifer; Fructuosus. 1. Fœcundus (from φύω, fœtus,) denotes the fruitfulness of a living and breeding being, in opp. to *effœtus*, like εὔτοκος; whereas fertilis and ferax (from φέρω) the fruitfulness of inanimate and productive nature, and of the elements, opposed to *sterilis*, like εὔφορος. Tac. Ann. xii. 63. Byzantium *fertili* solo *fœcundoque* mari, quia vis piscium hos ad portus adfertur. Germ. 5. Terra satis *ferax*, *frugiferarum* arborum impatiens, pecorum *fœcunda*, sed plerumque improcera. Mela. i. 9, 1. Terra mire *fertilis* et animalium *perfœcunda* genetrix. And ii. 7. 2. Fertilis denotes the actual fruitfulness which has been produced by cultivation; ferax, the mere capability which arises from the nature of the soil. Cicero uses *fertilis* in a proper, *ferax*, in a figurative sense.

3. Fertilis and ferax denote fruitfulness under the image of creative and productive power, as of the father and mother; uber, under the image of fostering and sustaining, as of the nurse, like εὐθηνής; frugifer, under the image of a corn-field; fructuosus, under that of a tree rich in fruit, like ἔγκαρπος. (iv. 331.)

FŒDUS; SOCIETAS. Fœdus (πεποιθός) is an engagement for mutual security, on the ground of a sacred contract; whereas societas, an engagement to some undertaking in common on the ground of a mere agreement. Liv. xxiv. 6. Hieronymus legatos Carthaginem mittit ad *fœdus* ex *societate* faciendum. Sall. Jug. 14. Cic. Phil. ii. 35. Neque ullam *societatem* . . . . *fœdere* ullo confirmari posse credidi. (vi. 132.)

FŒDUS, see *Tæter*. FŒMINA, see *Femina*.

FŒNUS; USURA. Fœnus (from φύω, fœtus,) denotes interest as the produce of capital, like τόκος; usura denotes what is paid by the debtor for the use of capital, like δάνος. (vi. 133.)

FŒTUS; FŒDUS, see *Prægnans*.

FORES, see *Ostium*. FORMA, see *Figura*.

FORMARE, see *Erudire*. FORMIDO, see *Vereri*.

FORMOSUS; PULCHER; VENUSTUS. 1. Formosus means beauty, as far as it excites pleasure and delight by fineness of form; pulchrum, as far as it excites admiration, is imposing, and satisfies the taste by its perfectness; venustum, as far as by its charms it excites desire, and captivates. Formositas works on the natural sense of beauty; pulchritudo, on the cultivated taste; venustas, on the more refined sensuality. Suet. Ner. 51. Fuit vultu *pulchro* magis quam *venusto;* that is, it had perfect and regular beauty rather than pleasing features, and possessed a cold, heartless sort of beauty, by which no one felt attracted. Comp. Catull. lxxxvi. Hor. A. P. 99. Cic. Off. i. 36. 2. Venustas, loveliness, is of higher import than *gratia*, grace ; the former transports, the latter only attracts. (iii. 29.)

FORS, see *Casus.*

FORTE, FORTUITO, FORTASSE, FORSITAN, see *Casu.*

FORTITUDO, see *Ferocia.* FORTUNA, see *Casus.*

FORTUNATUS, see *Felix.* FOVEA, see *Specus.*

FOVERE, see *Calere.*

FRAGOR ; STREPITUS ; CREPITUS ; SONITUS. F r a g o r (σφάραγος) is a hollow, discordant sound, as crashing, like δοῦπος ; s t r e p i t u s (θρέω, θορυβή ?) a loud noisy sound, as roaring, bawling, shrieking, like κτύπος ; c r e p i t u s (from κρέμβαλον ?) a single sound, or the frequent repeating of the same sound, as clapping, like κροῦσις, κρότος ; s o n i t u s (ἔνοσις Ἐννώ,) a sound consisting of the vibrations of elastic bodies, as ringing, clinking, like ἠχή. Cic. Top. 12. Quæruntur pedum *crepitus, strepitus* hominum. (v. 117.)

FRAGRARE, see *Olere.*

FRANGERE ; RUMPERE ; DIVELLERE. 1. F r a n g e r e (ῥῆξαι ? or σφαράξαι) denotes to break to pieces what is hard ; r u m p e r e (from ῥέπω, ῥόπαλον,) to rend to pieces what is flexible. Cato ap. Prisc. Si quis membrum *rupit*, aut os *fregit :* for by breaking a limb, not the invisible bones, but the visible flesh, is rent asunder. When, however, r u m p e r e is applied to any thing hard, it involves the notion of exertion employed, and of danger ; the *frangens* breaks to pieces what is entire ; the *rumpens* rends to pieces what is obstructive. 2. D i s r u m p e r e and d i f f r i n g e r e mean to rend to pieces, and break to pieces, what was originally entire ; whereas d i v e l l e r e (διέλκειν) to tear asunder what was at first joined together. (v. 321.)

FRAUDARE, see *Fallere.*

FRENUM ; HABENA ; OREÆ. 1. F r e n u m (from φράξαι ?) is the bridle with which the rider breaks the wild horse, like χαλινός ; whereas h a b e n a (from hebes, χαβός, κάμψαι,) the rein with which he turns the obedient horse, like ἡνίον. Hor. Ep. i. 15, 13. Læva stomachosus *habena* dicet eques; sed equi *frenato* est auris in ore; that is, he minds not the reins, and must feel the bit. Cic. Orat. i. 53. Senatum servire populo, cui populus ipse moderandi et regendi sui potestatem quasi quasdam *habenas* tradidisset: comp. with Tac. Dial. 38. Pompeius adstrinxit, imposuitque quasi *frenos* eloquentiæ. 2. O r e æ, a u r e æ, now only to be found in a u r i g a, were, perhaps, the generic term of *frenum* and *habena*, like harness. (v. 137.)

FREQUENTER, see *Sæpe*. FRETUS, see *Confisus*.

FRICARE, see *Lævis*.

FRIGERE; ALGERE; ALGIDUS; ALSUS; GELIDUS; FRIGUS; GELU; GLACIES. F r i g e r e (φρίξαι) means to be cold, in opp. to *calere*, Cic. Fam. viii. 8. Auct. Her. iv. 15. Sen. Ir. ii. 18; whereas a l g e r e (ἀλγεῖν) means to feel cold, in opp. to *æstuare*. Cic. Tusc. ii. 14, 34. Sen. Ir. iii. 12. Plin. H. N. xvii. 26. 2. A l g i d u s denotes cold, as an unpleasant chill; a l s u s, as a refreshing coolness. 3. F r i g i d u s denotes a moderate degree of coldness, in opp. to *calidus*; whereas g e l i d u s means on the point of freezing, in opp. to *fervidus*. 4. F r i g u s denotes, objectively, cold in itself, which attacks a man, and leaves him; whereas f r i g e d o denotes cold, subjectively, as the state of a man attacked by cold, which begins and ends; it is an antiquated word which has become obsolete by the general use of *frigus*. 5. G e l u, g e l u s, g e l u m, (γλοία) denote, like κρύος, cold that produces ice; g e l i c i d i u m, like κρυμός, a single attack of frost, a frosty night; and g l a c i e s, like κρύσταλλος, its effect, ice. (iii. 89.)

FRUCTUOSUS, see *Fœcundus*. FRUGI, see *Bonus*.

FRUGIFER, see *Fœcundus*.

FRUI, FRUNISCI, see *Uti*.

FRUSTRA; NEQUIDQUAM; INCASSUM; IRRITUS. 1. F r u s t r a (from ψύθος) means in vain, with reference to the subject, whose expectation and calculations have been disappointed; whereas nequidquam (that is, in nequidquam, in nihil), to no purpose, refers to the nullity in which the thing has ended. 2. Hence frustra, used adjectively, refers to the person; whereas irritus, the actual adjective, refers to the thing. 3. Frustra and nequidquam denote merely a failure, without imputing a fault, like μάτην; whereas incassum involves the accessory notion of a want of consideration, by which the failure might have been calculated upon, and foreseen, as in attempting any thing manifestly or proverbially impossible, εἰς κενόν. (iii. 100.)

FRUSTRARI, see *Fallere*. FRUTICETUM, see *Rami*.

FUGITIVUS, see *Perfuga*.

FULCIRI; NITI. Fulciri, fultus (φυλάξαι) means to prop one's self up in order to be secure against falling, generally by leaning against a pillar, etc.; whereas niti, nixus, in order to climb a height, or to get forward, generally by standing on a basis. (ii. 127.)

FULGUR; FULGURATIO; FULMEN. Fulgur, fulgetrum, and fulguratio, denote the shining of the lightning in the horizon, like ἀστραπή; fulgur, as momentary and single flashes; fulguratio, as continued and repeated; whereas fulmen means the lightning that strikes the earth, like κεραυνός. Liv. xl. 59. *Fulguribus* præstringentibus aciem oculorum, sed *fulmina* etiam sic undique micabant, ut petit viderentur corpora. Curt. viii. 4, 3. Ovid, Met. iii. 300. Cic. Divin. ii. 19. Plin. H. N. ii. 43. Si in nube erumpat ardens, *fulmina;* si longiore tractu nitatur *fulgetra;* his findi nubem, illis perrumpi. Sen. Q. N. i. 1. (iii. 318.)

FUNALE, see *Fax*.

FUNDAMENTUM, FUNDUS, see *Solum*.

FUNDUS, see *Villa*. FUNIS, see *Laqueus*.

FUNUS; EXSEQUIÆ; POMPA. Funus (from

φοινός, πεφνεῖν,) denotes the mere carrying out of the corpse, like ἐκφορά; whereas exsequiæ and pompa (πομπή) denote the solemn procession; exsequiæ, of the living, as relations and friends; pompa, of the inanimate, as the images of ancestors, and other pageants. Cic. Quint. 15. *Funus*, quo amici conveniunt ad *exsequias* cohonestandas. And Plin. H. N. x. 43. Flor. iii. 20. Nep. Att. 22. Elatus est in lecticula, sine ulla *funeris pompa*, comitantibus omnibus bonis, maxima vulgi frequentia. And Cic. Mil. 13. Tac. Ann. iii. 5. (iv. 408.)

FURARI, see *Demere*. FUROR, see *Amens*.

FUSTIS; FERULA; SUDES; TRUDES; RUDIS; SCIPIO; BACULUS. 1. Fustis and ferula denote sticks for striking; sudes, trudes, and rudis, for thrusting; scipio and baculus, for walking. 2. Fustus (πτορθός?) is a cudgel or club, large enough to strike a man dead; but ferula, a little stick, or rod for the chastisement of school-boys; sudes (ὄζος) and trudes (στορθή, the root of Trüssel, a weapon called the Morning-star) [a sort of truncheon with a spiked head], are used in battle; rudis (ὀρσός) only as a foil in the fencing-school; scipio (σκηπτίων, σκῆψαι), serves especially for ornament and state, as a symbol of superior power, or of the honor due to age; baculus, bacillum (βάκτρον), serve more for use and convenience to lean upon, and at the same time, when necessary, as a weapon. (iii. 265.)

## G.

GALEA, see *Cassis*. GANEUM, see *Deversorium*.

GANNIRE, see *Latrare*.

GARRIRE; FABULARI; BLATIRE; BLATERARE; LOQUAX; VERBOSUS. 1. Garrire (γηρύω) denotes talking, with reference to excessive fondness for speaking; fabulari, to the nullity; blatire, and the intensive blaterare, to the foolishness of what is said. 2. The *garrulus* is tiresome from the quality, the *loquax* from the quantity, of what he says. For garrulitas expresses childish or idle talkativeness, from the mere pleasure of talking and hearing one's self talk, without regard to the value and substance of what is said, and has its origin in a degeneracy of youthful vivacity, and even in the abuse of superior talents, like λαλιά; whereas loquacitas (λακάζειν) expresses a quaint talkativeness, from inability to stop short, which has its origin in the diminished energy of old age, like *ἀδολεσχία*. The *garrulus*, in his efforts to please and entertain by light conversation, is silly and imbecile; the *loquax*, in his efferts to instruct, and make himself clearly understood, is often tedious. 3. Garrulus and loquax denote qualities of persons, speakers; verbosus, of things, speeches, and writings. (iii. 81.)

Gaudere; Lætari; Hilaris; Alacer; Gestire; Exsultare. 1. Gaudere (from γαῦρος) denotes joy as an inward state of mind, in opp. to *dolor*, like ἥδεσθαι; whereas lætari and hilarem esse, the utterance of joy. Tac. Hist. ii. 29. Ut valens processit, *gaudium*, miseratio, favor; versi in *lætitiam* .... laudantes gratantesque. 2. The *lætus* (from λιλαίομοι) shows his joy in a calm cheerfulness, which attests perfect satisfaction with the present, in opp. to *mœstus*, Tac. Ann. xv. 23; the *hilaris* (ἱλαρός) in awakened mirth, disposing to jest and laughter, in opp. to *tristis;* the *alacer* (ἀλκή) in energetic vivacity, evincing spirit and activity, in opp. to *territus*. Cic. Cœl. 28. The *gaudens*, the *lætus*, the *hilaris*, derive joy from a piece of good fortune; the *alacer* at the same time from employment and action. Cic. Divin. i. 33, 73. Equum *alacrem lætus* adspexit. Lætitia shows itself chiefly in an unwrinkled forehead, and a mouth curled for smiling; hilaritas, in eyes quickly moving, shining, and radiant with joy; alacritas, in eyes that roll, sparkle, and announce spirit. Sen. Ep. 116. Quantam serenitatem *lætitia* dat. Tac. Agr. 39. Fronte *lætus*, pectore anxius. Cic. Pis. 5. Te *hilarioribus* oculis quam solitus es intuente. 3. Gaudere and lætari denote a moderate; exsultare and gestire, and perhaps the antiquated word vitulari, a passionate, uncontrolled joy, as to exult and triumph; the *gestiens* (γηϑεῖν) discovers this by an involuntary elevation of the whole being, sparkling eyes, inability to keep quiet, etc.; the *exsultans*, by a voluntary, full resignation of himself to joy, which displays itself, if not by skipping and jumping, at least by an indiscreet outbreak of joy, bordering on extravagance. 4. Jucundus denotes, like juvat me, a momentary excitement of joy; lætus, a more lasting state of joy; hence *lætus* is used as the stronger expression, in Plin. Ep. v. 12. Quam mihi a quocunque excoli *jucundum*, a te vero *lætissimum* est. (iii. 242.)

GAZÆ, see *Divitiæ*.

GELICIDIUM, GELIDUS, GELU, see *Frigere*.

GEMERE, see *Suspirare*. GEMINUS, see *Duplex*.

GENA, see *Mala*. GENERARE, see *Creare*.

GENS; NATIO; POPULUS; CIVITAS. 1. Gens and natio denote a people, in a physical sense, in the description of nations, as a society originating in common descent and relationship, without any apparent reference to civilization; whereas populus and civitas denote a people in a political sense, as a society formed by civilization and compact. Sall. Cat. 10, 1. *Nationes* feræ et *populi* ingentes subacti. Cic. Rep. i. 25. 2. Gens (γενετή) includes all people of the same descent, like φῦλον; natio (from γνήσιος) a single colony of the same, like ἔϑνος. Vell. P. ii. 98. Omnibus ejus *gentis nationibus* in arma accensis. Tac. G. 2, 38. But as *gens*, in this physical sense, as the complex term for several colonies, has a more comprehensive meaning than *natio*, so has it, at the same time, in its political accessory meaning, as a clan, γένος, or as the complex term for several families, a narrower meaning than *populus ;* hence sometimes *populus* forms, as a civilized *natio*, a part of the natural *gens*. Liv. iv. 49. Bolanis suæ *gentis populo*, and Virg. A. x. 202 ; sometimes g e n s, as a political society, forms a part of *populus* : Justin. vii. 1. Adunatis *gentibus* variorum *populorum*. 3. C i v i t a s (from κείω) denotes the citizens of a town collectively, πόλις, merely with regard to their interior connection, as including the inhabitants who are in the enjoyment of the full rights of citizenship, and the lawful possessors of the land ; p o p u l u s (redupl. of πόλις) means the people, δῆμος, more commonly in reference to their social relations, interior and exterior, and with the included notion of belonging to the state. A people can determine upon war as a *civitas ;* but can carry it on only as a *populus*. A *civitas* is necessarily stationary ; but a *populus* may consist of *Nomades*, or wanderers from one pasture to another.

GENS, GENUS, see *Stirps*.

GERERE, see *Ferre* and *Agere*.

GESTIRE, see *Velle* and *Gaudere*.

GIGNERE, see *Creare*. GILVUS, see *Luteus*.

GLABER, see *Lævus*. GLACIES, see *Frigere*.

GLADIUS ; ENSIS ; PUGIO ; SICA. 1. G l a d i u s (from κλάδος) is the usual, e n s i s (from ansa ?) the select and poetical name for a sword. Quintil. x. 1, 11. (v. 188.) 2. P u g i o (from pungere) is a dagger, as a fair and openly used soldier's weapon, on a level with the sword ; whereas s i c a (from secare) is the unfair and secret weapon of the bandit, on a level with poison. (vi. 291.)

GLOBUS ; SPHÆRA. G l o b u s is the popular term for any body that is round like a ball ; whereas s p h æ r a is the scientific term, derived from the Greek for a mathematical globe. (vi. 147.)

GLOBUS, see *Caterva*.

GLORIA ; CLARITAS. G l o r i a (from γέλως) denotes renown, under the image of something said, like κλέος; *claritas* (from γαληρός) under that of some thing bright, and that is seen, like δόξα. (v. 235.)

GLORIATIO, see *Jactatio*. GLUTUS, see *Faux*.

GNAVITAS, see *Opera*. GRACILIS, see *Exilis*.

GRADATIM, see *Paulatim*. GRADIRI, see *Ire*.

GRADUS; GRESSUS; PASSUS. 1. Gressus denotes a step subjectively, whereas gradus objectively. Gressus is a step that is being taken; gradus that is taken. 2. Gressus is a product of going, but passus, of standing also, if the feet are at the same distance from each other as in walking. Gressus denotes any separation of the feet, whether longer or shorter, quicker or slower, whether deserving the name of step or not; whereas passus means a regular measured step, which at the same time serves as a measure of length. Virg. Æn. i. 414. Tendere *gressus* ad mœnia: comp. with ii. 723. Iulus sequitur patrem non *passibus* æquis. (iv. 58.)

GRÆCI; GRAII; GRÆCULI; GRÆCANICUS. 1. Græci denotes the Greeks merely as a term in the description of different nations, and a historical name, without any accessory moral reference; whereas Graii, with praise, as the classical name for a nation of heroes in days of yore: Græculi, with blame, as the degenerate people, false and unworthy of trust, that existed in the times of the Roman writers. 2. Græcum means what is really Grecian, whether in or out of Greece; but Græcanicus, what is made after the Grecian manner, what is merely à la Grecque. (v. 304.)

GRANDÆVUS, see *Vetus*. GRANDIS, see *Magnus*.

GRATIA, see *Studium*.

GRATIAS AGERE, HABERE, REFERRE; GRATES; GRATARI; GRATULARI. 1. Gratiam or gratias habere means to feel thankful, like χάριν εἰδέναι; whereas gratias agere, to return thanks in words, like εὐχαριστεῖν; lastly, gratiam referre, to show one's self thankful by deeds, like χάριν φέρειν, ἀντιχαρίζεσθαι. Cic. Marc. ii. 33. Maximas tibi omnes *gratias agimus;* majores etiam *habemus.* Off. ii. 20. Inops etiamsi *referre gratiam* non potest, *habere* tamen potest. And Fam. v. 11. x. 11. Planc. 28. Balb. 1. Phil. iii. 2. 2. G r a t i a s a g e r e is the usual; g r a t e s a g e r e, a select and solemn form of speech. Cic. Somn. *Grates* tibi *ago*, summe Sol, vobisque reliqui cœlites. 3. In the same manner g r a t u l a r i denotes an occasional expression of thanks without oblation, and a congratulation without formality, whereas g r a t a r i, a solemn thanksgiving, or congratulation. Liv. vii. 3. Jovis templum *gratantes* ovantesque adire: comp. with Ter. Heaut. v. 1, 6. Desine deos *gratulando* obtundere. (ii. 213.)

GRATUS; JUCUNDUS; ACCEPTUS; GRATIOSUS. 1. G r a t u m (from κεχαρῆσθαι) means that which is acceptable only in reference to its value with us, as precious, interesting, and worthy of thanks; but j u c u n d u m (from juvare) in reference to the joy which it brings us, as delightful. Cic. Att. iii. 24. Ista veritas etiam si *jucunda* non est, mihi tamen *grata* est. Fam. v. 18. Cujus officia *jucundiora* scilicet sæpe mihi fuerunt, nunquam *gratiora.* And v. 15. xiii. 18. 2. G r a t u s refers to the feeling, as wished for; a c c e p t u s, to its expression, as welcome. 3. The *gratus alicui* meets with no antipathy, but is liked; the *gratiosus apud aliquem* is the object of distinguished favor, and enthusiastic attachment, as the favorite or darling. (iii. 254.)

GRAVIDUS, see *Prægnans.*

GRAVITAS, see *Moles* and *Severitas.*

GREMIUM; SINUS. G r e m i u m is the lap, or surface formed by the knees in a sitting posture, and figuratively the symbol of the fostering care of a mother; whereas s i n u s, the bosom, between the two breasts, especially in the female sex, and figuratively the symbol of protection and refuge. Cic. Pis. 37. Ætolia procul a barbaris disjuncta gentibus in *sinu* pacis posita medio fere Græciæ *gremio* continetur. (vi. 150.)

GRESSUS, see *Gradus*.

GREX, see *Caterva* and *Pecus*. GRUMUS, see *Collis*.

GULA, see *Faux*. GURGES, see *Virago*.

GURGULIO, see *Faux*.

GUSTUS, GUSTARE, see *Sapor*.

GUTTA; STILLA; STIRIA. G u t t a is a natural, s t i l l a (στίλη, σταλάξαι), an artificial measured drop. Further, the principal notion in g u t t a is that of smallness, hence g u t t a t i m means drop by drop; whereas in s t i l l a the principal notion is that of humidity, hence s t i l l a t i m means trickling or dripping. S t i l l a means a liquid; s t i r i a (στερεά) a frozen drop. (iii. 4.)

GUTTUR, see *Faux*. GYRUS, see *Orbis*.

## H.

HABENA, see *Frenum*. HABERE, see *Tenere*.

HABITARE, see *Incolere*. HABITUS, see *Vestis*.

HACTENUS, see *Adhuc*. HÆDUS, see *Caper*.

HÆRERE; PENDERE. H æ r e r e (χειρόω?) means to stick, and not to be loose, or able to get forwards; p e n d e r e (πέτεσθαι), to be suspended, and prevented from falling to the ground. Cic. Acad. ii. 39. Ut videamus terra penitusne defixa sit et radicibus suis *hæreat*, an media *pendeat*. (vi. 154.)

HÆSITARE, see *Cunctari*. HARENA, see *Sabulo*.

HARIOLARI; VATICINARI. H a r i o l a r i (from χρᾶν) means to foretell, with the accessory notion of charlatanism, like χρησμολογεῖν; whereas v a t i c i n a r i (from vates, ἠχέτης,) to foretell, with the accessory notion of inspiration, like μαντεύεσθαι. In Cic. Divin. i. 2, *Hariolorum* et *vatum* furibundæ prædictiones, it is only the *harioli*, who from their position and in public estimation already pass for charlatans; whereas the *vates* are charlatans only, as Cicero himself views them from his philosophical elevation. (iii. 76.)

HASTA, see *Missile*. HAUD SCIO AN, see *Casu*.

HELLUO, see *Prodigus*. HELVUS, see *Luteus*.
HEROS, see *Numen*. HILARIS, see *Gaudere*.
HIRCUS, see *Caper*.
HIRSUTUS, HIRTUS, HISPIDUS, see *Horridus*.
HISTORIÆ, see *Annales*. HISTRIO, see *Actor*.
HŒDUS, see *Caper*.

HOMICIDA; INTERFECTOR; PEREMTOR; INTEREMTOR; PERCUSSOR; SICARIUS. Homicida denotes the manslayer in a general sense, as far as manslaughter is a crime, like ἀνδροφόνος; whereas interfector, peremtor, and interemtor, only the slayer of a particular person, whether the deed be a crime or not, like φονεύς; percussor and sicarius denote the instruments of another's will, and mere mechanical executioners of another's decree; but the *percussor* executes a public sentence of condemnation, as the headsman, while the *sicarius* lends and hires out his hand to a secret assassination, like the bandit. Cic. Rosc. Am. 33, 93. Erat tum multitudo sicariorum . . et homines impune occidebantur . . . Si eos putas . . . quos qui leviore nomine appellant, *percussores* vocant, quæro in cujus fide sint et tutela. (iii. 191.)

HOMO; MAS; VIR; HOMUNCULUS; HOMUNCIO; HOMULLUS. 1. Homo (Goth. guma, from humus, χθών, ἐπιχθόνιος), means a human being, man or woman, in opp. to *deus* and *bellua*, like ἄνθρωπος; mas and vir mean only the man; mas in a physical sense, in opp. to *femina*, like ἄρσην; vir (Goth. wair, from ἱρῆνες), in a physical sense, in opp. to *mulier*, like ἀνήρ. Sen. Polyb. 36. Non sentire mala sua non est *hominis*, at non ferre non est *viri*. Ep. 103. Cic. Tusc. ii. 22. Fam. v. 17. Justin. xi. 13. 2. Homunculus denotes the weak and powerless being called man, with reference to the whole race, in opp. to the Deity, to nature in general, to the universe, etc.; homuncio and homullus denote the weak and insignificant man, as an individual, in opp. to other men; homunc i o, with a feeling of pity; h o m u l l u s, with a feeling of scorn. (v. 133.)

HONESTAS, see *Virtus*. HONESTUS, see *Bonus*.

HONORARE; HONESTARE. H o n o r a r e means to honor any body, by paying him singular respect, and yielding him honor; but h o n e s t a r e means to dignify, or confer a permanent mark of honor upon any body.

HORNUS; HORNOTINUS. H o r n u s (χθεσινός) that which is of this year, as a poetical, h o r n o t i n u s, as a prosaic word.

HORRIDUS; HIRTUS; HIRSUTUS; HISPIDUS; ASPER. H o r r i d u s (from χέρσος, χορταῖος), is the most general expression for whatever is rough and rugged, from want of formation; h i r t u s and h i r s u t u s refer particularly to what is covered with rough hair, in opp. to what is soft and smooth; h i s p i d u s and a s p e r, to rough elevations, in opp. to what is level; h i s p i d u s, to the roughness that offends the eye; a s p e r, to the roughness that causes pain. Vell. P. ii. 4. describes Marius as *hirtus et horridus; hirtus* referring to his neglected exterior, *horridus*, to his rough nature. (vi. 161.)

HORROR, see *Vereri*.

HORTARI; MONERE. The h o r t a t i o (ὄρθωσις, ἐρέθω), addresses itself immediately to the will and resolution; whereas the m o n i t i o, almost entirely to the consciousness and judgment. The h o r t a t i o has always an action for its object; the m o n i t i o, only a representation, and by the medium of that representation, an action for its object. Sall. Jug. 60. *Monere* alii, alii *hortari*. Cat. 60. Nequidquam *hortere* . . . Sed ego vos quo pauca *monerem*, convocavi. Sen. Ep. 13. Nimium diu te *cohortor*, cum tibi *admonitione* magis quam *exhortatione* opus sit. Cic. Fam. x. 40. Si aut aliter sentirem, certe *admonitio* tua me reprimere, aut si dubitarem, *hortatio* impellere posset. (i. 164.)

Hospes; Adventor. Hospes is the guest who visits his friend; adventor, the person who puts up at his host's. Sen. Benef. i. 14. Nemo se stabularii aut cauponis *hospitem* judicat. (iv. 392.)

Hospes, see *Externus*.

Hospitium, see *Deversorium*.

Hostis, see *Adversarius*. Hucusque, see *Adhuc*.

Humanitas; Comitas; Facilitas; Civilitas. Humanitas is a virtue of universal extent, which, like the mental cultivation, proceeding from intelligence, ennobles the whole man in mind and heart, and gives to his nature mildness and philanthropy, as a principle; in opp. to *feritas;* comitas (from κόσμος) is a moral virtue, which, like affability, without respect to higher rank in society, treats every man as a man; facilitas, a social virtue, which, like complaisance, by forbearance and meeting the views of others, facilitates mutual intercourse in life, and makes it pleasant; civilitas, a political virtue, which, like the republican feeling of a prince, makes the specific difference between a ruler and his people unfelt, and treats his subjects as fellow-citizens. Nep. Milt. 8. In Miltiade erat quum summa *humanitas*, tum mira *comitas*, ut nemo tam humilis esset cui non ad eum aditus pateret. (v. 6.)

Humanitus; Humane; Humaniter. Humanitus means in a human manner, in objective reference to the exterior condition of man, namely, that of weakness and mortality, like ἀνθρωπείως, ἀνθρωπίνως; whereas humane and humaniter, in subjective reference to man's capacity for and propensity towards cultivation; *humane facere* is the result of moral cultivation, like φιλανθρώπως; *humaniter facere* is the result of social cultivation, like ἐπιεικῶς. (v. 8.)

Humare, see *Sepelire*. Humerus, see *Armus*.

Humidus, see *Udus*. Humus, see *Tellus*.

## I & J.

JACERE, see *Cubare*.

JACTATIO; GLORIATIO; OSTENTATIO; VENDITATIO. Jactatio and gloriatio have their foundation in vanity and self-complacency; jactatio is making much ado of one's excellencies and merits, and shows itself in words and actions, with the accessory notion of folly; gloriatio is talking big, proclaiming one's excellencies and merits, with the accessory notion of insolence; whereas ostentatio and venditatio have their foundation in a crafty calculation of the effect to be produced, and a disregard to truth; ostentatio would conceal real emptiness under a false show; venditatio would, by exaggerating one's excellencies, pass them off for greater than they are.

JACTURA, see *Amittere* and *Damnum*.

JACULUM, see *Missile*. JANUA, see *Ostium*.

ICERE, see *Verberare*.

IDONEUS; APTUS. Idoneus denotes a passive, aptus an active fitness for any thing. F. A. Wolf. Or, the *idoneus* is fitted by his qualifications, and, through outward circumstances, for any particular destination, like the ἐπιτήδειος; the aptus (from potis, potens), by his worth and adequacy, like ἱκανός. The *idoneus* is in himself inactive, and suffers himself to be employed for a particular purpose, for which he is qualified; the *aptus* himself engages in the business, because he is adequate to it. (iii. 276.)

IGNARUS, see *Cognitio*.

IGNAVIA; INERTIA; SEGNITIA; DESIDIA; SOCORDIA; PIGRITIA. 1. Ignavia denotes the love of idleness, in an ideal sense, inasmuch as the impulse to action distinguishes the more noble from the ordinary man, and gives him an absolute value; in opp. to *industria*, Tac. Ann. xii. 12. xvi. 18; whereas inertia denotes the love of idleness in a *real tangible* sense, inasmuch as activity makes a man a useful member of society, and gives him a relative value. Ignavia is inherent in the temperament, and has no inclination for action; inertia lies in the character and habits, and has no desire to work. A lazy slave is called *inors;* a person of rank, that passes his time in doing nothing, is *ignavus*. 2. Segnitia, desidia, socordia, and pigritia, are the faults of a too easy temperament. Segnitia (from sequi, ὄκνος,) wants rousing, or compulsion, and must be conquered, before it resigns its ease, in opp. to *promptus*. Tac. Agr. 21. Desidia (from sedere) lays its hands on its lap, and expects that things will happen of themselves; socordia is susceptible of no lively interest, and neglects its duties from want of thought, like phlegm; pigritia has an antipathy to all motion, and always feels best in a state of absolute bodily rest, like slothfulness. (iv. 212.)

IGNAVIA, see *Vereri*.

IGNOMINIA; INFAMIA; DEDECUS; PROBRUM; OPPROBRIUM. 1. Ignominia deprives one of political honor, which is independent of the reports circulated concerning a man, and is the consequence of an official denunciation, the justice of which is supposed; that of the censor, for example, like ἀτιμία; whereas infamia deprives one of moral honor, of one's good name, has a reference to public scorn, and is the consequence of shameless and dishonorable conduct, like δυσφημία. 2. Ignominia and infamia are abstract, and denote subjective states; dedecus and probrum are concrete, and denote, objectively, disgrace itself; dedecus is a deviation from the conduct that becomes a man of honor, from whom noble actions are expected; probrum is a stain on the morality of a man, from whom, at least, irreproachable conduct is expected. Dedecus is incurred generally in our public relations, by abjectness of spirit, etc.; probrum, in our private relations, by licentiousness, etc. 3.

P r o b r u m (from *προφέρω*) is reproach, as far as it can justly be made; o p p r o b r i u m, reproach, as far as it actually is made. In *probrum* the disgrace itself is more considered; in *opprobrium*, the open proclamation of it.

IGNOSCERE; VENIAM DARE. I g n o s c e r e (*ἀναγιγνώσκειν*) is a moral act; as, to forgive from one's heart; to forgive and forget, in opp. to retaining anger, *συγγιγνώσκειν*; whereas v e n i a m d a r e (*ἀνίαν* or *ἄνεσιν δοῦναι*) is a political act, to allow clemency to take place of justice, in opp. to punishment, like *μεθιέναι*. The friend *ignoscit* a person of his own rank; one who is of higher rank and greater power *veniam dat*. Cic. Man. 3. Illis imperatoribus laus est tribuenda quod egerunt; *venia danda* quod reliquerunt; comp. with Att. xvi. 16. *Ignosce* mihi quod eadem de re sæpius scribam. (v. 170.)

ILIA, see *Caro*. ILLICO, see *Repente*.

ILLUSTRIS, see *Celeber* and *Luculentus*.

IMAGO; SIMULACRUM; STATUA; SIGNUM. 1. I m a g o and s i m u l a c r u m denote, as the most general terms, any representation, whether a work of statuary or of painting; i m a g o (*μηχανή*) is allied to the original, as to a pattern, by a striking likeness of form, like *εἰκών*; s i m u l a c r u m is opposed to the original, as a real being, by a deceptive imitation of its form, like *εἴδωλον*; whereas s t a t u a, s i g n u m, and e f f i g i e s, are merely plastic works; t a b u l a and p i c t u r a, merely pictures. 2. S i m u l a c r u m and s t a t u a denote the copying of the whole figure, consequently, in the plastic art, standing figures; e f f i g i e s and i m a g o, principally the copying of the characteristic parts, namely, the features; e f f i g i e s, in staturary, as busts; i m a g o, in painting, as half-length portraits. Tac. Ann. i. 74. Alia in *statua* amputato capite Augusti *effigiem* Tiberii inditam. Hist. ii. 3. *Simulacrum* deæ *effigie* humana. Cic. Tusc. iii. 2, 3. Optimus quisque consectatur nullam eminentem *effigiem* (virtutis) sed adumbratam *imaginem* gloriæ. Signum (from sequo, to proclaim,) means any plastic work, in opp. to *tabulæ* and *picturæ*. Sal. Cat. 11. Cic. Orat. i. 35. Man. 14. Suet. Cæs. 47. Quintil. ix. 2. Cic. Verr. iv. 1; simulacrum means the sacred statue of a god, like *ἄγαλμα;* statua, the profane statue of a man, like *ἀνδριάς*. Cic. Cat. iii. 8. *Simulacra* deorum immortalium depulsa sunt et *statuæ* veterum hominum dejectæ. Tac. Ann. i. 73. Suet. Tib. 26. Cic. Verr. i. 22. Legati deorum *simulacra* venerabantur, itemque cætera *signa* et ornamenta lacrimantes intuebantur. (v. 237.)

Imber, see *Pluvia*.

Imitatio; Æmulatio; Certatio; Rivalitas; Simulatio. 1. Imitari means merely the effort to produce something like some other thing, without any accessory moral notion; æmulari (from *αἴσιμος*) means, at the same time, to do something which shall gain equal or superior consideration, honor, and approbation, when compared with the thing imitated. Imitatio has in view only the thing itself, and is generally moderate and laudable; æmulatio has in view chiefly the person, who is already in possession of the quality worthy of imitation, and always seems more or less a passion, which deserves praise or blame, according as it has its foundation in the lover of honor, or in immoderate ambition. Plin. Ep. vii. 30. Demosthenis orationem habui in manibus, non ut *æmularer* (improbum enim ac pæne furiosum) at tamen *imitarer* ac sequerer tantum. Comp. i. 2, 2. viii. 5, 13. Quintil. i. 2, 26. Cic. Tusc. iv. 8, 17. 2. The æmulus is at first behind his opponent, and strives for a time only to come up to him, and be like him; whereas the certator and concertator are already on a par with their opponent, and strive to outdo him, and conquer him. 3. Æmulatio contends for superiority in any art; rivalitas, only for preference in estimation. Cic. Tusc. iv. 26, 56. Illa vitiosa *æmulatione*, quæ *rivali-*

*tati* similis est, quid habet utilitatis? 4. Imitatio is an effort to become something which a man at present is not, but fain would be, and really can become; whereas simulatio, an effort to pass for something which a man properly and naturally is not, nor ever can be. Imitatio is the means of attaining to an actual or presumptive ideal; whereas simulatio remains for ever a mere counterfeit. (iii. 64.)

IMPAR, see *Æquus*. IMPENSÆ, see *Sumptus*.

IMPERARE, see *Jubere*.

IMPERTIRE; TRIBUERE; PARTICIPARE; COMMUNICARE. Impertire and tribuere denote giving a portion, without reference to any share, which the giver is to retain for himself; impertire means giving, as an act of free will and of goodness; tribuere, as an act of justice, or of judiciousness; whereas participare and communicare, the giving a share of something of which one also retains a share one's self; participare has generally the receiver for its object, who is to share a possession; but communicare, generally the thing shared, in the use of which the receiver is to have a share. (iv. 158.)

IMPIETAS, see *Delictum*. IMPIUS, see *Scelestus*.

IMPONERE, see *Fallere*.

IMUS; INFIMUS. Imum (superl. from in) denotes the lowest part of a whole; infimum (superl. from inferus) either the lowest part of all the parts, that is, the basis, or the lowest in a discrete magnitude, that is, a magnitude consisting of distinct parts. The *imum* is the lowest extremity of a part; then the *infimum*, the lowest part, with reference to the other parts. Cic. Rosc. Com. 7. Ab *imis* unguibus usque ad summum verticem: compare with Divin. i. 33. Ut ab *infima* ara subito anguis emergeret; and with N. D. ii. 20. Luna *infima* est quinque errantium. Further, imus denotes the lowest in a purely local relation; infimus, with the accessory notion of the lowest rank. (iv. 377.)

INAMBULARE, see *Ambulare*.

INANIS; VACUUS. Inanis (from ἰνάω) means the emptiness of that which has been full, but is now without its contents, in opp. to *plenus*, Cic. Orat. i. 9, 37. Parad. 6, 1. Brut. 8, 34; whereas vacuus denotes the emptiness of that which may be filled, but is at present vacant, in opp. to *occupatus*, Tac. Hist. iv 17; or to *obsessus*, Cic. N. T. i. 24. Tac. Ann. vi. 34. Jason post avectam Medeam genitosque ex ea liberos *inanem* mox regiam Æetæ *vacuosque* Colchos repetivit; that is, the palace deserted and desolate, and the people without a governor. Figuratively, inane means a nullity; vacuum, a vacancy. (i. 100.)

INCASSUM, see *Frustra*. INCASTUS, see *Inficetus*.
INCEDERE, see *Ire*. INCENDERE, see *Accendere*.
INCESTUS, see *Inficetus*. INCHOARE, see *Incipere*.
INCIENS, see *Prægnans*.

INCIPERE; ORDIRI; INCHOARE; CŒPISSE. 1. Incipere denotes the beginning, in opp. to the state of rest, which precedes and follows, consequently it is in opp. to *cessare* and *desinere*, *desistere*, *finire;* whereas ordiri (from ἔρδειν, radix,) in opp. to an advancement; consequently in opp. to *continuare*, and its intransitive *pergere;* lastly, inchoare (from conari) in opp. to ending and accomplishing, consequently in opp. to *perficere*, *consummare*, *peragere*, *absolvere*, etc. Cic. Off. i. 37. Ut *incipiendi* ratio fuerit, ita sit *desinendi* modus. Tusc. i. 49. Sen. Ep. 116. Plin. H. N. xi. 51. Plin. Pan. 54, 6. 57, 2. Ep. ix. 4. Quintil. xi. 3, 34. Tac. Agr. 32. Varro R. R. iii. 16. Apes cum evolaturæ sunt, aut etiam *inciperunt*, consonant vehementer. Cic. Fin. iv. 6. Hoc *inchoati* cujusdam officii est, non *perfecti*. Brut. 33. Liv. xl. 9. Plin. Ep. iii. 8, 7. Plin. H. N. x. 63. Tac. Dial. 33. Suet. Claud. 3. Cic. Fr. ap. Non. *Perge*, quæso, nec enim imperite exorsus es. 2. Cœpi has nearly the same words in opp. to it as *incipere* has; Sen. Cons. Polyb. 20. Quicquid *cœpit*, et desinit. Cic. Rab. Post. 2. Ovid, Ep. ix. 23; cœpi refers more to the action which is begun; in c e p i, more to the beginning which has been made. C œ p i is a sort of auxiliary verb; i n c e p i is emphatic; hence c œ p i has an infinitive, i n c i p e r e a substantive, for its object. Cic. Verr. v. 10. Quum ver esse *cœperat* (sed cum rosam viderat, tum ver *incipere* arbitrabatur), dabat se labori. (iii. 157.)

INCITARE; INSTIGARE; IRRITARE; INSTINCTUS. 1. I n c i t a r e (from ciere) denotes to urge an inactive person by merely bidding, speaking to, and calling upon him, to an action, generally of a laudable kind, synonymously with *hortari;* i n s t i g a r e (from στίξαι) to spur on a reluctant person by more vehement exhortations, promises, threatenings, to an adventurous act, synonymously with *stimulare;* i r r i t a r e (ἀνερεθίζω) to incite a quiet person by rousing his passions, ambition, revenge, to a violent action, synonymously with *exarcerbare.* Ter. And. iv. 2, 9. Age, si hic non insanit satis sua sponte, *instiga.* Lucr. iv. 1075. Et stimuli subsunt qui *instigant* lædere id upsum. 2. I n s t i g a t u s means spurred on by an exterior and profane power, by words, commands, etc.; i n s t i n c t u s means impelled by an interior and higher power, by inspiration, love, the voice of the gods. (iii. 314.)

INCLYTUS, see *Celeber.*

INCOLERE; HABITARE; INCOLA; INQUILINUS; COLONUS. 1. I n c o l e r e is transitive, as to inhabit; h a b i t a r e, intransitive, as to dwell. At the same time i n c o l e r e has reference to the country, to which a man, as a citizen or inhabitant, belongs; whereas h a b i t a r e has reference to the house, in which a man, as owner or tenant, has his stationary residence. 2. I n c o l a is the inhabitant, in opp. to the citizen, Cic. Off. i. 34, like μέτοικος; i n q u i l i n u s, the tenant, in opp. to the owner of the house, *dominus,* Cic. Phil. ii. 41, like σύνοικος; c o l o n u s, the farmer, in opp. to the landowner, Cic. Cæc. 32; something like θής.

INCOLUMIS, see *Salvus.* INCURIOSUS, see *Tutus.*

INCUNABULA, see *Cunae.*

INCURVUS, see *Curvus*. INCUSARE, see *Arguere*. INDAGARE, see *Quærere*. INDIGERE, see *Carere*. INDIGNARI, see *Succensere*. INDOLES, see *Ingenium*. INDULGERE, see *Concedere*. INDUSTRIA, see *Opera*. INEDIA, see *Fames*. INERTIA, see *Ignavia*. INFAMIA, see *Ignominia*. INFANS, see *Puer*. INFENSUS, INFESTUS, see *Adversarius*.

INFICETUS; INFACETUS; INCESTUS; INCASTUS. 1. Inficetus involves positive blame, a tasteless and heavy fellow; whereas infacetus only negative, a man not remarkable for wit. 2. In the same manner incestus denotes an incestuous person; whereas incastus only an unchaste person. Sen. Contr. ii. 13. (ii. 83.)

INFIDELIS, INFIDUS, see *Fidus*. INFIMUS, see IMUS. INFITIARI, INFITIAS IRE, see *Negare*. INFLAMMARE, see *Accendere*.

INFORTUNIUM; CALAMITAS; INFELICITAS; MISERIA. Infortunium and calamitas denote a single misfortune; infortunium, more as a vexatious accident, like malheur, for example, the loss of a purse, receiving blows, etc.; calamitas (from κολούω) a tragic accident, as the loss of a beloved person, of power, etc.; whereas infelicitas and miseria denote an unfortunate state of considerable duration; infelicitas, merely as the absence of success; miseria (from μυσαρός ?) as an actual, pressing state of affliction.

INGENIUM; NATURA; INDOLES. Ingenium and natura denote the disposition, as far as it constitutes the immovable ground of human individuality, and is susceptible of no change; ingenium, more with reference to the faculties of the mind, natura to the feelings of the heart; whereas indoles denotes the disposition, as far as it constitutes only the beginning of individuality, and is susceptible of improvement. (vi. 172.)

INGLUVIES, see *Faux*. INGREDI, see *Inire* and *Ire*.

INGRUERE, see *Irruere*. INIMICITIA, see *Odium*. INIMICUS, see *Adversarius*.

INIRE; INTRARE; INTROIRE; INGREDI. 1. Inire denotes almost always only a figurative entering, as to engage in any thing, for example, *inire pugnam*, *numerum*, etc.; whereas intrare, introire, ingredi, a literal entering; intrare is usually transitive, as to enter, and has an emphasis on the verbal part of the word; whereas introire is intransitive, as to step in, and has an emphasis on the adverbial part of the word. In the phrase *intrare curiam* one thinks more of the mere threshold, which is to be stepped over; in the phrase *introire* one thinks more of the four walls by which one is to be enclosed. 2. Intrare and introire suppose a space distinctly limited by walls, boundaries, marks; whereas ingredi supposes, generally, any limited space, for example, *viam*, *pontem*, etc. (iv. 521.)

INITIUM; PRINCIPIUM; PRIMORDIUM. 1. Initium denotes the beginning in an abstract sense, as the mere point from which a thing begins, in opp. to *exitus*. Cic. Rosc. Com. 13, 39. Tusc. i. 38. Brut. 34. Sen. Ep. 9. N. Q. iii. 29; whereas principium denotes the beginning as a concrete notion, as that part of the whole which stands before the other parts in things, and goes before them in actions, in opp. to *extremum*. Cic. Cleunt. 4. Orat. 61, 204. Cæc. 15, 44. In *initium* the beginning is made only with reference to time; in *principium* the foundation also is laid with reference to space. The *initium* is pushed out of the way by that which follows; the *principium* serves as a basis for that which follows. The *initia philosophiæ* are the rudiments over which the scholar goes, and which are superseded by further studies; the *principia* are the fundamental principles, to which he must always recur. Initio usually means "at the beginning, but differently (or, not at all) afterwards;" whereas principio means from the very beginning, and so onwards. 2. Priordium is a more solemn and comprehensive term than *principium*, and supposes a whole of great extent, the beginning of which is so far removed that one can distinguish a merely apparent beginning from the actual and primeval source and origin. (iii. 163.)

INJURIA, see *Contumelia*. INNOCENTIA, see *Virtus*.

INNUMERUS; INNUMERABILIS. Innumerus is a poetical and choice expression, like numberless, ἀνήριθμος; innumerabilis, a prosaic and usual expression, like innumerable, ἀναρίθμητος. (vi. 173.)

INOPIA, see *Paupertas*. INQUAM, see *Dicere*.

INQUILINUS, see *Incolere*.

INQUINARE, s. *Contaminare*. INSANUS, see *Amens*.

INSCENDERE, see *Scandere*. INSCIUS, see *Cognitio*.

INSIGNIS, see *Eminens*.

INSIMULARE, see *Arguere*.

INSOLENTIA, see *Superbia*. INSOMNIS, see *Vigil*.

INSOMNIUM, see *Somnus*. INSTIGARE, see *Incitare*.

INSTITUERE; INSTAURARE; RESTITUERE; RESTAURARE. Instituere means to establish a profane, instaurare, a sacred, or honorable, or generally important institution, such as sacrifices, sacred games, wars and battles. Hence is *instituere* itself a usual, *instaurare*, a solemn, select expression. In the same manner *restituere* is distinguished from *restaurare*. (iv. 300.)

INSTITUERE, see *Erudire*.

INSTRUCTUS, see *Præditus*.

INSUPER, see *Præterea*. INTEGER, see *Salvus*.

INTEGRARE, see *Iterum*.

INTELLIGERE; SENTIRE; COGNOSCERE. Intelligere denotes a rational discernment, by means of reflection and combination; sentire, a natural discernment, by means of the feelings, immediate images, or perceptions, whether of the senses or of the mind; lastly, cognoscere denotes an historical discernment, by means of the senses and of tradition. Sen. Ir. iii. 13. Quidni gauderet, quod iram suam multi *intelligerent*, nemo *sentiret?* Cic. N. D. iii. 24 Quare autem in his vis deorum insit, tum *intelligam* quum *cognovero.* (vi. 175.)

INTERCAPEDO; INTERRUPTIO; INTERPELLATIO; INTERLOCUTIO. Intercapedo and interruptio are any interruption of another person's business; intercapedo, a quiet, often even a benevolent interruption; interruptio, a violent and turbulent interruption; whereas interpellatio and interlocutio are only the interruption of a speech by speaking between; the *interpellator* will nearly prevent the speaker from going on; the *interlocutor* will make himself also heard in the midst of another's speech. (vi. 176.)

INTERDICERE, see *Vetare.* INTERDIU, see *Dies.*

INTERDUM, see *Nonnunquam.*

INTEREA; INTERIM. Interea refers to a business of some duration, which takes place in a space of time, as in the mean time; interim, to a momentary business, as in the midst of this. They have the same relation to each other, as a point of time to a space of time. Cic. Quint. 6. Hæc dum Romæ geruntur . . . Quintius *interea* de agro detruditur; that is, gradually; comp. with Fam. x. 12. *Interim* ad me venit Manutius noster. Tac. Ann. xi. 32. Non rumor *interea*, sed undique nuntii incedunt . . . Atque *interim* Ostiensem viam intrat. (iv. 271.)

INTEREMTOR, see *Homicida.* INTERESSE, see *Adesse.*

INTERFECTOR, see *Homicida.*

INTERFICERE; PERIMERE; INTERIMERE; NECARE; OCCIDERE; JUGULARE; OBTRUNCARE; TRUCIDARE; PERCUTERE. Interficere and perimere are the most general expressions for putting to death, in whatever manner, and from whatever motive, *fame, veneno, suspendio, ferro, suppliciis, dolo,* like κτείνειν; but interficere as a usual, perimere as an old, forcible, poetical expression. Interimere involves the accessory notion of privacy, as to remove out of the way; ἀναιρεῖν; n e c a r e, that of injustice, or, at least, cruelty, to murder, φονεύειν. Cic. Tusc. v. 20. Dionysius alterum jussit *interfici*, quia viam demonstravisset *interimendi* sui. Curt. ix. 7, 8. Boxum protinus placuit *interfici;* Biconem etiam per cruciatus *necari.* 2. O c c i d e r e, j u g u l a r e, t r u c i d a r e, o b t r u n c a r e, p e r c u t e r e, denote a sanguinary death-blow; o c c i d e r e means by cutting down, especially the business of the soldier in honorable open battle; j u g u l a r e, by cutting the throat or neck, or rather by a skilfully-directed thrust into the collar-bone, especially the business of the bandit, after the pattern of the gladiator, like σφάξαι; o b t r u n c a r e means to butcher, massacre, and cut to pieces, after the manner of the awkward murderer; t r u c i d a r e, to slaughter as one would a steer, after the manner of the blood-thirsty miscreant, who, without meeting with resistance, plays the hero on the defenceless; p e r c u t e r e, to execute, as a mere mechanical act, after the manner of the headsman, or other executioner of a sentence of condemnation, or, at least, of a death-warrant. Senec. Contr. iii. 21. Nec dominum *occidit*, nec domino venenum dedit. Hor. Ep. i. 2. Ut *jugulent* hominem, surgunt de nocte latrones. Sallust. Fr. Cæteri vice pecorum *obtruncantur;* so that you may see a mangled mass of limbs, as in the heap of slain in a battle. Tac. Hist. . . . Juberet *interfici;* offerre se corpora iræ; *trucidaret.* Cic. Cat. iv. 6. and Rosc. Am. 34. Cujus consilio *occisus* sit invenio; cujus manu *percussus* sit non invenio. (iii. 181.)

INTERITUS, see *Lues* and *Mors.*

INTERLOCUTIO, see *Intercapedo.*

INTERMITTERE; OMITTERE. I n t e r m i t t e r e means merely to leave off for a time, — in tempus mittere cum spe consilioque resumendi; whereas o m i t t e r e, to leave out altogether. Varro Fr. Studia tantum *intermittantur*, ne *omittantur.* (i. 3.)

INTERMORI, see *Mors.*

INTERPELLATIO, see *Intercapedo.*
INTERROGARE, see *Rogare.*
INTERRUPTIO, see *Intercapedo.*
INTESTINA, see *Caro.*
INTRARE, INTROIRE, see *Inire.*
INTUERI, see *Videre.* I NUNC, see *Agere.*
INVADERE, see *Irruere.* INVALETUDO, see *Æger.*

INVENIRE; REPERIRE; DEPREHENDERE; NANCISCI; ADIPISCI; CONSEQUI; ASSEQUI. Invenire donotes, as a general term, to find; reperire and deprehendere suppose a previous concealment of the thing found, and an intention, and pains employed on the part of the finder; but the *reperiens* (from πεπαρεῖν) merely discovers what was concealed, and now lies before his eyes, like ἀνευρεῖν; the *deprehendens*, what desired to hide itself, or to escape, and now is in his power. Tac. Ann. i. 74. Perniciem aliis ac postremo sibi *invenere:* comp. with xiv. 3. Cædes quonam modo occultaretur nemo *reperit.* 2. Invenire, reperire, deprehendere, imply a concealed object, which is discovered; whereas nancisci, adipisci, assequi, and consequi, only a distant object, which is reached; the *nanciscens* (from ἐνεγκέσθαι) arrives at his object with or without trouble, sometimes even against his wish, as to light upon; the *adipiscens* (from potiri) only by exertion, as to achieve; the *consequens* arrives at the object of his wish with or without assistance; the *assequens*, at the object of his endeavors, by means of exertion. Suet. Tib. 10. Titus ad primam statim mansionem febrim *nactus:* comp. with Dom. 15. Nero in *adipiscenda* morte manu Epaphroditi adjutus est. Cic. Att. x. 12. *Nactus* Curionem omnia me *consecutum* putavi. Rosc. Com. 4. Ut neque nihil neque tantum quantum postulavimus *consequamur.* In Cic. Mil. 11. Nihil dico quid resp. *consecuta* sit, nihil quod vos, nihil quod omnes boni; namely, by the death of Clodius, to which certainly nobody but Milo had contributed; *assecuta sit* could not be substituted; and, on the other hand, in Sen. Brev. 17. Operose *assequuntur* quæ volunt, anxii tenent quæ *assecuti* sunt; the word *consequuntur* would be too weak. Cic. Fam. i. 7, 10. Omnia quæ ne per populum quidem sine seditione *assequi* arbitrabantur, per senatum *consecuti* sunt (iii. 142.)

Invertere, see *Vertere.*

Investigare, s. *Quærere.*

Invicem, see *Vicissim.*

Invidia; Livor; Invidentia; Malignitas; Obtrectatio; Detrectatio. Invidia denotes looking askance, as a sign that a man grudges something to another, from moral or immoral motives, not *necessarily*, though especially, from self-love, like *ὑποψία*; whereas livor (from χλεύη, or χλοιά), denotes the self-tormenting envy, which poisons the whole soul, and deprives the body itself of its fresh healthy color. 2. Invidia is the usual term for envy, whether active, as that which a man harbors, or passive, as a state in which a man stands; whereas invidentia is a new term of Cicero's for the envy which a man harbors. 3. Invidia and livor denote envy as a temporary state, whereas malignitas as an habitual quality and disposition, in opp. to goodness of heart. The *invidus* and *lividus* grudge particular persons particular advantages, in particular cases; but the *malignus* wishes well to nobody but himself. 4. Invidia, livor, malignitas, denote a feeling and state of mind, whereas obtrectatio denotes an action, or manner of acting, proceeding from this feeling, inasmuch as it seeks to injure the envied person by dishonorable means, namely, detraction. *Obtrectatio* can scarcely be conceived as existing without *invidia*, but *invidia* may without *obtrectatio*, if the envious person is too cowardly to enter into conflict with the envied. 5. Obtrectatio supposes a rival, and has its origin in jealousy; whereas detrectatio only an enemy in general, and proceeds principally from antipathy. (iii. 65.)

Invidia, see *Odium.*

JOCUS, see *Ludus.*

IRASCI, see *Succensere*

IRE; MEARE; GRADIRI; INGREDI; INCEDERE; VADERE. 1. Ire and meare denote to go, in the most general sense, as motion from one place to another; ire especially applies to persons, in consequence of an act of the will, like ἰέναι; but meare (from ἀμεύω) especially to beasts, ships, rivers, stars, as mere mechanical motion, in which reason has no share, like φοιτᾶν; whereas gradiri and ingredi, incedere and vadere, with particular accessory notions in regard to the manner of going; gradiri and ingredi, in a quiet manner, and with a regular measured step, in opp. to *serpere, currere, stare;* Cic. N. D. ii. 47. Att. ii. 23, like βαδίζειν; incedere, in a proud manner, and with a graceful measured step, as in a procession and march, in opp. to *ambulare;* Sen. N. Q. vii. 31, like ἐμβαίνειν; and vadere (ἐλθεῖν?) with alacrity and a quick step, as in travelling, and in attacking the enemy, in opp. to repere? like χωρεῖν; Thuc. v. 70. 2. Ingressus means going in general; incessus a manner of going peculiar to the individual, and by which he is known as well as by his physiognomy. Ingressus is purely physical; incesus is moral and characteristic. (iv. 53.)

IRRIDERE, see *Ridere.*

IRRITARE, see *Incitare* and *Lacessere.*

IRRITUS, see *Frustra.*

IRRUERE; IRRUMPERE; INGRUERE; INVADERE. Irruere (εἰσρεῦσαι) means to rush on hastily and inconsiderately; irrumpere, to force one's way with violence; ingruere (ingravare) to press on with threats and importunity; invadere, to fall upon with boldness, and without regard to consequences. (vi., 180.)

ITER; VIA; TRAMES; SEMITA; CALLIS. 1. Iter and meatus denote the progress which a person makes, the going, the journey, in an abstract sense;

.ter, that which a rational being makes; meatus, that which a being void of reason and of will makes; via, the path on which a person goes, in a concrete sense. Hor. Od. iii. 2, 22. Virtus negata tentat *iter via*. Cic. Att. v. 14. *Iter* conficiebamus æstuosa et pulverulenta *via*. 2. Iter in a concrete sense, denotes a way which leads directly to a particular point, whether beaten and trodden, or not, like κέλευθος; whereas via (from the old word veha, way), a way, which, if not beaten, is the ordinary and usual way, like ὁδός. Cæs. B. G. vi. 27, means by *viarum atque itinerum duces*, the guides, who partly point out the frequented roads and paths, partly give information as to where they lead out. 3. Via and iter may be narrow or wide; whereas, trames, callis, and semita, denote only a narrow way or path; trames (τρῆμα) a by-road in a plain and town, by which one may arrive, partly in a shorter time, partly without being so much observed as in the open road, to a given point; semita (from secare, segmen), a foot-path, which often runs by the side of the high-road, like οἶμος; callis (from κέλευθος) a path over a mountain or through a wood, which is scarcely passable except for cattle, like ἀτραπός. Plaut. Cas. iii. 5, 42. De *via* in *semitam* degredi; and Liv. xliv. 43. Cic. Phil. xiii. 9, 19. Egressus est non *viis*, sed *tramitibus* paludatus; and Rull. ii. 35. Virg. Æn. ix. 383. Rara per occultos lucebat *semita calles;* and Curt. vii. 11, 2. (iv. 64.)

Iter facere, see *Proficisci*.

Iterum; Rursus; Denuo; De integro; Repetere; Integrare. 1. Iterum (ἕτερον) means, like δεύτερον, a second time; rursum or rursus, (revorsus) like αὖθις and πάλιν, again, once more; denuo (de novo) like νεόθεν, anew; de integro, like αὖθις ἐξ ὑπαρχῆς, quite afresh. Justin. xxi. 4, 6. Hoc consilio præventus *iterum* servitia concitat, statutaque *rursus* cædium die, quum *denuo* se proditum videret. 2. In the same manner pugnam iterare, Liv. vi. 32, means to join battle a second time; pugnam repetere, x. 36, to repeat the battle; pugnam renovare, Cæs. B. G. iii. 20, to renew the battle; and pugnam integrare, Liv. vii. 7, to begin the battle again quite from the beginning. Aut. Herenn. ii. 3, 47. Enumeratio est per quam colligimus et commonemus quibus de rebus verba fecerimus, breviter, ut *renovetur*, non *redintegretur* oratio. (i. 184.)

JUBERE; IMPERARE; PRÆCIPERE; MANDARE. Jubere (from ἰότης) means to bid, merely in consequence of one's own wish and will, in opp. to *vetare*, like κελεύειν; imperare, to command, by virtue of a military supreme authority, like ἄρχειν; præcipere to enjoin, by virtue of an authority as a teacher, etc., something like ἐντέλλεσθαι; mandare (from μήδομαι) to charge, in consequence of thorough confidence in a person, like ἐφίεσθαι.

JUCUNDUS, see *Gratus*. JUGULARE, see *Interficere*.

JUGUM, see *Mons*. JUMENTUM, see *Pecus*.

JURGIUM, see *Disceptatio*.

JUSJURANDUM; JURAMENTUM; SACRAMENTUM. Jusjurandum, and the later word juramentum, denote a civil oath, by which a man confirms or promises something; sacramentum denotes a military oath, by which the soldier solemnly pledges and binds himself not to forsake his standard. Liv. xxii. 38. Milites tunc quod nunquam antea factum erat, *jurejurando* a tribunis militum adacti jussu consulum conventuros neque injussu abituros; nam ad eam diem nihil præter *sacramentum* fuerat. And xxxv. 19. (vi. 183.)

JUVARE, see *Auxilium*.

JUVENIS, see *Puer*.

JUVENTA; JUVENTUS; JUVENTAS; JUVENALIS; JUVENILIS. 1. Juventa (from ζέω, ζόη), is the season of youth; juventus, a collection of young men; Juventas, the goddess of youth. 2. Juvenalis denotes youthful, either indifferently, as that which belongs to young people, or with praise, in opp. to the weakness of old age; whereas juvenilis donotes youthful, with the accessory moral notion of what is in conformity with the character of young people, mostly with blame, in opp. to the maturity of age. (v. 46.)

## L.

Labare; Titubare; Vacillare; Nutare. Labare (the ancient Gothic word, slipan, from λωφᾶν), denotes tottering, with reference to the whole body, which rests on no firm basis; titubare (from ταφεῖν τυφλός), with reference to the feet, which refuse their service, and stagger; vacillare (ἧκα) with reference to the upper part of the body, which wants its upright, steady, secure position; lastly, nutare (from νεύειν) with reference to the head, which seems ready to fall off. The *titubans* threatens to sink to the ground; the *vacillans*, to fall over. Titubatio betrays bodily weakness; vacillatio, want of external dignity, and a steady carriage. (iii. 62.)

Labes, see *Vitium*.

Labi; Cadere. Labi (from λείβω) means to fall, with reference to the point from which, and to the space through which, any one glides or sinks down, like ὀλισθεῖν; whereas cadere means to fall, with reference to the point which a man reaches by his fall, as to come to the ground, like πεσεῖν. Virg. Æn. vi. 310. *Lapsa cadunt* folia. Cic. Brut. 49. Quibus vitiis *labatur* aut *cadat* orator. (i. 128.)

Labor; Molestia; Ærumna. 1. Labor is the toil which requires strength and causes weariness, like πόνος; molestia (from μόλις, μαλερός,) the trouble which, by its greatness or unseasonableness, dispirits, like χαλεπότης; ærumna (αἰρομένη) the hardship that almost exceeds human strength, and bows down even the hero, like ταλαιπωρία; an antiquated, half poetical expression, in Cic. Fin. ii. 35, and Quintil. viii. 3, 26. Cic. Fin. v. 32. Ut ubi virtus sit resque magnæ et summe laudabiles virtute res gestæ, ibi esse miseria et *ærumna* non possit, tamen *labor* possit, possit *molestia*. (iv. 422.) 2. Laborare denotes, as an intransitive verb, to be in a state of trouble and toil; but elaborare, as a transitive verb, to produce something by trouble and toil. (i. 116.)

Labor, see *Opera*.

Lacerare; Laniare. Lacerare (from λακίς) denotes to tear by mere force, which may be done by the hands, claws, teeth; whereas laniare denotes the effect of a *cutting* instrument, under which *teeth* and *claws* may be included. Appul. Met. iv. p. 84. Morsibus *laceratus*, ferroque *laniatus*. Liv. xxii. 51. (v. 176.)

Lacertus, see *Ulna*.

Lacessere; Irritare; Sollicitare. 1. Lacessere (λακίζειν) means to excite the reason and will of another to resistance; irritare (ἀνερεθίζω) to provoke his feelings or passions to anger. Cic. Mil. 31. Ut vi *irritare* ferroque *lacessere* fortissimum virum auderet. 2. Lacessere means to excite, when a man in a coarse manner disturbs the peace of another; sollicitare, when a man disturbs the quiet of another in a refined manner. (v. 176.)

Lacrimare; Plorare; Flere; Lamentari; Ejulare; Deflere; Deplorare. 1. Lacrimare (from δάκρυ) denotes the physical consequence of a certain emotion of the mind, whether joyful or sorrowful, like δακρύειν, to shed tears; whereas plorare (from pluere) denotes a passionate expression of grief, like θρηνεῖν, to wail and cry. Between the two stands flere (φλέω) in opp. to *ridere*, partaking of the passionless feeling denoted by *lacrimare*, and of the feeling of grief denoted by *plorare*, like κλαίειν, to weep. Sen. Ep. 63. Nec sicci sint oculi amisso amico, nec fluant; *lacrimandum* est, non *plorandum*. 2. Lamentari and e j u l a r e denote a higher degree of *ploratus;* but l a m e n t a t i o (from κλαῦμα?) is, like κωκύειν, a longer continued wailing; e j u l a r e (from εἶα) a wailing interrupted by cries and sobs, like ὀλολύζειν. 3. P l o r a r e and f l e r e are intransitive verbs, as to weep; d e p l o r a r e and d e f l e r e transitive, as to deplore.

LACUNA; LACUS; STAGNUM; PALUS; ULIGO; LAMA; LUSTRUM. L a c u n a denotes, in poetical language, any standing water, from a sea to a pool; l a c u s and s t a g n u m are collections of standing water kept sound and fresh by their own springs, or by ebbing and flowing; l a c u s (liquere) is large enough to bring to mind the image of the open sea, in opp. to the main sea, like λίμνη; s t a g n u m, like a pond, not so large as to resemble a lake, in opp. to a stream, like τέναγος; whereas p a l u s and u l i g o are collections of standing water corrupted and grown foul; p a l u s (πλυδᾶν) is, like a marsh, a district covered with a surface of foul water, like ἕλος; u l i g o (from ὀλός) like a moor, a district soaked through with foul water. The p a l u s appears as a mass of water made thick by mud and bog-earth, in which a person may be drowned; u l i g o only as ground thoroughly soaked with water, in which a man may sink down. Lastly, l a m æ and l u s t r a denote standing waters of small extent; l a m a, a mere dirty and filthy puddle on a high road; l u s t r a, an ill-smelling and noisome quagmire in woods, etc. (v. 30.)

LÆDERE; VIOLARE; OFFENDERE. L æ d e r e denotes a physical injury, as to hurt; v i o l a r e, an injury to a person's rights, as to offer violence; o f f e n d e r e (from πένθος) an injury to a person's feelings, as to affront. L æ d e r e refers to whatever object is capable of receiving injury; v i o l a r e, to one that has a just claim to protection; o f f e n d e r e, to a rational and feeling being. Cic. Off. i. 28, 99. Justitiæ partes sunt non *violare* homines, verecundiæ non *offendere.*

Fin. iii. 11. Sen. Ir. iii. 18. Pleraque eorum propter quæ irascimur *offendunt* nos magis quam *lædunt.* Const. 4. Contumelia tantum delicatis gravis est, qua non *læduntur*, sed *offenduntur*. Ovid, Am. iii. 3, 31. Formosa superi metuunt *offendere* læsi. (iii. 138.)

LÆTARI, see *Gaudere.*

LÆVIS; GLABER; FRICARE; TERERE. 1. Lævis, levis, (λεῖος) means smooth, in opp. to rough and rugged, and gives a pleasant impression of elegance; whereas glaber (γλαφυρός) in opp. to rough, covered with hair, and grown up, and gives an unpleasant impression of deficiency. 2. Fricare means to rub, and thereby make smooth, like ψήχειν; whereas terere (τείρειν) means to rub, and thereby make less, like τρίβειν.

LÆVUS, see *Sinister.*

LAMA, see *Lacuna.*

LAMBERE; LINGERE. Lambere means to lick, inasmuch as one uses the tongue, like the hand, as an instrument to take hold of, or to touch anything, whether eatable, and possessing a taste, or not; lingere (λείχειν) when one uses the tongue as the organ of the sense of taste, in order to ascertain the flavor of any thing. Plin. H. N. xxxv. 7. Canem ex ære vulnus suum *lambentem;* compare with xxxi. 4. Pecoribus sal-datur *lingendus.* (v. 152.)

LAMENTARI, see *Lacrima.*

LANCEA, see *Missile.*

LANIARE, see *Lacerare.*

LANIENA; Macellum. Laniena is the butcher's stall, where the *lanius* sells slaughtered and ready-jointed meat; macellum, the market in which the *macellarius* sells all sorts of meat, including poultry and fish.

LAPIS, see *Saxum.*

LAQUEUS; FUNIS; RESTIS. 1. Laqueus (from ἑλίξαι) is the noose at the end of a rope; whereas funis and restis mean the rope itself; funis, a thicker rope, which is meant more for drawing and pulling, and on that account must have a proper length, like σχοῖνος; r e s t i s, a thinner rope, which serves more for fastening and hanging up, and therefore may be short, like σπάρτη. The trace by which the *equus funalis* is attached; the rope on which the *funambulus* balances himself; the tow which draws the boat to the ship, are never rendered in prose by *restis;* whereas the rope with which the self-murderer hangs himself, or the slave is whipped, or the garment girded, is seldom rendered by *funis*, unless the poet gives the preference to the last word as a more elevated term. (v. 36.) 2. R u d e n t e s are the sail ropes; r e t i n a c u l a, and o r æ, the cables or anchor-ropes; r e t i n a c u l a, as a more general and popular term; o r æ, o r a s, s o l v e r e, as more technical expressions in nautical language.

Largitio, see *Donum*.

Largus; Benignus; Liberalis; Munificus. L a r g u s means any one who makes a rich present, to whomever he makes it, and from whatever motive, in opp. to *parcus*. Ter. Heaut. iii. 1, 31; whereas b e n i g n u s, l i b e r a l i s, and m u n i f i c u s, denote virtuous qualities in the giver. The *benignus* follows a pure impulse of humanity, love towards his fellow men; the *liberalis*, a noble pride, or feeling of self-respect; the *munificus*, a princely feeling, or, at any rate, a feeling of laudable ambition. *Benignitas* gives richly, because it has no wish to possess and enjoy alone, like goodness; *liberalitas* gives as much as, and not less than, a man of noble sentiment believes suitable to his own rank and to another's merits, without scrupulous mercantile calculation, like a gentlemanly spirit; *munificentia* gives rather too much than too little, from the pleasure of making people happy, and causing an agreeable surprise, like generosity. (iv. 146.)

Larva; Persona. L a r v a (from lar?) is a caricatured, frightful mask; p e r s o n a (παρισῶν) an ingeniously formed, characteristic mask.

LASCIVUS, see *Petulans*.

LASSUS, see *Fatigatus*.

LATEBRA; LATIBULUM. Latebra is a retired or obscure place, where a man can conveniently remain concealed; latibulum, a lurking-hole, into which a man must creep like a beast. (vi. 189.)

LATRARE; GANNIRE; BAUBARI. Latrare means the hostile bark of a great dog, and, figuratively, to wrangle, like ὑλακτεῖν; whereas gannire, the harmless bark of a little dog, and, figuratively, to chatter, like κυνζᾶσθαι; lastly, baubari, the whining and howling of a dog, like βαΰζειν. Lucret. v. 1064—1070.

LATRO, see *Præda*. LATUS, see *Coxa*.
LECTUS, see *Cubile*. LEGARE, see *Mittere*.
LEMBUS, see *Navigium*. LEMURES, see *Spectrum*.
LENIS, see *Mitis*. LENTUS, see *Tardus*.

LEPIDUS; FACETUS; FESTIVUS; SALSUS; DICAX; CAVILLATOR. Lepos facetiæ, and festivitas, denote the harmless wit, which, like humor, is only opposed to seriousness, and is the attribute of a benevolent mind; lepos (from λέπω, λεπτός,) the lightest wit, in opp. to dull gravity; festivitas (from σπαθᾶν) the more cheerful sort of wit, in opp. to gloomy seriousness; facetiæ, the jocund wit, in opp. to sober seriousness; whereas sales, dicacitas, and cavillatio, denote the more pungent wit, which is a sign of an acute intellect; sales (ἅλες) the piquant wit, in opp. to what is flat and trivial, which aims at a point, whether others may be pleasantly or painfully affected by it; dicacitas (from δακεῖν) the satirical wit, which is exercised at the cost of others, yet so that the jest is still the principal aim,— the pain inflicted, only an accidental adjunct; cavillatio, the scoffing wit, in which the mortification of others is the principal aim, the jest only a means and unimportant form. Cic. Orat. 30. Demosthenes non tam *dicax* fuit, quam *facetus*. Est autem illud acrioris ingenii, hoc majoris artis. (v. 21).

LETUM, see *Mors*. LEVIS, see *Lævis*.
LIBARE, see *Sapor*. LIBENTER, see *Sponte*.
LIBERALIS, see *Largus*. LIBERALITAS, see *Donum*.

LIBERTUS; LIBERTINUS. Libertus means the freed-man, with reference to his master, in opp. to *servus;* Cic. Mil. 33. Sext. 35. Tac. G. 25. Suet Cæs 75; libertinus, with reference to his rank, in opp. to *civis* and *ingenuus*. Liv. x. 21. xli. 8. Suet. Cl. 54. Senec. Contr. iii. 21. Quærendus mihi gener erat aliquis *libertinus*; quid ergo? alieno potius *liberto?* Cic. Verr. i. 47. Trebonius fecit heredem *libertum* suum . . . Equiti Romano *libertinus* homo fit heres. Suet. Cl. 25. Tac. H. iii. 58. (vi. 194.)

LIBIDO, see *Cupido*.

LIBRA; PONDO. Libra pondo is the full expression, literally a balance in weight, that is, a scale, filled so as to balance a pound; libra (λεῖος) is a less definite expression, inasmuch as leaving out the *pondo*, makes it doubtful whether the balance itself be not understood; pondo is an elliptical expression, in which the principal notion, weight, is expressed, and the accessory notion left out; the scale that is filled must balance the definite weight. In a similar manner *operæ pretium est*, is distinguished from *operæ est*, and from *pretium est*. (vi. 195.)

LIBRARE; VIBRARE. Librare hastam (from λεῖος) means to raise the spear in a horizontal direction, in order to hurl it with greater force, and with a surer aim; vibrare (ὑφή) to brandish it backwards and forwards, or up and down, that is, either in a horizontal or perpendicular direction, in order to testify an eager desire for the combat. (v. 196.)

LIBURNA, see *Navigium*. LICET, see *Concessum est*.

LIGARE; VIERE; VINCIRE; NECTERE; OBLIGARE; OBSTRINGERE; DEVINCIRE. 1. Ligare and viere denote to bind, in order to prevent things falling asunder, synonymously with *copulare*, like δέειν; whereas vincire and nectere mean to fetter, in order to hinder free movement, synonymously with *coercere*, like δεσμεύειν. 2. Ligare is the general, viere (ὀχεῖν) the technical expression for binding fast, etc. 3. Obligare means to oblige by acts of kindness; obstringere, to oblige by benefits; devincire, to rivet to one's self by a lasting intimate connection. The *obligatus* feels himself bound by the conventional duties of social life; the *obstrictus*, by the duties of morality or religion; the *devinctus*, by the duties of piety. (iv. 282.)

LIMA; SCOBINA. Lima is a tool for filing smooth; scobina, for filing off. (vi. 197.)

LIMES, see *Finis.*

LIMUS, see *Lutum.*

LINGERE, see *Lambere.*

LINGUA; SERMO. Lingua denotes the speech of any, even the most uncultivated people, gens or natio, in as far as they possess proper words to express their notions; whereas sermo, only the speech of a cultivated people, populus, in as far as it is adapted for the expression of connected thoughts. Lingua is, like the tongue, born with us, and refers more to the mere gift of speech; sermo requires voluntary activity, and involves the rules of grammar and of style. Cic. Fin. i. 3, 10. Sæpe disserui Latinam *linguam* non modo non inopem, sed locupletiorem etiam esse quam Græcam: comp. with Off. i. 31. *Sermone* debemus uti eo, qui notus est nobis. (iv. 22.)

LINTER, see *Navigium.*

LIQUERE, see *Fluere* and *Constat.*

LIRA, see *Porca.*

LITERA; ELEMENTUM. Litera is a letter, as the most indivisible part of writing, like γράμμα; elementum (ἄλημα) as the most indivisible part of language or of knowledge in general, like στοιχεῖον. (iii. 210.)

LITERÆ; EPISTOLA; CODICILLI. Literæ is the most general expression for a letter; epistola is one directed to a distant friend, and sent by a messenger;

c o d i c i l l i, an address to one within the same walls, as a note. Sen. Ep. 55. Adeo tecum sum ut dubitem an incipiam non *epistolas* sed *codicillos* tibi scribere. Cic. Fam. vi. 18. Simul accepi a Seleuco tuo *literas;* statim quæsivi e Balbo per *codicillos* quid esset in lege. (vi. 198.)

LITERÆ; ARTES; DOCTRINÆ; DISCIPLINÆ. L i t e r æ and a r t e s denote the sciences as the general objects of scientific education; l i t e r æ, in a narrower sense, only as literature, or the sciences so far as they are laid down in books, and, together with other branches of knowledge, enrich the mind, and are the means of sharpening the understanding and forming the taste; a r t e s (ἀρεταί?) in the widest sense, so far as the knowledge of them immediately attests intellectual cultivation, and readiness in the practical application of the sciences; whereas d o c t r i n æ and d i s c i p l i n æ denote particular parts of the general objects of knowledge formed into systems; d o c t r i n æ, more the speculative and abstract parts of philosophical and learned education; d i s c i p l i n æ, more the practical parts, that are conducive to the purposes of life. (v. 269.)

LITIGATIO, see *Disceptatio.* LITUS, see *Rpia.*

LIVOR, see *Invidia.* LOCUPLES, see *Divitiæ.*

LOCUS; TRACTUS; REGIO; PLAGA. L o c u s (λόχος) denotes a space, as a single point, like τόπος; t r a c t u s (from trahere) as a line, with the notion of extension to a distance, as a tract of country, something like κλίμα; r e g i o (from ῥῆχος, ὄρχος,) as a circle, with the included notion of the environs, like the surrounding country, χῶρος; p l a g a (πλάξ) principally as a surface or plain.

LONGÆVUS, see *Vetus.* LONGE, see *Procul.*

LOQUAX, see *Garrire.* LOQUI, see *Fari, Dicere.*

LUCERE; FULGERE; SPLENDERE; NITERE; RENIDERE; CORUSCARE; MICARE; RADIARE. 1. L u c e r e, f u l g e r e, s p l e n d e r e, n i t e r e, denote a steady and continued brightness; f u l g e r e (φλογεῖν) through a glaring light, or a dazzling fiery color, like φλέγω; lucere (from λευκός) through a beneficial light, and a soft fiery color, like φαίνω, φέγγω; splendere (from φάλανθος) as the consequence of a clear and pure light, in opp. to *sordere*; Cic. Sext. 28. Sen. Ep. 5. Martial, Ep. ii. 36. Tac. A. i. 84. Suet. Aug. 35; like λάμπω; nitere (from νίζω) as the consequence of humidity, oiling or washing, to glisten, in opp. to *squalere*. Cic. Fin. iv. 3. Orat. 32. Sen. Q. N. i. 17. Quintil. ii. 5, 23; like στίλβω. 2. Whereas coruscare, micare, radiare, mean an unsteady, tremulous light; coruscare (from κορύσσω) to shine like forked lightning; micare, to sparkle, like metal placed in the sun; radiare, to beam, like the shooting rays of the sun. Cic. Cat. ii. 3. qui *nitent* unguentis, qui *fulgent* purpura. Auct. ad Herenn. iv. 33. Tantus erat in armis *splendor*, ut solis *fulgor* obscurior videretur. Plin. H. N. xxxvii. 2. *Splendor* murrhinis sine viribus: *nitor*que verius quam *splendor*; for *splendor* denotes brightness, with regard to its intensity; *nitor*, with regard to its beauty. Auct. ad Herenn. iv. 50. Gemmæ *nitore* et auri *splendore*: hence, figuratively, splendor denotes pomp; nitor, only neatness. (ii. 76.)

Lucerna, see *Candela*.

Lucrum; Emolumentum; Quæstus; Compendium. Lucrum and emolumentum denote gain, in any condition of life; lucrum (from lucar, locare,) gain deserved and earned by one's self, in opp. to *damnum;* Cic. Fin. v. 30, etc.; like κέρδος; emolumentum (from molere) gain falling to one's share without any exertion of one's own, in opp. to *detrimentum;* Cic. Fin. i. 16, like ὠφέλημα; whereas quæstus and compendium denote gain in the course of trade; quæstus, rather the steadily continued gains of a regular occupation, *earnings*, in opp. to *sumptus;* Cic. Parad. vi. 3. Hor. Sat. i. 2. 19, like χρηματισμός; compendium, more a single gain of considerable amount, in opp. to *dispendium*. (v. 257.)

LUCTUS, see *Dolor*.

LUCULENTUS; ILLUSTRIS. Luculentus means, what may be seen, and need not shun the light, synonymously with *probabilis;* whereas illustris (from λεύσσω) what makes itself seen, attracts the eye, and spreads its rays, synonymously with *excellens*. Hence *luculentus* never implies emphatic praise. Cic. Off. iii. 14, 60. Hoc quidem satis *luculente*, that is, it is probable enough. And Fin. ii. 5, 15. Cum Græce ut videor *luculenter* sciam, without presumption; just like, sic satis. (ii. 84.)

LUCUS, see *Silva*.

LUDIO, see *Actor*.

LUDUS; SCHOLA. Ludus is a lower school for boys, who are compelled to learn; schola, a higher school for youths and men, who wish to learn. Ludus supposes *discipulos*, *ludi-magistrum*, and school-discipline; schola supposes *auditores*, *doctorem*, and academical regulations. (vi. 203.)

LUDUS; LUSUS; LUDICRUM; JOCUS. 1. Ludus (from λοίδορος) denotes play in an objective sense, inasmuch as it is at hand for a man's entertainment; whereas lusus, in a subjective sense, inasmuch as a man carries it on and produces it himself; further, ludus denotes play, as a means of recreation, in opp. to exertion; lusus, as a childish, useless pastime, in opp. to real business. Plin. Ep. ix. 33. 3. Pueri quos otium *ludus*que sollicitat: comp. with ix. 25. *Lusus* et ineptias nostras legis. Or, Cic. Flacc. 5, 12. Græci quibus jusjurandum *jocus* est, testimonium *ludus;* that is, to whom it is a mere trifle to bear false witness; compare with Sen. Contr. i. 2. Piratas . . . quibus omne fas nefasque *lusus* est; that is, to whom the distinction between right and wrong is a mere sporting with words. 2. The plur. ludi assumes the special meaning of public spectacles, and in this sense has a singular peculiar to itself in the word *ludicrum*. 3. Ludus and lusus have more a negative character, as mere pastimes and amusements, as a guard against ennui; whereas jocus more a positive character, as an utterance of humor and wit. The *ludens* wishes merely to be free from exertion, to do nothing serious, and to amuse himself; the *jocans* will be as active at the command of mirth, as others at the command of seriousness. (ii. 33.)

LUES; CONTAGIUM; PESTILENTIA; PESTIS; PERNICIES; EXITIUM; INTERITUS; EXITUS. 1. Lues (from λοιμός) denotes epidemic disease, as proceeding from an impure morbid matter; contagium (from contingere? or κατατήκειν?) as contagious; pestilentia, as a disease reigning in the land, and especially as a pestilence. Sall. Cat. 10. Post ubi *contagia* quasi *pestilentia* invasit. Plin. H. N. xxiii. 28. Laurus folia *pestilentiæ contagia* prohibent. Lucan. vi. 86. Fluidæ *contagia* pestis. 2. Pestis is used for pestilence itself only by the poets; otherwise it denotes, like *exitium* and *pernicies* (from necare), that which destroys in general, without reference to disease; but pestis is, according to rule, used as a concrete, exitium and pernicies as abstract terms. Sen. N. Q. iii. pr. Philippi aut Alexandri . . . . qui *exitio* gentium clari non minores fuere *pestes* mortalium quam inundatio. 3. Pernicies has an active meaning, and denotes the destruction of a living being by murder; whereas exitium has a passive meaning, and denotes the destruction even of lifeless objects by annihilation; lastly, interitus has, like *exitus*, a neutral meaning, the destruction of living or lifeless objects by decay. Tac. Ann. xiv. 65. Poppæa non nisi in *perniciem* uxoris nupta; postremo crimen omni *exitio* gravius: and ii. 68. Cic. Cat. iv. 3. Cum de *pernicie* populi Romani, *exitio* hujus urbis cogitarit. Rull. ii. 4, 10. Extremi *exitiorum exitus*. 4. Exitium is a violent, exitus a natural end. Cic. Rull. ii. 4, 10. Qui civitatum afflictarum perditis jam rebus extremi *exitiorum* solent esse *exitus*, is, as it were, the last breath of a state that is being destroyed; like Verr. v. 6, 12 *Exitus* exitiales. (ii. 62. iii. 176.)

LUMEN; LUX. Lumen (λευσσόμενον) is a luminous body, like φέγγος; l u x (λευκή) a streaming mass of light, like φάος. Cic. Fin. iii. 14, 45. Ut obscuratur et offunditur *luce* solis *lumen* lucernæ. Curt. viii. 2, 21. Sed aditus specus accipit *lucem;* interiora nisi allato *lumine* obscura sunt. Cic. Acad. iv. 8, 28. Si. ista vera sunt, ratio omnis tollitur quasi quædam *lux lumen*que vitæ; that is, reason alone is in itself bright and light, and at the same time spreads brightness and light over life. Also, in a figurative sense, l u m e n denotes distinction, l u x only clearness. Cicero (Man. 5.) calls Corinth, Græciæ totius *lumen*, but Rome (Catil. iv. 6.) *Lucem* orbis terrarum; Corinth is compared to a glimmering point of light; Rome is distinguished as that city in comparison with which all other cities lie in darkness. (ii. 66.)

LURIDUS, see *Luteus.*

LUSTRUM, see *Lacuna.*

LUSUS, see *Ludus.*

LUTEUS; GILVUS; HELVUS; FLAVUS; LURIDUS. L u t e u s (from λωτός) denotes a decided yellow, as the yolk of an egg; g i l v u s, (ἀγλαός) and h e l v u s, a fainter reddish yellow, like that of honey; f l a v u s and l u r i d u s, a lighter whitish yellow; f l a v u s (from φλεύω) a glossy beautiful yellow, like that of light auburn hair; l u r i d u s (from χλωρός) a wan unpleasant yellowishness, like that of pale death.

LUTUM; LIMUS; CŒNUM; SORDES; SQUALOR; PÆDOR; SITUS; STERCUS; FIMUS; OLETUM; MERDA. 1. L u t u m, l i m u s, c œ n u m, all denote impurity, as a substance, and as of a wet sort; l u t u m (from λύϑρον) is the dirt of the streets or roads, like πηλός; l i m u s (λειβόμενος) the mud of a river, like ἰλύς; c œ n u m (from cunire) the mire of a moor or morass, like βόρβορος. Tac. Ann. i. 63. Cætera *limosa*, tenacia gravi *cœno* aut rivis incerta erant; whereas s o r d e s, s q u a l o r, p œ d o r, s i t u s, denote impurities as a form, and of a dry sort; s o d e s (from ἄρδα) in opp. to *splendor*, through indigence, or niggardliness and vulgarity, for example, clothes dirty from long wear, like ῥύπος; s q u a l o r (from σκέλλω) in opp. to *nitor*, through want of civilized habits, and of delicacy in the senses, for example uncombed hair, like αὐχμός; p æ d o r (from ψοῖθος) in opp. to *munditiæ*, through neglect of the person, for example, through *pædiculos*, vermin, itch, etc., like πίνος; s i t u s (ἄσις) in opp. to *usus*, in consequence of long disuse, for example, through mould, rust, etc., like ἄζη. Hence the different forms of the adjectives lutosus, limosus, cœnosus, that is, full of lutum, etc.; and of sordidus, squalidus, pædidus, that is, resembling sordes, etc., and in circumlocution, *oblitus luto, limo, cœno*, but *obsitus sordibus, squalore, pædore.* 2. S t e r c u s (from τάργανον) denotes in dung its disgusting sense, as filth, like κόπρος; whereas f i m u s (opimus ?) in its useful sense, as manure. 3. For offensive excrements c œ n u m is the most general; o l e t u m denotes human; m e r d a (μίνθος) animal excrements.

LUX, see *Lumen*.

LUXUS; LUXURIA. L u x u s denotes luxury as an act or as a condition, and sometimes even objectively, as an object of luxury; whereas l u x u r i a, always subjectively, as a propensity and disposition, as the desiderative of *luxus*. Sen. Ir. i. 11. Animis delicias, *luxus*, opes ignorantibus: and further on; Opinionem *luxuriæ* segnitiæque. Sall. Cat. 13. Romani famem aut si tim . . . . *luxu* antecapere; that is, by the arts of lux ury: compare with Jug. 90. *Luxuria* atque ignavia pessimæ artes: that is, as proceeding from voluptuousness. (ii. 23.)

LYMPHATUS, see *Amens*.

## M.

MACELLUM, see *Laniena*.

MACERIA, see *Murus*.

MACER, see *Exilis*.

MACULA, see *Vitium*.

MADIDUS, see *Udus*. MAGISTER, see *Doctor*.
MAGNOPERE, see *Perquam*.

MAGNUS; GRANDIS; AMPLUS; INGENS; IMMANIS; VASTUS. 1. Magnus, grandis, and amplus, denote a becoming greatness; ingens, immanis, and vastus, an overwhelming greatness. Sen. Ir. i. 16. Nec enim *magnitudo* ista est, sed *immanitas*. Cic. Læl. 26. 2. Magnus (from μέγα, mactus,) denotes greatness without any accessory notion, in opp. to *parvus*, like μέγας; whereas grandis, with the accessory notion of intrinsic strength and grandeur, in opp. to exilis, Sen. Ep. 100; subtilis, Quintil. xii. 10, 58; tumidus, in the same book, § 80; minutus, Cels. ii. 18; exiguus, Quintil. xi. 3, 15; lastly, amplus (adj. from ambi) with the accessory notion of comeliness, and of an imposing impression. 3. Ingens (ἄγονος) denotes excessive greatness merely as extraordinary, like ἄπλετος; immanis (ἀμήχανος) as exciting fear, like πελώριος; vastus (from vagus?) as wanting regularity of form like ἀχανής. (iii. 228.)

MALA; MAXILLA; GENA. 1. Mala (from μέμαχα, or from Mandere) denotes the upper, maxilla, the under jaw. Cels. Med. viii. 1. 2. Mala denotes the cheek as a usual expression, and in a merely physiological sense; gena (from γένυς) as a more ancient and select expression, and with an *æsthetic* reference. (vi. 208.)

MALEDICTUM; PROBRUM; CONVICIUM. Maledictum is any utterance of what is injurious to another, whether to bring him ill-luck by cursing, or disgrace by verbal injuries, like κακηγορία; probrum (from προφέρω) an invective, like ὄνειδος, consisting of attacks and assertions wounding the honor of another; convicium (καταικία) the abusive word, like λοιδορία, consisting of single words and appellations wounding the honor of another. For example, *fur!* is a *convicium*, *fur es*, a *probrum*; each of them a *maledictum*. (iv. 198.)

MALEFACTUM, MALEFICIUM, see *Delictum*.

MALITIA; MALIGNITAS; MALEVOLENTIA; MALUS; NEQUAM; PRAVUS. 1. Malitia denotes the baseness which shows itself in the love of lying and deceiving, from want of conscience; malignitas, the ill-will which grudges good to another, and wishes it only to itself, from pure selfishness; malevolentia, the ill-will which wishes evil to another rather than good, from personal aversion. Malitia is a way of thinking and acting deserving of punishment as endangering the security of society; malignitas is a despicable disposition, which implies the want of philanthropy; lastly, malevolentia, a detestable quality, as connected with deriving pleasure from the misfortunes of others. 2. Malus homo is a morally bad man, but nequam a good-for-nothing man, whose faultiness shows itself in aversion to useful labor, and a propensity to roguish tricks, in opp. to *frugi*. Plaut. Pseud. i. 5. 53. Cic. Font. 13. Or. ii. 61. Fin. ii. 8. Sen. Contr. ii. 21; pravus (περαῖος) a man whose character has taken a vicious direction, in a physical, or intellectual, or moral point of view in opp. to *rectus*. Plaut. Bacch. iii. 3, 8. Cic. Fin. ii. 8. Acad. i. 10. Quintil. viii. 3, 48. Nec parricidam *nequam* dixeris hominem, nec meretrici forte deditum *nefarium;* quod alterum parum, alterum nimium est. Afric. ap. Gell. vii. 11. (i. 62.)

MALIGNITAS, see *Invidia*.

MAMMA; MAMILLA; UBER; PAPILLA. 1. Mamma and uber denote the breast in the female body; mamma (μάμμη) denotes the visible breast as a fleshy part of the body, particularly of a female body; whereas uber (οὐαρόν) the nourishing breast as filled with milk, which is only found in the female body, like οὖθαρ. 2. Papilla and mamilla denote the nipples of the breast, common to the male and female; papilla (redupl. of πάλλα) with reference to their spherical shape, without distinction of the sexes, like μαζός; mamilla (redupl. from ἀμέλγω) with reference to their adaptation for suckling, and therefore belonging only to the female sex, like τίτθη, and teats. (iv. 133.)

MANARE, see *Fluere*. MANCIPARE, see *Vendere*.

MANCIPIUM, see *Servus*. MANDARE, see *Jubere*.

MANE; CREPUSCULO; DILUCULO. Mane (from μηνύειν) denotes in the morning, in the early course of the bright day, in opp. to the night, and the forenoon hours, like ὄρθρῳ; crepusculo (from creperus, κρύψαι,) in the twilight, in opp. to the bright day; diluculo, in the twilight, in opp. to the dark night, like λυκόφως.

MANERE; MORARI; TARDARE; DETINERE. 1. Manere (from μένειν) denotes remaining, in opp. to going away; whereas morari (from βραδύς) denotes tarrying, as an interruption of motion, in opp. to going forwards. Cic. Sen. 23. *Commorandi* natura deversorium nobis, non habitandi dedit. Hence in Tac. H. ii. 48. Irent propere neu *remanendo* iram victoris asperarent,— the reading *remorando* deserves the preference. 2. Morari *aliquem* means, to prevail upon any one to stay of his own free will by proposing conditions, like διατρίβειν; tardare, to prevent a person's hastening on his way by opposing difficulties, like βραδύνειν; detinere, to hinder him from going forwards by force, like κατέχειν. Tardare has generally an action for its object[1]; detinere, a person; morari, either. (iii. 298.)

MANERE; EXSPECTARE; PRÆSTOLARI; OPPERIRI. 1. Manere (from μένειν) denotes a mere physical act to remain in a place, till something has happened; whereas exspectare, præstolari, and opperiri, denote a mental act, to wait for, to wait in conscious expectation of some event, or of some person. 2. Exspectare denotes waiting for, almost as a mere mental act, as a feeling, without practical reference or ac-

[1] [But: *nos* Etesiæ valde *tardarunt.*]

cessory meaning; whereas præstolari and opperiri, with the accessory notion that the person waiting intends, after the arrival of the object waited for, to do something. 3. The præstolans (from παραστέλλεσθαι) waits for a person in order to perform services for him; the opperiens, for an occurrence, in order not to be taken by surprise. The præstolans stands in subordinate relation to the person waited for; the opperiens, in co-ordinate, whether as friend or foe. Lastly, præstolari is a prose expression; opperiri, a poetical, or at least, a select expression. For the German distinction between *warten* and *harren*, the former denoting calm, passionless waiting for, the latter, eager, impatient longing for, the Latins have no correspondent synonymes. (iii. 57.)

MANES, see *Spectrum*. MANICÆ, see *Vincula*.

MANIFESTO, see *Aperire*. MANNUS, see *Equus*.

MANSUETUDO; CLEMENTIA. Mansuetudo (from manui suetus) is the mildness and magnanimity of a private individual, who does not take vengeance for a mortification suffered, in opp. to *iracundia;* whereas clementia (from ἀκαλός, κηλεῖν, and mens,) the mercifulness and humanity of the ruler, or the judge, who does not inflict upon the malefactor the punishment which he deserves, in opp. to *crudelitas*. Sen. Clem. 2. Cic. Lig. 3. Att. viii. 9. Plin. Pan. 3. (v. 11.)

MANSUETUS, see *Cicur*.

MANUBIÆ, see *Præda*.

MARE; ÆQUOR; PONTUS; PELAGUS. 1. Mare (from μύρω) denotes the sea, as a mass of water, in opp. to *terra* and *aër*, like ἅλς, θάλασσα; æquor, pelagus, and pontus, with reference to its dimensions; æquor and pelagus, with reference to its horizontal dimension, the surface of the sea, like πέλαγος, whence πελαγίζειν, to float on the sea; pontus (from πεσεῖν, πίτνειν,) with reference to its perpendicular dimension, the depth of the sea; like πόντος, whence ποντίζειν, to sink into the sea. Colum. viii. 17. Ut in solo piscinæ posita libella septem pedibus sublimius esset *maris æquor.* Ovid, Met. ii. 872. Mediique per *æquora ponti* fert prædam. 2. Æ q u o r (from æquus) denotes the surface of the sea in a merely physical sense; whereas p e l a g u s (from πλάξ) with the accessory notion of its great extent and immensity. (iv. 72.)

MARGO; ORA. M a r g o (ἀμέργων) denotes the brink, the natural boundary of a surface, considered almost as a mere mathematical line, and only improperly as including an exterior portion of the surface; whereas o r a (ὦα, οὖρος, ὅρος) denotes the brim, or border, the artificial edging of a surface, generally for the sake of ornament, and therefore necessarily including a certain portion of the surface. Hence we say, *ora togæ,* but not *margo;* and, on the other hand, *margo fluminis* and *ripæ,* if the mere line of shore is meant, without any portion of the bank. (iii. 212.)

MARITA, see *Femina.* MAS, see *Homo.*

MATRIMONIUM, see *Conjugium*

MAXILLA, see *Mala.* MEARE, see *Ire.*

MEDERI; MEDICARI; SANARE; MEDICAMEN; MEDICINA; REMEDIUM. 1. M e d e r i and the poetical word m e d i c a r i (μέδειν) denote healing, as the act of the physician, who heals with humane sympathy, judgment, and art, synonymously with *curare,* like ἰᾶσθαι; s a n a r e, as the effect of the physic, which in a mechanical way makes the sick well again, synonymously with *restituere,* like ἀκεῖσθαι. 2. M e d i c a m e n t u m means a remedy, with reference to its material substance, as it is prepared by the apothecary, like φάρμακον; m e d i c i n a, with reference to its healing virtues, as ordered by the physician; each with reference to an illness; whereas r e m e d i u m denotes a remedy for any of the evils to which we are subject, like ἄκος. Cic. N. D. ii. 53. *Medicamentorum* salutarium plenissimæ terræ: comp. with Divin. ii. 51. Quam a medico petere *medicinam.* (v. 198.)

Meditari, see *Cogitare.*

Medius; Modicus; Mediocris. Medius (μέσος) is purely local, in the middle, in opp. to the extremes; modicus denotes quantity, with reference to number and magnitude, as moderate, in opp, to over-measure; mediocris denotes quality, with reference to worth, as middling, in opp. to distinction; hence *modicæ facultates* and *mediocre ingenium* are identical. Cic. Rep. ii. 31. Haud *mediocris* vir fuit, qui *modica* libertate populo data facilius tenuit auctoritatem principum. (v. 202.)

Medius dies, see *Meridies.*

Membrum; Artus. Membrum (redupl. of μέρος) denotes a limb of the body itself, like μέλος and κῶλον; whereas artus (ῥέϑος, ἄρϑρον,) properly only a joint of a limb, like ἄρϑρον and ἅψος. Senec. Contr. ii. 13. Differebatur distortis *articulis;* nondum in sua *membra artus* redierant. Virg. Æn. v. 422. Magnos *artus membrorum.* Quintil. Decl. ult. Ut per singulos *artus membra* laxaret. Further, membra denotes the limbs collectively, including the head and trunk, as parts of the body; whereas artus only the extremities, which *per commissuras* with the body, properly so called, namely, the head and trunk, hang together. Gell. N. A. i. 14. (iv. 150.)

Meminisse; Reminisci; Recordari. Meminisse denotes remembrance as a state of mind, like μεμνῆσϑαι, in as far as one has retained something in memory, without ever having forgotten it, like *memorem esse;* whereas reminisci and recordari denote remembrance as an act of the mind, in as far as one again brings to one's mind what had already been driven out of one's thoughts, like ἀναμιμνήσκεσϑαι. But reminisci denotes this act of the mind as momentary, like *in memoriam revocare;* whereas recordari denotes it as of some duration, like *revocata in memoriam contemplari.* Cic. Lig. 12, 35. Equidem, cum tuis omnibus negotiis interessem, *memoria teneo,* qualis

T. Ligarius, quæstor urbanus, fuerit erga te et dignitatem tuam; sed parum est, me hoc *meminisse;* spero etiam te, qui oblivisci nihil soles, nisi injurias, quoniam hoc est animi, quoniam etiam ingenii tui, te aliquid de hujus illo quæstorio officio cogitantem, etiam de aliis quibusdam quæstoribus *reminiscentem recordari.* This passage shows, that *memoria tenere* is only a circumlocution for *meminisse:* there is another passage where *recordari* is employed as the consequence of *reminisci,* but there is no instance of the converse; for *reminisci* and *recordari* have the same relation to each other as *intueri* and *conspicere.* Cic. Sen. 21. Pueri . . . . ita celeriter res innumerabiles arripiunt, ut eas non tum primum accipere videantur, sed *reminisci* et *recordari:* he might have added, Quæ non satis *meminerint,* sed in aliquantum temporis obliti sint. Tusc. i. 24, 58. Animus, quum se collegit atque recreavit, tum agnoscit illa *reminiscendo;* ita nihil aliud est discere, quam *recordari.* Senec. Ep. 100. Magis *reminiscor* quam teneo. (i. 166.)

MENDA, MENDUM, see *Vitium.*

MENDICITAS, see *Paupertas.* MENS, see *Anima.*

MERACUS, see *Purus.* MERCARI, see *Emere.*

MERCENARII; OPERARII; OPERÆ. Mercenarii mean laborers as far as they work, not for their own interest, but for pay, in opp. to the proprietor, who hires their services; whereas operarii and operæ, as far as they undertake to perform for others, a mere mechanical work, in opp. to the principal or director, who gives out the plan. Mercenarii refer to the motive; operarii, to the art employed being of an inferior sort. (vi. 217.)

MERCES, see *Præmium.* MERCIMONIUM, see *Merx.*

MERDA, see *Lutum.*

MERERE; DIGNUM ESSE; MERERI. 1. Merere and Mereri (μείρεσθαι) suppose an activity, as to deserve; whereas dignum esse (from *decet,* δίκη,) only a quality, as to be worthy. 2. Merere is usually a transitive verb, as to deserve, and is in construction with an accusative, or with a sentence, as its complement; whereas m e r e r i, an intransitive verb, as to be deserving, and is in construction with an adverb. Cic. Rosc. Com. 15. Fructum, quem *meruerunt*, retribuam: comp. with Catil. ii. 2, 4. Si illum, ut erat *meritus*, morte mulctassem. Cæs. B. G. vi. 5, with B. Civ. iii. 53. Suet. Cal. 40, with Aug. 56. 3. M e r e r e as an intransitive, or without an object, denotes to serve as a warrior, by the ellipsis of *stipendia*; whereas m e r e r i as a transitive, or with an object, means to earn something for one's self, without any stress being laid upon the worthiness. (v. 213.).

MERETRIX, see *Pellex*.

MERIDIES; MEDIUS DIES. M e r i d i e s denotes noon, as a point of time, which separates the forenoon from the afternoon; m e d i u s d i e s, the middle of the day, as a space of time which lies between the morning and the evening.

MERUS, see *Purus*.

MERX; MERCIMONIUM. M e r x means wares, in as far as they are already wrought up, as an article of trade; m e r c i m o n i u m, in as far as they can become so, like the materials of wares. Tac. A. xi. 5. Nec quidquam publicæ *mercis* tam venale fuit: comp. with xv. 38. *Mercimonium* quo flamma alitur.

METIRI; METARI; DIMETIRI; DIMETARI. 1. M e t i r i means to measure a space in order to know its magnitude; whereas m e t a r i, to mark the boundaries of the space that has been measured, that they may be known to others. 2. By d i m e t i r i and d i m e t a r i, the measuring and marking out of sub-divisions is especially meant; wherefore *metari castra* refers merely to the whole circumference of the entrenchments; when, therefore, Liv. viii. 38. uses the phrase *locum castris dimetari*, it is evident of itself that he expressly means, to mark the boundaries of the *principia* and of the *prætorium*, etc., that are within the camp. (ii. 169.)

METUERE, see *Vereri.*
MICARE, see *Lucere.*
MINIME, see *Neutiquam.*
MINISTER, see *Servus.*
MINUTUS, see *Parvus.*

[*Mirari* is indifferent: *admirari* usually involves praise, *demirari* blame.]

MISERERI; MISERARI; MISERET ME. Misereri means to feel pity in the heart, to compassionate, like ἐλεεῖν; whereas miserari, to express pity in words, to commiserate, like οἰκτείρειν. For the German word *erbarmen*, to show pity by actions, the Latins have no separate word. 2. By misereor tui, pity is represented as an act of the free-will, and thereby the noble nature of the compassionate is depicted; whereas by miseret me tui, pity is represented as a suffering, which cannot be resisted, whereby all moral merit is taken away, and the greatness of another's misfortune more strongly expressed. Miserere is a causative, like οἰκτίζειν. (ii. 171.)

MISERIA, see *Infortunium.*

MISSILE; HASTA; LANCEA; JACULUM; VERUTUM; TRAGULUM; PILUM. Missile is the most general name for a weapon used in fighting at a distance, from the spear to the arrow; hasta and lancea serve both for thrusting and hurling; hasta (from σχαστήριον, σχάζω,) as a genuine Roman weapon, δόρυ; lancea, as a foreign weapon, supposed to have come originally from the Suevi, λόγχη; pilum, jaculum, verutum, are more for hurling; jaculum, as the most general expression, including the hunting spear, βέλος; verutum (from ὀρυχή) and tragulum (τρώγλη) military weapons for hurling, ἄκων; pilum (from πῆλαι) in the singular, as the peculiar weapon for hurling used by the Roman legion. Liv. ix. 19. Romano *pilum* haud paulo quam *hasta* vehementius ictu *missu*que telum.

MITIS; LENIS; PLACIDUS. Mitis means mild, in opp. to *acerbus*, like μείλιχος; lenis (from lana? or from the Goth, latjan, lassus?) gentle, in opp. to *ve-*

*hemens*, like πρᾶος; placidus, composed, in opp. to *turbidus*, like ἤπιος.

MITTERE; LEGARE; AMITTERE; DIMITTERE; OMITTERE. 1. Mittere (μεθεῖναι) is the general expression, to send; legare (from λέγω) has a special political meaning, to delegate. The *missus* makes his appearance as a servant or messenger; the *legatus*, as a representative. 2. Amittere and dimittere mean to let go any thing already in one's possession; amittere, against one's will, as to lose; dimittere, after having used it, as to dismiss; whereas omittere means to let anything pass by, without taking possession of it; to speak with precision, *Amittimus inviti et casu, omittimus volentes et sponte.* Hence *amittere occasionem* means, to let slip an opportunity, so as not to be able to take advantage of it, from negligence; whereas *omittere occasionem* means, to renounce an opportunity, so as not to wish to take advantage of it, from attaching little value to it. *Vitam amittere* means, to lose one's life; *vitam omittere*, to sacrifice it. (iii. 285.)

MODERATUS, MODESTIA, see *Modus*.

MODICUS, see *Medius*.

MODO-MODO; NUNC-NUNC. Modo-modo is properly applicable only to transactions of the past and of the future; nunc-nunc only to those of the present. This distinction is neglected, yet nunc-nunc gives a livelier color to description, and belongs to poetry, or to the more elevated style of prose; modo-modo, like 'just now,' is the proper prose expression, which Cicero always uses. (iv. 276.)

MODO, see *Nuper*.

MODUS; MODESTIA; MODERATIO; TEMPERATIO; CONTINENTIA; ABSTINENTIA. 1. Modus, in a moral sense, denotes the *μέτριον*, or the included notion of the *μηδὲν ἄγαν* in objective relation; modestia and moderatio, in subjective relation; Modestia is the feeling of preference for this *modus;* moderatio, the habit of acting in conformity to this feeling. 2.

Moderatio is moderation, as springing from the understanding, from calculation and reflection, akin to *prudentia;* temperatio and temperantia are qualities pervading the whole man, and ennobling his whole being, akin to *sapientia.* Moderatio supposes, like self-government, a conflict between the passions and reason, in which reason comes off conqueror; in temperatio, as in tranquillity of mind, the reason is already in possession of superiority, whether through nature or moral worth. 3. Temperatus, temperatio, denote merely a laudable property, which may belong even to things; whereas temperans, temperantia, a virtue of which reasonable beings alone are capable. 4. Moderatio denotes moderation in *action*, in opp. to *cupiditas;* whereas continentia, moderation in enjoyment, in opp. to *libido;* Cic. Cat. ii. 11, 25. Verr. iv. 52. 5. Continentia denotes command over sensual desires, continence; abstinentia, over the desire for that which belongs to another, firm integrity; the translation of *abstinentia* by 'disinterestedness,' is not precise enough, for this virtue is required by morality only, *abstinentia*, by *law* also. Quintil. v. 10, 89. Cic. Sext. 16. 6. Modestia shuns overstepping the right measure, out of regard to the morals which the *modus* prescribes; whereas verecundia and reverentia out of regard to persons, whom the *verecundus* is afraid of displeasing, and whom the *reverens* thinks worthy of respect; lastly, pudor, out of self-respect, that one may not bring one's self into contempt. Varro, ap. Non. Non te tui saltem *pudet*, si nihil mei *revereare*. Terent. Phorm. i. 5, 3. or ii. 1, 3. Non simultatem meam *revereri?* Saltem *pudere?* (ii. 203.)

MŒNIA, see *Murus*.

MŒSTITIA, see *Dolor*.

MOLES; ONUS; PONDUS; GRAVITAS. Moles and onus denote the heaviness of an object in its disadvantageous sense; moles (from μῶλος or μόχλος) abso lutely, as unwieldiness, so far as through its greatness it is inconvenient to move, like ὄγκος; o n u s, relatively to its pressure, so far as it is irksome to the person carrying it, as a burden, φόρτος; whereas p o n d u s (from pendere) in an advantageous sense, as force and strength, like weight, ἄχθος; lastly, g r a v i t a s (from γεραός) unites both senses, and sometimes denotes the irksome heaviness, sometimes the effective weightiness, like βάρος. (iv. 223.)

MOLESTIA, see *Labor*. MOLIRI, see *Audere*.

MONERE, see *Hortari*. MONETA, see *Pecunia*.

MONS; JUGUM. M o n s (from minari, eminere,) denotes the mountain with reference to its dimension of height; whereas j u g u m, with reference to its breadth and length, sometimes as the uppermost ridge, which, according as it is flat or pointed, is with yet greater precision called either *dorsum* or *cacumen*, in opp. to *radices montis;* sometimes as a range of mountains, particularly in an ascending direction, by which several mountains become joined, so as to form a chain, or pile of mountains, in opp. to the mountain itself. Liv. xxii. 18. Sub *jugo montis* prœlium fuit: comp. with xli. 18. Petilius adversus Balistæ et Leti *jugum*, quod eos *montes* perpetuo *dorso* conjungit, castra habuit. Or, Tac. G. 10, with 43, and Agr. 10. Or, Virg. Ecl. v. 76, with Ovid, Met. iv. 657. (v. 225.)

MONSTRA, see *Auguria*. MONSTRARE, see *Ostendere*.

MORARI, see *Tardare*.

MORBIDUS, MORBUS, see *Æger*.

MORIGERARI, see *Parere*. MOROSUS, see *Austerus*.

MORS; LETUM; NEX; OBITUS; INTERITUS; PERIRE; OPPETERE; DEMORI; INTERMORI; EMORI. 1. M o r s and l e t u m denote a natural death; m o r s (μόρος) the usual expression in a merely physical sense, as the way to corruption, like θάνατος; l e t u m (from λαχεῖν, λάχεσις,) the select and solemn expression, as the lot of death, like οἶτος; whereas n e x (from νεκρός) a violent death, as the passive of *cædes*. 2. M o r s, letum, nex, are proper, whereas obitus and interitus only softer, expressions. Obitus, decease, denotes, like *exitus*, a natural death; whereas interitus, together with perire, usually denotes, like *exitium*, a violent death. Plin. Ep. iii. 7. Silius ultimus ex Neronianis consularibus *obiit*, quo consule Nero *periit*. Plaut. Epid. iii. 4, 56. Malo cruciatu *pereas*, atque *obeas* cito. 3. Perire represents death as destruction and corruption; interire as a vanishing, so that the former applies more to the body, the latter to the soul. Plaut. Capt. iii. 5, 32. Qui per virtutem *periit*, at non *interit*; that is, he who dies a noble death, though his body perishes, still lives in name and posthumous renown. Further, perire denotes a sudden and violent death, particularly by self-murder; interire, a gradual and painful, but, it may be, also a peaceful, death. Tac. Ann. xv. 44. Et *pereuntibus* Christianis addita ludibria, ut ferarum tergis contecti laniatu canum *interirent*. Serv. ap. Cic. Fam. iv. 5. Si quis nostrum *interiit*, aut occisus est. 4. Obire mortem denotes to die, as a physical event, by which one ends all suffering; whereas oppetere mortem denotes to die, as a moral act, in as far as a man, if he does not seek death, at any rate awaits it with firmness and contempt of it. 5. Demori denotes to die off, as one belonging to a society, and thereby to occasion a vacancy; intermori, to be apparently dying, to be sick of a lingering disease, like ἐκθανεῖν; emori, to die entirely, in opp. to a mere semblance of life in misfortune, slavery, and disgrace, like πανδίκως θανεῖν. Cic. Pis. 7. Ut *emori* potius quam servire præstaret. (iii. 182.)

Mos, see *Consuetudo*. Mostellum, see *Spectrum*.
Mucro, see *Acies*. Mulcare, see *Verberare*.

Mulcere; Palpare. Mulcere (μύλλειν, μαλακός) means to stroke any thing in itself rough, as the hair, for instance, in order to make it smooth; thence, figuratively, to pacify an enraged person, like καταψῆν;

whereas palpare (ψηλαφᾶν, ἁπαλός,) to stroke any thing already smooth, in order to excite a pleasant sensation; thence, figuratively, to caress and coax, like ψηλαφᾶν. (v. 109.)

MULCTA, see *Vindicta*.

MULIER, see *Femina*.

MUNDUS, see *Purus*.

MUNIFICUS, see *Largus*.

MUNIMENTA, see *Murus*.

MUNUS, see *Donum* and *Officium*.

MURUS; PARIES; MŒNIA; MACERIA; PARIETINÆ; MUNIMENTA. 1. Murus (μοῖρα, μείρω,) denotes any sort of wall, merely with reference to its form, without reference to its use, like τεῖχος; paries (πείρω) especially a wall, as the side of a building, or as a partition to separate the rooms, like τοῖχος; mœnia (ἀμύνω) the walls of a city, as a defence against the enemy, like περίβολος? maceria, the wall of an enclosure, to mark the boundaries and to exclude thieves, the garden or vineyard wall, like θριγκός. Virg. Æn. vi. 549. *Mœnia* lata videt triplici circumdata *muro*. And Flor. i. 4. Vitruv. viii. 4. Tac. Ann. xv. 43. Nero instituit, ut urbis domus non communione *parietum*, sed propriis quæque *muris* ambirentur. 2. Muri, mœnia, etc., are walls in a good condition; parietinæ, walls that are falling into ruins. 3. Mœnia denote walls as a defence of a city against a first assault; munimenta, the proper fortifications of fortresses and camps, which are of themselves a bulwark against being taken by storm. (v. 350.)

MUTILARE; TRUNCARE. Mutilare denotes smaller mutilations, such as the breaking off of horns, the cutting off of a finger, the nose, etc.; truncare denotes greater mutilations, such as the chopping off of arms, feet, hands. The *mutilata membra* may be compared to twigs and shoots broken off; the *truncata membra*, to principal branches chopped off. (iv. 325.)

MUTUO, see *Vicissim*.

Mutuum dare, see *Commodare*.
Mysteria, see *Arcana*.

## N.

Nancisci, see *Invenire*.
Nares, see *Nasus*.

Nasus; Nares. Nasus is the exterior of the nose, as a prominent part of the face, like *ῥίν*; nares (*ναρός*) the interior of the nose, as the organ of smell, like *μυκτῆρες*. (vi. 231.).

Natio, see *Gens*.

Navigium; Navis; Celox; Lembus; Liburna; Scapha; Cymba; Linter. Navigium is the most general expression, like vessel; navis (*ναῦς*) an ordinary ship for distant voyages; celox, lembus, and liburna, are boats which may be manned and armed for service in war; scapha, cymba, and linter, are only skiffs and wherries, intended merely for short distances and for crossing over; scapha and cymba, of the broader sort, in the form of small barges; linter, long and narrow, like a canoe. (vi. 232.)

Necessarius; Propinquus; Cognatus; Consanguineus; Affinis. 1. Necessarius means any one to whom one is bound by a permanent connection, whether of an official kind, as *collega*, *patronus*, *cliens*, or of a private nature, as *familiaris*, *amicus*, like *προσήκοντες*; propinquus, any one to whom one is bound by a family connection, a relation, like *ἀγχιστεῖς* and *ἔται*, as a species of *cognatus* and *consanguineus*, related by blood; affinis, a relation by marriage, or in law, like *κηδεστής*. 2. Cognatio is the relationship by blood existing among members of the same family, like *σύναιμος*; consanguinitas, the relationship of nations by derivation from a common origin, like *συγγενής*. Cæs. B. G. vii. 32. Hominem summæ potentiæ et magnæ *cognationis*: comp. with i. 11. Ambarri necessarii et *consanguinei* Æquorum. Liv. vii. 9. Suet. Cl. 25. Justin, xviii. 5. (v. 179.)

Necesse est; Oportet; Opus est; Debere. 1. Necesse est (ἀναγκάζω) denotes an obligation of nature and necessity, like ἀνάγκη ἐστίν; oportet, an obligation of morality and of honor, like χρή; opus est (πόθος, optare?) an obligation of prudence, like δεῖ. Cic. Orat. ii. 25. Jure omnia defenduntur quæ sunt ejus generis, ut aut *oportuerit* aut licuerit aut *necesse fuerit* Att. iv. 6. Si loquor de republica quod *oportet*, insanus; si, quod *opus est*, servus existimor. And xiii. 25. Cat. ap. Sen. Ep. 94. Emo non quod *opus est*, sed quod *necesse est;* quod non *opus est*, asse carum est. And Cic. Or. ii. 43. 2. Oportet denotes objectively, the moral claim which is made upon any man; debere (δεύεσθαι, δεῖν? or, dehibere?) subjectively, the moral obligation which any man is under, like ὀφείλειν. Tac. Hist. iv. 7. Accusatores etiamsi puniri non *oporteat*, ostentari non *debere*. (v. 323.)

Nectere, see *Ligare*.

Nefandus, Nefarius, see *Scelestus*.

Nefastus, see *Delictum*.

Negare; Infitiari; Infitias ire; Denegare; Pernegare; Recusare; Abnuere; Renuere; Repudiare. 1. Negare means to deny, from objective motives, when a man has, or professes to have, the truth in view, like ἀποφάναι, οὐ φάναι; whereas infiteri, infitiari, and infitias ire, mean to disown from subjective motives, when personal interest is in some way implicated, like ἀρνεῖσθαι. 2. Infiteri is an obsolete expression; infitiari (ἀνα-φατίζειν,) the usual and general expression; infitias (ἀμφασίας) ire is only connected with a negation, and answers to the phrase, not to assent to. 3. Negatio is a denial, merely conveying information to the hearer; pernegatio, or negitatio, to convince him, when he is incredulous; denegatio, to get rid of his importunity, when his request is useless. Martial, Ep. iv

82. *Negare* jussi, *pernegare* non jussi. Cic. Phil. xi. 8, 19. In quo maximum nobis onus imposuit, assensero, ambitionem induxero in curiam; *negaro;* videbor suffragio meo tanquam comitiis honorem amicissimo *denegasse.* 4. Negare supposes a question only, whether actual or possible, which is denied; whereas recusare, a request which is refused; hence negare is a more general and mild expression than *recusare;* for the *negans* merely denies the possibility of granting what he is asked or requested; whereas the *recusans* also calls in question the justice of the request, which he protests against as a threat, or as an encroachment. Hence negare, denegare, are more used in private transactions; recusare, in public affairs. 5. Negare and recusare take place by means of words and speeches; abnuere and renuere, mostly by signs and gestures; abnuere, by waving a person from one with the hand, like ἀπονεύω; renuere, by drawing back the head, like ἀνανεύω. 6. Abnuere is a more friendly, renuere a haughtier manner of denying. 7. Recusare refers to an object which is considered as a burden, and claims resignation, in opp. to *suscipere*, Suet. Ner. 3; whereas repudiare (from repedare?) refers to an object which is considered as a good, and promises profit or pleasure, in opp. to *assumere.* Cic. Orat. 62. Cic. Fin. i. 10, 33. Sæpe eveniet ut et voluptates *repudiandæ* sint, et molestia non *recusanda.* (iv. 40.)

NEGLIGERE, see *Spernere*, NEMUS, see *Silva.*

NEPOS, see *Prodigus.* NEQUAQUAM, s. *Neutiquam.*

NEQUIDQUAM, see *Frustra.* NEQUITIA, see *Malitia.*

NESCIUS, see *Cognitio.*

NEUTIQUAM; NEQUAQUAM,; MINIME. Neutiquam means, in no case, in opp. to *utique*; nequaquam, by no means; minime, not in the least.

NEX, see Mors.

NIGER, see *Teter* and *Ater.*

NIHIL AGERE, see *Vacare.*

Nihil est; Nihili est; Nullus est. Nihil est denotes the entire want of virtue and efficacy; as, he is good for nothing; whereas nihili est, the entire want of value and usefulness, as he is of no use; lastly, nullus est, the negation of existence in general, as it is all over with him. (i. 56.)

Nitere, see *Lucere*. Niti, see *Fulciri*.

Nobilis, see *Celeber*. Nocens, see *Culpa*.

Nominare; Nuncupare; Vocare; Appellare. Nominare and nuncupare mean, to call anybody by his name; nominare, to call him by the name which he already possesses; nuncupare, to give a name to an object that has hitherto been without a name; whereas appellare and vocare mean to designate a person by any name, title, or appellation belonging to him. (v. 105.)

Nonnunquam; Interdum; Aliquando. Nonnunquam, sometimes in opp. to *nunquam* and *semper*, approximates to the meaning of *sæpius*, like ἔσθ' ὅτε; interdum, at times, is in opp. to *crebro*, and approximates to the meaning of *rarius*, like ἐνίοτε; lastly, aliquando, now and then, is in opp. to *semel*, and approximates to the meaning of *prope nunquam*, like ποτέ. The *interdum facta* denotes actions repeated at considerable intervals of time; the *nonnunquam facta*, actions repeated at shorter intervals; the *aliquando facta*, actions repeated at very distant intervals of time. Cic. Sext. 54. Comitiorum et concionum significationes *interdum* veræ sunt, *nonnunquam* vitiatæ et corruptæ. And Acad. i. 7. Off. ii. 18. Brut. 67. Mur. 30. (iv. 273.)

Notare, see *Animadvertere*.

Notitia, see *Cognitio*.

Novissimus, see *Extremus*.

Novus; Recens; Novicius. 1. Novus means new, as that which did not exist in former times, in opp. to *antiquus*, like νέος; whereas recens (from candere) new, as one that has not long been in existence, in opp. to *vetus*. Cic. Verr. ii. 2. Mur. 7. 16. Tusc. iv. 17. Tac. Ann. ii. 88. iv. 12. Colum. vi. 12; like καινός. 2. N o v u s denotes new, indifferently; n o v i c i u s (from νέαξ) with the accessory notion of being a novice, who must accustom himself, or be instructed by others, before he is qualified for something, in opp. to *vetustus?* (iv. 95.)

NOXIA, NOXIUS, see *Culpa*.

NULLUS SUM, see *Nihil sum*.

NUMEN; DEUS; DIVUS; SEMO; HEROS. N u m e n (πνεῦμα) in a wider sense is any divine being, like δαίμων; in a narrower sense it is used as a species of *Deus*, or ancient *Divus*, θεός; and for *semideus*, a half-god; or *semo*, a half-man; for which last, besides the foreign word *heros*, *numen* also is used. Plin. Pan. 2, 3. Nusquam ut *deo*, nusquam ut *numini* blandimur. (vi. 239.)

NUMMUS, see *Pecunia*.

NUNC-NUNC, see *Modo-modo*.

NUNCUPARE, see *Nominare*.

NUPER; MODO. N u p e r (νέον, πέρι) means several days, months, also, years since, lately, like νεωστί; whereas m o d o, a few moments since, just now, like ἄρτι. Cic. Verr. iv. 3, 6. *Nuper* homines nobiles ejusmodi; sed quid dico *nuper?* imo vero *modo* ac plane paulo ante vidimus. Tusc. i. 24. Quanta memoria fuit *nuper* Charmadas! quanta qui *modo* fuit Scepsius Metrodorus!

NUPTIÆ, see *Conjugium*.

NUTARE, see *Labare*.

NUTRIRE, NUTRICARE, see *Alere*.

## O

*ıbula*

OBJICERE; EXPROBRARE. O b j i c e r e means to

M*

charge a person with something, from which he must vindicate himself as against an accusation; whereas e x p r o b r a r e means to upbraid a person with something, which he must let remain as it is. The *objiciens* will call a person to account; the *exprobrans* only put him to the blush. (iv. 198.)

OBITUS, see *Mors*.

OBLECTATIO; DELECTATIO. O b l e c t a t i o (from ἀλέγειν ?) is a pleasant occupation, conversation, amusement, which disperses ennui, and confers a relative pleasure; whereas d e l e c t a t i o is a real delight, which procures positive enjoyment, and confers absolute pleasure. Cic. Orat. i. 26. In iis artibus, in quibus non utilitas quæritur necessaria, sed animi libera quædam *oblectatio*. And Ep. Q. Fr. ii. 14. Satis commode me *oblectabam:* comp. with Fam. ix. 24. Magna te *delectatione* et voluptate privavisti. Or, Suet. Dom. 21. with Aug. 29. Plin. Ep. iv. 14. with iv. 8. (v. 10.)

OBLIGARE, see *Ligare*.

OBLIQUUS, see *Transversus*.

OBLITUS, see *Delibatus*.

OBSCURUM; TENEBRÆ; CALIGO; TENEBRICOSUS; OPACUS; UMBROSUS. 1. O b s c u r u m (σκοτερόν) denotes darkness as an obstruction of light, like σκότος, in opp. to *illustre*. Auct. ad Her. iii. 19, 32. Plin. Pan. 69; whereas t e n e b r æ (δνοφεραί) as the absence of light,) like ζόφος, κνέφας,) in opp. to *lux*. Cic. Ep. ad Q. Fr. i. 2; lastly, c a l i g o (from celare) as the positive opposite to light and brightness, like ἀχλύς. C a l i g o denotes a greater degree of darkness than *tenebræ;* t e n e b r æ than *obscuritas;* o b s c u r i t a s than *opacum* and *umbrosum*. Cic. Acad iv. 23, 72. Sensus quidem non *obscuros* facit sed *tenebricosos*. Plin. Ep. vii. 21. Cubicula obductis velis *opaca*, nec tamen *obscura* facio. Tac. H. ii. 32. Senatum et populum nunquam *obscurari* nomina, etsi ali quando *obumbrentur*. Hence, figuratively, o b s c u r u s denotes only an insignificant person, of whom nobody takes notice; whereas tenebricosus something positively bad, which seeks darkness that it may remain unobserved. 2. Opacus denotes shady, with reference to a pleasant and beneficial coolness, in opp. to *apertus* and *apricus*, like εὔσκιος; whereas umbrosus (umbra, ἀμαυρός,) implies a depth of shade approaching to darkness, like σκιόεις. (iii. 168.)

OBSECRARE, see *Rogare*.

OBSECUNDARE and OBSEQUI, see *Parere*.

OBSERVARE, see *Vereri*.

OBSTINARE, s. *Destinare*.

OBSTINATIO, s. *Pervicacia*.

OBSTRINGERE, s. *Ligare*.

OBTEMPERARE, see *Parere*.

OBTESTARI, see *Rogare*.

OBTINGERE, see *Accidere*.

OBTRECTATIO, s. *Invidia*.

OBTRUNCARE, s. *Interficere*.

OBTUTUS, see *Invidia*.

OBVENIRE, see *Accidere*.

OCCASIO; OPPORTUNITAS; POTESTAS; COPIA; FACULTAS. Occasio and opportunitas are the opportunities which fortune and chance offer; occasio, the opportunity to undertake something in a general sense, like καιρός; opportunitas, the opportunity to undertake something with facility and the probability of success, like εὐκαιρία; whereas potestas and copia are opportunities offered by men, and through their complaisance; potestas denotes the possibility of doing something with legal authority; copia the possibility of doing something with convenience; lastly, facultas, as the most general expression, the possibility to do something in a general sense.

OCCIDERE, see *Interficere*.

OCCULERE, OCCULTARE and OCCULTE, see *Celare*.

OCULI, see *Facies*.

ODIUM; INVIDIA; INIMICITIA; SIMULTAS. 1. Odium and invidia denote the feeling of aversion; inimicitia and simultas, the exterior state arising from this feeling. 2. Invidia has a negative character, like disaffection, like δύσνοια, and is a temporary feeling, in opp. to *gratia* or *favor;* whereas odium (from ὀδύσασθαι) has a character thoroughly positive, like hatred, μῖσος, and is a deep-rooted feeling, in opp. to *amor*. Plin. Pan. 68, 7. Hence, invidia is the beginning of *odium*. Invidia has merely persons; odium, persons and things for its objects. Tac. Ann. ii. 56. Armenii . . . sæpius discordes sunt, adversus Romanos *odio*, et in Parthum *invidia*. xiii. 15. Nero intellecta *invidia odium* intendit. Plin. Pan. 84, 2. Exardescit *invidia*, cujus finis est *odium*. 3. Inimicitia denotes any enmity which has its foundation in antipathy or disagreement, like δυσμένεια, ἔχθρα; whereas simultas (ὁμαλότης) denotes a political enmity, which has its foundation in rivalship, like φιλονεικία. Suet. Vesp. 6. *Simultas* quam ex æmulatione non obscuræ gerebant. (iii. 73.)

ODORARI, ODORUS, see *Olere*.

OFFENDERE, see *Lædere*.

OFFENSIO, see *Contumelia*.

OFFICIUM; MUNUS. Officium means an employment, as imposing a moral obligation, undertaken from conscientious feelings; munus, as imposing a political obligation, undertaken merely as a charge or office. Cic. Mur. 35. Hæc sunt *officia* necessariorum, commoda tenuiorum, *munia* candidatorum. (v. 352.)

OLERE; OLFACERE; FRAGRARE; ODORARI; OLIDUS; ODORUS; REDOLERE; PEROLERE. 1. Odor and olere (ὄδωδα) denote, objectively, the smell which a thing has in itself, in opp. to *sapor*, etc., like ὀσμή; whereas olfactus and olfacere denote, subjectively, the sensation caused by this smell, or the sense of smell, in opp. to *gustus*, etc., like ὄσφρησις. 2. Olere means to smell, in opp. to being without smell, and especially denotes a rank and bad smell; whereas fragrare (from βρέχειν) denotes a good smell. Redolere and perolere are used as frequentatives; redolere denotes a strong smell in an indifferent sense; perolere, a penetrating smell, in a bad sence. 3. Olfactus is a smell, as far as it is an involuntary effect of the sense of smell; o d o r a t u s, as far as it is an intentional exertion of that sense. 4. O l f a c e r e, to smell, is of a passive nature, like *audire*, the smell mounting up to the nose of itself; o d o r a r i, to smell at, to sniff, ῥινηλατεῖν, is of an active nature, like *auscultare*, the man drawing up the smell into his nose of himself. *Olfaciens* sentit odorem, *odorans* captat. 5. O l i d u s denotes smelling, and particularly with a bad smell; o d o r u s, with a good smell. Hence, b e n e o l i d u s denotes merely the negative of a stench; o d o r u s, a positive good smell; and the antiquated word o l o r denoted a stench, like *oletum;* but o d o r denotes only a smell. (iii. 131.)

OLETUM, see *Lutum.*

OLFACERE, OLIDUS, see *Olere.*

OMINA, see *Auguria.*

OMITTERE, see *Intermittere*, *Mittere*, and *Relinquere.*

OMNES, see *Quisque.* OMNINO, see *Plane.*

ONUS, see *Moles.* OPACUS, see *Obscurum.*

OPEM FERRE, see *Auxilium.*

OPERA; LABOR; INDUSTRIA; GNAVITAS; ASSIDUITAS; DILIGENTIA. 1. O p e r a (from περᾶν, πράσσειν,) denotes activity without intense exertion, as merely doing, or turning one's hand to, something, in opp. to momentary inactivity; and also in opp. to thinking, speaking, advising, like ἐργασία; whereas l a b o r denotes strenuous exertion, which is followed by fatigue, labor, in opp. to pleasure, like πόνος. Plaut. Aul. iii. 3. 7. *Opera* huc est conducta vestra, non oratio: comp. with Bacch. iii. 6, 11. Cic. Rep. i. 9. Otiosiorem *opera* quam animo. Liv. xxii. 22. Ut *opera* quoque impensa consilium adjuvem meum. And Liv. v. 4. *Labor* voluptasque dissimillima natura, societate quadam naturali inter se sunt conjuncta: comp. with Cic. Mur. 35. Plin. Ep. ix. 10. Senec. Tranq. 2. 2. I d u s t r i a, g n a v i t a s, and s e d u l i t a s, denote activity as an habitual quality, in opp. to the love of idleness; i n d u s t r i a, of an elevated sort, the impulse to activity that animates the hero or the statesman, in opp. to *ignavia*, *gnavitas* (γενναιότης) of a useful sort, the diligence of ordinary men, and of the industrious citizen; s e d u l i t a s (sine dolore) an activity that shows itself in small matters, often even of a comic sort, the indefatigable bustling of the busy housewife, of the good-natured nurse, of any one who pays officious court to another. Colum. xii. præf. 8. Ut cum forensibus negotiis matronalis *sedulitas industriæ* rationem parem faceret. 3. A s s i d u i t a s and d i l i g e n t i a denote industry; a s s i d u i t a s (from sedere) like *συνέχεια*, more in an extensive sense with continued and uninterrupted efforts; d i l i g e n t i a, (ἀλέγειν) more in an intensive sense, with careful and close application, in order to attain the end of one's industry. 4. S t u d i u m denotes inclination and love towards the object of one's industry, and an inward impulse. (i. 111.)

OPERÆ, see *Mercenarii.*
OPES, see *Divitiæ.*
OPIFEX, see *Faber.*
OPIMUS, see *Pinguis.*
OPINARI, see *Censere.*
OPINIO, see *Sententia.*
OPITULARI, see *Auxilium.*
OPORTET, see *Necesse est.*
OPPERIRI, see *Manere.*
OPPETERE, see *Mors.*
OPPORTUNITAS, s. *Occasio.*
OPPRIMERE, s. *Vincere.*
OPPROBRIUM, s. *Ignominia.*
OPTARE, see *Velle.*
OPTIMATES, see *Primores.*
OPULENTIA, see *Divitiæ.*
OPUS EST, see *Necesse est.*
OPUS, see *Agere.*
ORA, see *Margo* and *Ripa.*
ORARE, see *Rogare.*
ORATIO, see *Sermo.*

ORBIS; CIRCULUS; GYRUS. O r b i s (from ῥαιβός) denotes a circular motion, and the periphery described by it; whereas c i r c u l u s denotes a circular level; lastly, g y r u s (from γυρός) a curved, and especially a serpentine line. The phrase *in orbem consistere* could not be changed into *in circulum*, and a limited social circle, *circulus*, could not be expressed by orbis. Tac. G. 6. Equi nec variare *gyros* nostrum in modum docentur; in rectum aut uno flexu dextros agunt, ita conjuncto *orbe* ut nemo posterior sit. (v. 182.)

ORDIRI, see *Incipere*. ORDO, see *Series*.
OREÆ, see *Frenum*. ORNARE, see *Comere*.
ORNATUS, see *Prœditus*. OS, see *Facies*.

OSCULUM; SUAVIUM; BASIUM. Osculum is a friendly; suavium, a tender; basium, an ardent kiss. (vi. 251.)

OSTENDERE; MONSTRARE; DECLARARE. Ostendere means to show, as far as one makes something observable, lets it be seen, and does not keep it secret, like φῆναι, ἐμφανίσαι; monstrare (intensive from μανϑάνειν) means to show, as far as one imparts information thereby; lastly, declarare, to make evident, as far as one makes a thing clear, and dispels doubt, like δηλῶσαι.

OSTENTA, see *Auguria*. OSTENTATIO, see *Jactatio*.

OSTIUM; JANUA; FORES; VALVÆ. Ostium and janua denote the door, as the opening through which one goes in and out; ostium, as the most general expression for any door, like ϑύρα; janua, as a particular expression only for a house-door; whereas fores and valvæ denote the leaves of a door, which serve to close the opening; fores, of ordinary doors, like ϑυρίδες; valvæ, of stately buildings and temples, as double or folding doors. Tac. Ann. xiv. 8. Anicetus refracta *janua* obvios servorum adripit, donec ad *fores* cubiculi veniret. (v. 214.)

OTIARI, see *Vacare*.

OTIUM; PAX; CONCORDIA. Otium (αὔσιος, αὔτως,) denotes quiet times in general, as a species of *pax* (πῆξαι), with reference to foreign relations; concordia, with reference to internal relations. (v. 246.)

## P.

PÆDOR, see *Lutum*.

PÆNE: PROPE; FERE; FERME. Pæne and prope serve to soften an expression that is much too strong, and as a salvo to an hyperbole; p æ n e, in opp. to *plane*, is translated 'almost;' p r o p e, 'nearly;' whereas f e r e and f e r m e serve only as a salvo to the accuracy of an expression, like 'about.'

PÆSTUS, see *Strabo*.
PALAM, see *Aperire*.
PALARI, see *Errare*.
PALPARI, see *Mulcere*.
PALUS, see *Lacuna*.
PALUS, see *Stipes*.
PANDUS, see *Curvus*.
PAR, see *Æquus*.
PARATUS, see *Instructus*.
PARERE, see *Creare*.

PARERE; OBEDIRE; DICTO AUDIENTEM ESSE; OBSEQUI; OBSECUNDARE; MORIGERARI; OBTEMPERARE.

P a r e r e, o b e d i r e and d i c t o a u d i e n t e m e s s e, denote obedience as an obligation, and a state of duty and subjection; p a r e r e, in a lower relation, as that of a servant to his master, a subject to his sovereign, in opp. to *imperare*, Cic. Fam. ix. 25; o b e d i r e, o b œ d i r e, in a freer relation, as that of an inferior to his superior, of a citizen to the law and magistrate; d i c t o a u d i e n t e m e s s e, in a relation of the greatest subordination, as that of a soldier to his general, as to obey orders; whereas o b s e q u i, o b s e c u n d a r e, o b t e m p e r a r e, and m o r i g e r a r i, as an act of free will. The *obsequens* and *obsecundans* obey from love and complaisance, showing their readiness to obey; the *morigerans* and *obtemperans*, from persuasion, esteem, or fear, evincing their conformity to another's will. Hirt. B. Afr. 51. Jubæ barbaro potius *obedientem* fuisse quam nuntio Scipionis *obtemperasse*. Cic. Cæc. 18. Man. 16. Tac. H. ii. 14. Parata non arma modo sed *obsequium* et *parendi* amor; that is, readiness to obey, from respect and love to the general, and from taking a pleasure in obedience, from a feeling that without order and subordination their cause could not be upheld. Cic. Orat. 71. Dum tibi roganti voluerim *obsequi;* comp. with Fam. ix. 25. *Obtemperare* cogito præceptis tuis. (v. 271.)

PARIES, PARIETINÆ, see *Murus*.

PARILIS, see *Æquus*.

PARMA, see *Scutum.*

PARS; PORTIO. Pars (from πείρω) denotes a part, with reference to a whole; whereas portio, a part or share with reference to a possessor. Plin. H. N. xi. 15. Æstiva mellatione decimam *partem* apibus relinqui placet, si plenæ fuerint alvi; si minus, pro rata *portione.* (iv. 148.)

PARTES; FACTIO. Partes denote the party, which is formed of itself by difference of principles and interests; whereas factio (from σφηκόω) the clique of partisans, formed by narrow differences of the members of a party with each other, and who act together with a blind party-spirit, in order necessarily and by force to give the upper hand to their own cause. Sall. Jug. 31. Inter bonos amicitia, inter malos *factio* est.

PARTICEPS, see *Socius.*

PARTICIPARE, see *Impertire.*

PARTIRI, see *Dividere.*

PARUMPER; PAULISPER. Parumper means in a short time; paulisper, during a short time. Hence acts of the mind are particularly in construction with *parumper;* acts of the body, with *paulisper;* for with the former is necessarily connected the glance at the future, which *lies* in *parumper;* in *paulisper*, duration of time only is considered; for example, we use the expression *paulisper morari*, but *parumper dubitare.* (i. 145.)

PARVUS; MINUTUS; EXIGUUS; PUSILLUS. Parvus and minutus denote littleness, quite indifferently, and in a purely mathematical sense, without any accessory notion; parvus (παῦρος) a natural and intrinsic littleness, in opp. to *magnus*, like μικρός; minutus (μινύθω) an artificial and fabricated littleness; whereas exiguus and pusillus with a contemptuous accessory notion; exiguus from (egere) in a pitiable sense, as paltry and insignificant, in opp. to *amplus.* Planc. ap. Cic. Fam. x. 24; or in opp. to *grandis*, Quintil. xi. 3, 15; but pusillus (ψιλός?) in a ludicrous sense, as petty, nearly in opp. to *ingens*, like τυτθός. (v. 28.)

PASCERE, see *Alimenta*.

PASSI; PROLIXI; SPARSI. Passi capilli denotes loose hair, in opp. to *cohibiti nodo;* whereas prolixi capilli denotes hair suffered to hang down, in opp. to *religati in verticem;* lastly, sparsi capilli denotes dishevelled hair, in opp. to *pexi*. (vi. 258.)

PASSUS, see *Gradus*.

PATEFACERE, see *Aperire*.

PATERNUS; PATRIUS. Paternus denotes, like πατρῷος, what belongs to a father, and is derived from him, like paternal; whereas patrius, what belongs to and is derived from one's ancestors or native country, like πάτριος.

PAULATIM; SENSIM; GRADATIM; PEDETENTIM. Paulatim and sensim represent gradual motion under the image of an imperceptible progress; paulatim, by little and little, in opp. to *semel*, at once, Sen. Q. N. ii. 8. Cœl. Aurel. Acut. ii. 37; sensim, (ἀνεσίμως) imperceptibly in opp. to *repente;* Cic. Off. i. 33. Suet. Tib. 11; — whereas gradatim and pedetentim, under the image of a self-conscious progress; gradatim, step by step, like βάδην, in opp. to *cursim*, *saltuatim*, etc.; whereas pedetentim denotes at a foot's pace, in opp. to *curru*, *equo*, *volatu*, *velis*. (iii. 97.)

PAULISPER, see *Parumper*.

PAUPERTAS; INOPIA; EGESTAS; MENDICITAS. Paupertas (redupl. of parum) denotes poverty only as narrowness of means, in consequence of which one must economize, in opp. to *dives*, Cic. Parad. 6. Quintil. v. 10, 26, like πενία; whereas inopia and egestas denote galling poverty, in consequence of which one suffers want, and has recourse to shifts; inopia, like ἀπορία, objectively, as utterly without means, so that one cannot help one's self, in opp. to *copia* or *opulentia;* Cic. Parad. 6. Sen. Vit. B. 15. Tac. Hist. iii. 6;

e g e s t a s, like ἔνδεια, subjectively, as penury, when a man feels want, in opp. to *abundantia;* lastly, m e n d i c i t a s (from μαδίζειν,) as absolute poverty, in consequence of which one must beg, like πτωχεία. The *pauper* possesses little enough; the *inops* and *egenus*, too little; the *mendicus*, nothing at all. In the kingdom of Plutus, according to the order of rank, the *pauperes* would occupy the middle station, who must live the life of citizens, and economize; the *inopes* and *egeni*, if not in a state of overwhelming necessity, would occupy the station of the poor, who live from hand to mouth, and must occasionally starve; the *mendici*, the station of the beggars, who, without property of any sort, or the means of earning it, live on alms. Cic. Parad. 6. Istam *paupertatem* vel potius *egestatem* et *mendicitatem* tuam nunquam obscure tulisti. Sen. Ep. 17. 50. Ovid, Rem. 748. Suet. Gr. 11. Vixit in summa *pauperie*, et pæne *inopia.* Plin. Ep. iv. 18. *Inopia* vel potius, ut Lucretius ait, *egestas* patrii sermonis. Cic. Inv. i. 47. Propter *inopiam* in *egestate* esse. (iii. 111.)

PAVIRE, see *Verberare.* PAX, see *Otium.*

PECCATUM, see *Delictum.* PECULARI, see *Vastare.*

PECULIARIS, see Privus.

PECUNIA; NUMMUS; MONETA. P e c u n i a (from παχύνω) is money, as a collective expression; n u m m u s (νόμιμος) a piece of money, in reference to its value and currency; m o n e t a, a coin in reference to its coinage and appearance. (vi. 240.)

PECUS; JUMENTUM; ARMENTUM; GREX. 1. P e c u s, p e c o r i s, is the most general expression for domestic beasts; j u m e n t a and a r m e n t a denote the larger sort, bullocks, asses, horses; p e c u s, p e c u d i s (from the Goth. faihu) the smaller sort, swine, goats, and especially sheep. 2. J u m e n t a denotes beasts used in drawing carriages, bullocks, asses, horses; a r m e n t a (ἀρόματα) beasts used in ploughing, oxen and horses, with the exclusion of cows, pack-asses, riding-horses, etc., which are neither fit for drawing carriages, nor for the plough. 3. As a singular and collective noun, armentum denotes a herd or drove of the larger cattle, like ἀγέλη; grex (from ἀγείρω) a herd or flock of the smaller animals, like ποίμνη, πῶϋ. Plin. Ep. ii. 16. Multi *greges* ovium, multa ibi equorum boumque *armenta* (iv. 298.)

PECUS, see *Animal*. PEDETENTIM, see *Paulatim*.
PEDICA, see *Vincula*. PEJERARE, see *Perlucidus*.
PEJOR, see *Deterior*. PELAGUS, see *Mare*.
PELLEGERE, PELLICERE, see *Perlucidus*.

PELLEX; CONCUBINA; MERETRIX; SCORTUM. 1. Pellex and the foreign word pallaca (παλλακή, παραλέγεσθαι,) mean the bed-fellow of a married man with reference to his wife, and in opp. to her, as her rival; whereas concubina means any bed-fellow, without further limitation than that she does not live in a state of lawful wedlock. Suet. Cæs. 49. *Pellicem* reginæ Dolabella Cæsarem dixit: comp. with Ner. 44. *Concubinas*, quas secum educeret. 2. Pellex and concubina are bound to one man; meretrix, scortum, lupa, prostibulum, are common prostitutes. 3. The meretrices and scorta are not *so low* as *lupæ, prostibula*. They exercise some choice and selection, and support themselves by the work of their own hands, from which *meretrices* derive their name (from mereri); meretrices are considered with ref. to the *class* they belong to; scorta (κόρη, κοράσιον), with ref. to their moral character, as enticing men to sin, like ἑταῖραι, filles de joie. The meretrices are common; the scorta, lascivious and dissolute. (v. 241.)

PELLIS, see *Tergus*. PELLUCIDUS, see *Perlucidus*.
PENDERE, see *Hærere*. PENITUS, see *Plane*.
PENNA, see *Ala*. PENUS, see *Alimenta*.
PERCONTARI, s. *Rogare*. PERCUSSOR, see *Homicida*.
PERCUTERE, see *Interficere*.

PERDERE; PESSUNDARE; PERVERTERE; EVERTERE.

Perdere and pessundare denote complete destruction; perdere, by breaking to pieces, or by any other mode of destroying; pessundare (πεζὸν θεῖναι) by sinking, or any other mode of getting rid of; whereas evertere, pervertere, and subvertere merely denote throwing down; evertere, by digging up and tearing up what is fastened in the ground, in opp. to *fundare*, Plin. Pan. 34. Cic. Acad. iv. 10. Fin. ii. 25. Verr. iii. 18. Pis. 35; pervertere, by pushing down what stands fast; subvertere, by secretly digging under, and withdrawing the basis. Cic. Pis. 24. Provincia tibi ista manupretium fuerit non *eversæ* per te sed *perditæ* civitatis. Ad. Att. v. 16.

PERDERE, see *Amittere*. PEREGRINARI, s. *Proficisci*.
PEREGRINUS, s. *Externus*, PEREMTOR, see *Homicida*.
PERFERRE, see *Ferre*. PERFICERE, see *Finire*.
PERFIDIOSUS, PERFIDUS, see *Fidus*.

PERFUGA; TRANSFUGA; PROFUGUS; FUGITIVUS; EXTORRIS; EXUL; PERFUGIUM; SUFFUGIUM; REFUGIUM. 1. Perfuga and transfuga denote the deserter who flees from one party to another, like αὐτομόλος; but the perfuga goes over as a delinquent, who betrays his party; the transfuga, as a waverer, who changes and forsakes his party; whereas profugus and fugitivus denote the fugitive, who forsakes his abode, but profugus is the unfortunate man, who is obliged to forsake his home, and, like a banished man, wanders in the wide world, like φυγάς; fugitivus, the guilty person, who flees from his duty, his post, his prison, his master, like δραπέτης. The perfuga and transfuga are generally thought of as soldiers; the profugus, as a citizen; the fugitivus, as a slave. Liv. xxx. 43. De *perfugis* gravius quam de *fugitivis* consultum. 2. Perfugium is an open secure place of shelter in serious dangers; suffugium, if not a secret, is at least an occasional and temporary place of shelter from inconveniences; refugium is a place of shelter prepared, or at least thought of beforehand in case of a retreat. 3. Profugus denotes a merely physical state, something like fugitive; extorris, a political state, like homeless, or without a country; exul, a juridical state, like banished. The extorris suffers a misfortune, as not being able to remain in his native land; the exul, a punishment, as not being allowed. Appul. Met. v. p. 101. *Extorres* et . . . velut *exulantes*. (iv. 239.)

PERICLITARI, PERICULUM, see *Tentare*.

PERIMERE, see *Interficere*. PERIRE, see *Mors*.

PERLUCIDUS; PELLUCIDUS; PERLEGERE; PELLEGERE; PERLICERE; PELLICERE; PERJURARE; PEJERARE. 1. Perlucidus means very bright, whereas pellucidus, transparent. Cic. Civ. i. 57. 2. Perlegere means to read through, that is, from beginning to end; whereas pellegere, to read over, that is, not to leave unread. Plaut. Pseud. i. 1. 3. Perlicere means completely to inveigle, Liv. iv. 15. Tac. Ann. xiii. 48; whereas pellicere, to lead astray. 4. Perjurare means to swear faslely; pejerare, to violate an oath. (ii. 82.)

PERMITTERE, see *Concedere* and *Fidere*.

PERNEGARE, see *Negare*.

PERNICIES, see *Lues*. PERNIX, see *Citus*.

PERPERAM; FALSO; FALSE; FALLACITER. 1. Perperam (redupl. of παρά) denotes that which is not true, objectively, with reference to the object, as incorrect; whereas falso, subjectively, in reference to the person, as mistaken. 2. Falso agere has its foundation in error and self-deceit; whereas false and fallaciter happens against better knowledge and conscience; false, through fear and weakness of character; fallaciter, like deceitfully, with the wicked intention of deceiving and betraying. Comp. Tac. Ann. i. 1. Tiberii res . . . ob metum *false* compositæ sunt, according to Wolf's reading; comp. with Germ. 36. Inter impotentes et validos *falso* quiescas. 3. The adjective falsus combines the notions of *falso* and of the participle *falsus*, and is distinguished only from *fallax*. Cic. Phil. xii. 2. Spes *falsa* et *fallax*. Tac. Ann. xvi. 33. Specie bonarum *falsos* et amicitiæ *fallaces*. (i. 66.)

PERPETI, see *Ferre*. PERPETUUS, see *Continuus*.

PERQUAM; VALDE; ADMODUM; MAGNOPERE. Perquam means, in an extraordinary degree, with an indication of astonishment on the part of the speaker; whereas valde, very, admodum, tolerably, and multum, are a simple and quiet enhancing of the attributive, or of the verb; magnopere, only of the verb. (v. 262.)

PERSEVERANTIA, see *Pervicacia*.

PERSONA, see *Larva*.

PERTINACIA, see *Pervicacia*.

PERVERTERE, see *Vertere* and *Perdere*.

PERVICACIA; PERSEVERANTIA; PERTINACIA; CONTUMACIA; DESTINATIO; OBSTINATIO. 1. Pervicacia and perseverantia denote adherence to what is once resolved upon as a virtue; pervicacia (from vincere? vigere?) has its foundation in natural energy of disposition; perseverantia, in earnestness of character, formed by cultivation; whereas pertinacia and contumacia as a fault; pertinacia has its foundation in a stiff-necked adherence to what is once resolved upon, like obstinacy and stubbornness, in opp. to condescension; contumacia (from temere, contemnere) in a haughty maintenance of one's free-will, even against proper and legitimate superiority,[1] like insolence and refractoriness, in opp. to complaisance, *obsequium*. Tac. Ann. iv. 20. Hist. iv. 74. Accius apud Non. Tu *pertinacem* esse, Antiloche, hanc prædicas, ego *pervicaciam* esse aio et a me uti volo, etc. Cic. inv. ii. 54. Unicuique virtuti finitimum vitium reperietur, ut *pertinacia*, quæ finitima *persever-*

1 [But, adhibere *liberam* contumaciam. Cic. Tus. 1, 29.]

*antiæ* est: comp. with Balb. 27. Marc. 10. 2. Pervicacia, etc. denote persisting in a resolution once made; destinatio and obstinatio are more immediately connected with the making of the resolution; destinatio, the making of an unalterable resolution, decidedness; obstinatio, adhering to it in spite of insurmountable obstacles and reasonable remonstrances, obstinacy. (iv. 176.)

Pessulus, see *Sera*. Pessumdare, see *Perdere*.

Pestilentia, Pestis, see *Lues*.

Petere; Rogare; Postulare; Exigere; Poscere; Flagitare. 1. Petere and rogare are the most general expressions for asking any thing, whether as a request or as a demand, and stand therefore in the middle between poscere and orare, yet somewhat nearer to a request; petere (from ποθεῖν) generally refers to the object which is wished for; whereas rogare to the person who is applied to; hence we say, *petere aliquid ab aliquo*, but *rogare aliquem aliquid*. Cic. Verr. * * Iste *petit* a rege, et cum pluribus verbis *rogat*, uti ad se mittat. Planc. 10, 25. Phil. ii. 30. Fam. ix. 8. and ii. 6. Ne id quod *petat*, exigere magis quam *rogare* videatur. Pseudoquintil. Decl. 286. Curt. iv. 1, 8. 2. Postulare and exigere denote simply a demand, without any enhancing accessory notion, as a quiet utterance of the will; postulare (diminutive of πόθος) more as a wish and will; exigere, more as a just claim; whereas poscere and flagitare, as an energetic demand; poscere (from πόθος) with decision, with a feeling of right or power; flagitare, with importunity, in consequence of a passionate and impatient eagerness. Tac. Hist. ii. 39. Othone per literas *flagitante* ut maturarent, militibus ut imperator pugnæ adesset *poscentibus*; plerique copias trans Padum agentes acciri *postulabant*. Cic. Verr. iii. 34. Incipiunt *postulare*, *poscere*, minari. Planc. 19. *Poscere* atque etiam *flagitare* crimen. Legg. i. 5. *Postulatur* a te jamdiu vel *flagitatur* potius historia. (v. 230.)

PETRA, see *Saxum*.

PETULANS; PROCAX; PROTERVUS; LASCIVUS. The p e t u l a n s (σπαταλῶν) sins against *modestia* through wantonness, raillery, and needless attack; the p r o c a x, through importunity and boisterous forwardness; the p r o t e r v u s (from proterere? or ταράξαι?) from impetuosity and haughty recklessness; the l a s c i v u s, through unrestrined frolicksomeness and inclination for play. Hence p e u t l a n t i a has its foundation in aversion to rest and quietness, or in the love of mischief; p r o c a c i t a s, in assurance or complete impudence; p r o t e r v i t a s, in a feeling of strength, or in insolence; l a s c i v i a, in high spirits, or the want of seriousness. (iii. 40.)

PIETAS, see *Diligere*.

PIGET; TÆDET; PŒNITET. P i g e t (from παχύς) means, what one can neither do nor suffer, in general terms; t æ d e t (from tardus?) what one can no longer do or suffer; p œ n i t e t, what one would fain never have done or suffered. (vi. 269.)

PIGRITIA, see *Ignavia*. PILUM, see *Missile*.

PILUS, see *Crinis*.

PINGUIS; OPIMUS; OBESUS; CORPULENTUS. 1. P i n g u i s (παχύς, πάνχυ,) denotes fat, indifferently, or, on its dark side, as that component part of the body that is most without sensation and strength; thence, figuratively, sluggish: whereas o p i m u s (from πιμελής) on its bright side, as a sign of plenty and good living; thence, figuratively, opulent. 2. O b e s u s denotes fatness, on its dark side, with reference to the unwieldiness connected with it, in opp. to *gracilis*, Cels. i. 3. ii. 1. Suet. Dom. 18; whereas c o r p u l e n t u s, on its bright side, with reference to the portliness connected with it. (v. 222.)

PINNA, see *Ala*. PIRATA, see *Præda*.

PLACIDUS, see *Mitis*.

PLAGA, see *Locus*, *Rete*, and *Vulnus*.

PLANCÆ, see *Axis*.

PLANE; OMNINO; PRORSUS; PENITUS; UTIQUE. Plane means completely, in opp. to *pæne*, Cic. Brut. 97, 33; or *vix*, Att. xi. 9; omnino, altogether and generally, in opp. to partly, in some instances, with some exceptions; in opp. also to *magna ex parte*, Cic. Tusc. i. 1. Fam. ix. 15, or *separatim*, Plin. Ep. viii. 7, ὅλως; prorsus, exactly, in opp. to in some measure, or almost; penitus, thoroughly, deeply, in opp. to in a certain degree, or superficially, πάντως; utique [related to *utcunque*, as *quisque* to *quicunque*: opp. *neutiquam*], at any rate, in opp. to at all events, or *perhaps* ὁπωσδήποτε. (v. 260.)

PLANUS, see *Æquus*.

PLERIQUE; PLURIMI. Plerique means a great many, in an absolute sense; plurimi, most, in a superlative sense. Tac. Ann. xiii. 27. *Plurimis* equitum, *plerisque* senatorum non aliunde originem trahi. (vi. 273.)

PLORARE, see *Lacrimare*. PLUMA, see *Ala*.

PLURIMI, see *Plerique*.

PLUVIA; IMBER; NIMBUS. Pluvia (from πλεῦσαι) denotes rain as a beneficial natural phenomenon, which, as it falls on the land, the thirsty ground absorbs, like ὑετός; imber and nimbus involve the notion of an unfriendly phenomenon, which, falling in a particular district, disperses the fine weather; imber (ὄμβρος, from μύρω) so far as the rain is attended by cold and stormy weather; nimbus (from *nivere*, νίφα, νίπτω) so far as it is attended with cloudy weather. (ii. 88.)

POCULUM; CALIX; SCYPHUS; SIMPUVIUM; CYATHUS; CRATER. 1. Poculum and calix denote, as old Latin words, any sort of drinking vessel, merely with reference to its use; poculum, a usual cup for meals; calix, a rarer chalice, or goblet, for feasts; whereas scyphus, cantharus, cymbium, culigna, are foreign words, of Greek origin, denoting particular sorts of cups, with reference to their form. 2.

P o c u l u m, etc. all serve as drinking cups; whereas the old Roman word s i m p u v i u m, and the modern c y a t h u s, are ladles to fill the *pocula* from the *crater*, as with the punch-ladle we fill the punch-glasses from the punch-bowl. (v. 318.)

POEMA, see *Canere*. PŒNA, see *Vindicta*.
PŒNITET, see *Piget*. POETA, see *Canere*.
POLLERE, see *Posse*.

POLLICERI; PROMITTERE; SPONDERE; RECIPERE. P o l l i c e r i (from pro and loqui, λακεῖν) means to promise, generally from a free impulse, and as an act of obliging courtesy, like ἐπαγγέλλεσθαι; p r o m i t t e r e, to promise, generally, at the request of another, as an act of agreement, and in reference to the fulfilment of the promise, like ὑπισχνεῖσθαι; s p o n d e r e and d e s p o n d e r e (μετὰ σπονδῶν) to promise in a solemn manner, as the consequence of a stipulation with judicially binding strength, as to pledge one's self, ἐγγυᾶν; r e c i p e r e, to take upon one's self, and pass one's word of honor, as an act of generosity, inasmuch as one sets at ease the mind of a person in trouble, like ἀναδέχεσθαι. The *pollicens* makes agreeable offers, the *promittens* opens secure prospects; the *spondens* gives legal security; the *recipiens* removes anxiety from another. Cic. Att. xiii. 1. Quoniam de æstate *polliceris* vel potius *recipis;* for the *pollicens* only engages his good-will, the *recipiens* undertakes to answer for consequences. Sen. Ep. 19; Jam. non *promittunt* de te, sed *spondent.* Cic. Fam. vii. 5. Neque minus ei prolixe de tua voluntate *promisi*, quam eram solitus de mea *polliceri;* for with regard to Trebatius, Cicero could only express his hope, with regard to himself he could actually promise. (iv. 109.)

POLLUERE, s. *Contaminare*. POMPA, see *Funus*.
PONDO, see *Libra*. PONDUS, see *Moles*.
PONTUS, see *Mare*. POPINA, s. *Deversorium*.
POPULARI, see *Vastare*. POPULUS, see *Gens*.

PORCA; SULCUS; LIRA. P o r c a (from σπαράξαι)

is the ridge between two furrows, the soil thrown up; s u l c u s (ὁλκός) the furrow itself, the trench made by the plough; l i r a (λέχριος ?) sometimes one; sometimes the other, (vi. 277.)

PORCUS, see *Sus*. PORTARE, see *Ferre*.

PORTENTA, see *Auguria*. PORTIO, see *Pars*

POSCERE, see *Petere*.

POSSE; QUIRE; VALERE; POLLERE. 1. P o s s e and q u i r e were originally transitive; p o s s e (from πότνιος) denotes being able, as a consequence of power and strength, like δύνασθαι; q u i r e (κοεῖν) as the consequence of complete qualification, like οἷόν τ' εἶναι. Cic. Tusc. ii. 27. Barbari ferro decertare acerrime *possunt*, viriliter ægrotare non *queunt;* whereas v a l e r e and p o l l e r e are intransitive. Hence we say, *possum* or *queo vincere*, but *valeo* or *polleo ad vincendum*. 2. V a l e r e (from ἑλεῖν) means to possess the right measure of strength, and thereby to match another, in opp. to insufficient strength, like σθένειν; whereas p o l l e r e (πολλός) means to have very considerable strength and means, and thereby to distinguish one's self from others, in opp. to an ordinary degree of strength, like ἰσχύειν. iv. (160.)

POSSIDERE, see *Tenere*. POSTERITAS, see *Stirps*.

POSTREMUS, see *Extremus*. POSTULARE, see *Petere*.

POTARE, see *Bibere*.

POTENTIA; POTENTATUS; POTESTAS; VIS; ROBUR. P o t e n t i a, p o t e n t a t u s, and p o t e s t a s (πότνιος) denote an exterior power, which acts by means of men, and upon men; whereas v i s and r ó b u r denote an interior power and strength, independent of the cooperation and good-will of others. P o t e n t i a denotes a merely factitious power, which can be exerted at will, like δύναμις; p o t e n t a t u s, the exterior rank of the ruler, which is acknowledged by those who are subject to him, like δυναστεία; p o t e s t a s, a just and lawful power, with which a person is entrusted, like ἐξουσία. Tac. Ann. xiii. 19. Nihil tam fluxum est quam fama *potentiæ* non sua *vi* nixæ. V i s (ἴς) is the strength which shows itself in moving and attacking, as an ability to constrain others, like κράτος; r o b u r (from ἐῤῥῶσθαι) the strength which shows itself in remaining quiet, as an ability to resist attack, and remain firm, like ῥώμη. (v. 83.)

POTESTAS, see *Occasio*.

PRÆBERE; EXHIBERE; PRÆSTARE; REPRESENTARE. P r æ b e r e and e x h i b e r e denote a voluntary act of the giver, by which a want or wish of the receiver is satisfied; the *præbens* (præhibens) is considered in relation to the receiver, to whom he gives up what he himself before possessed; the *exhibens*, in relation to the world at large, and generally gives to him who has the best claim, what he himself before possessed; whereas p r æ s t a r e and r e p r æ s e n t a r e denote an involuntary act of the giver, who only fulfils a duty, as to perform or discharge; the *præstans* releases himself from an obligation by discharging it, in opp. to being longer in a state of liability; the *repræsentans* fulfils a promise, in opp. to longer putting off. (iv. 132.)

PRÆCEPTOR, see *Doctor*.

PRÆCIPERE, see *Jubere*.

PRÆCLARUS, see *Eminens*.

PRÆDA; MANUBIÆ; SPOLIA; EXUVIAE; RAPINA. 1. P r æ d i a and m a n u b i æ denote booty only as a possession and gain that has been made by conquest; whereas s p o l i a and e x u v i æ, at the same time, as signs of victory and of honor. 2. P r æ d a denotes any sort of booty; whereas m a n u b i æ only the honorable booty of the soldier, taken in war; and r a p i n a, the dishonorable booty of the *prædo*, who violates the peace of the country, robbery. (iv. 337.) 3. P r æ d o is the robber in general, in as far as he commits the robbery with his own hands, like ληστής, as a species of *latro* (from ὀλετήρ) the highwayman, who lays wait for travellers, like σίνις, and *pirata* (πειρατής) the sea-robber; whereas r a p t o r means the robber of some particular person or thing, like ἁρπακτήρ.

PRÆDICERE, see *Divinare*.

PRÆDITUS; INSTRUCTUS; EXSTRUCTUS; ORNATUS. 1. Præditus (præ-θετός) refers to a distinction which sheds lustre; instructus and exstructus to a qualification which attests usefulness; ornatus refers to both, for *ornamentum* is not, on the one side, that which is merely of use, like *instrumentum*, nor, on the other, that which is merely for show, like *decus*, but that which is of such eminent utility as to be prized even as an ornament. Instructus paints the qualification, etc., as a perfection which protects and secures; ornatus, as an accomplishment of an imposing nature. It is only in a higher point of view, and with reference to ideal claims, that *ornatus* is considered as a want; but, according to ordinary pretensions, it passes for a distinction of life. Cic. Phil. x. 4. Græcia copiis non *instructa* solum, sed etiam *ornata*. Sen. Tranq. 9. Sicut plerisque libri non studiorum *instrumenta*, sed cœnationum *ornamenta* sunt. 2. Instructus refers to persons and things, which act either offensively or defensively; exstructus to things which are for the most part only destined to be acted upon; for example, we say, *instructæ naves* but *exstructæ mensæ*. The *exstructa* are absolutely ready; the *instructa* are only relatively so, only fully prepared to be employed according to their destination. (iii. 260.) 3. Istructus refers to the possession of the means; paratus to the readiness of the possessor to employ them. (vi. 175.)

PRÆDIUM, see *Villa*.

PRÆGNANS; GRAVIDUS; FŒTUS; FORDUS; INCIENS. Prægnans (from γενέσθαι, gnasci) denotes pregnancy quite in a general sense; gravidus, that of human beings; fœtus, fordus, inciens, that of animals, as with young; fœtus (from φύω) that of all animals; fordus or hordus (φοράς) that of cows; inciens (ἔγκυος) that of small animals, and particularly of swine. Varro, R. R. ii. 5. Quæ sterilis est vacca, taura appellatur; Quæ *prægnans*, *horda*. *Gravida mulier* is the physical and medical expression, like ἔγκυος; *prægnans*, the more select and decorous expression, something like 'in a family way.' (v. 226.)

PRÆMIUM; PRETIUM; MERCES. Præmium is a prize of honor, that confers distinction on the receiver, as a reward, in opp. to *pœna;* Tac. Ann. i. 26. Cic. Rep. iii. 16. Rabir perd. 11. Liv. xxxvi. 40, like ἆθλον, γέρας; whereas pretium and merces are only a price, for the discharge of a debt, as a payment; pretium, as a price for an article of merchandise, in opp. to *gratia*, Cic. Verr. ii. 36. Suet. Galb. 15. Appul. Apol. p. 296, like ὦνος; merces denotes wages for personal services of some duration, or hire for something hired, like μισθός. (iv. 139.)

PRÆS, see *Sponsor*. PRÆSAGIRE, see *Divinare*.

PRÆSENTEM ESSE, see *Adesse*.

PRÆSENTIRE, see *Divinare*.

PRÆSTANS, s. *Eminens*. PRÆSTOLARI, see *Manere*.

PRÆTEREA; INSUPER; ULTRO. Præterea intimates something that completes what is gone before, as πρὸς τούτοις; insuper, something in addition to what is gone before, like προσέτι; lastly, ultro, something that exceeds what has gone before, so striking as to cast it into the back-ground. (iii. 108.)

PRÆVIDERE, see *Divinare*. PRAVITAS, see *Malitia*.

PRECARI, see *Rogare*. PREHENDERE, s. *Sumere*.

PRETUM, see *Præmium*.

PRIDEM; DIU; DUDUM; DIUTURNUS; DIUTINUS. 1. Pridem (πρὶν δή) denotes a point of time, as long before; diu and dudum, a space of time as long since; diu denotes many days, months, years ago; dudum (δαρόν?) several minutes or hours since. *Jam pridem mortuus est* means, he died long ago, as an aorist; *jam diu mortuus est*, he has already long been in his grave as a perfect. Cic. Cat. i. 1. Ad mortem te duci *jam pridem* oportebat; in te conferri pestem illam quam tu in nos omnes *jamdiu* machinaris. Tac. Ann. xv. 64. Seneca Annæum *diu* sibi amicitiæ fide et arte medicinæ probatum orat, proviram *pridem* venenum promeret. 2. Diutunus denotes long duration indifferently, as something long in a general sense, or with praise, as something lasting and possessing durability, in opp. to that which quickly passes away, like *χρόνιος*; whereas diutinus, with blame, something protracted and wearisome, like *αἰανός*. Cic. Senect. 19. Nihil mihi *diuturnum* videtur, in quo est aliquid extremum: comp. with Fam. xi. 8: Libertatis desiderio et odio *diutinæ* servitutis.

PRIMORDIUM, see *Initium*.

PRIMORES; PRINCIPES; PROCERES; OPTIMATES. Primores and principes denote the most eminent persons in a state, as a class of the most influential and respectable citizens, in opp. to insignificant persons; primores, so far as they are so by their connections, birth, power, and credit; principes, so far as they have raised themselves by their intellect, commanding talent, and activity to take the lead in debates, to be at the head of parties, to be the first men even among the *primores*, and in the whole state; whereas proceres, as far as they are so from their natural position, as the nobility, in opp. to the commonalty; optimates, as a political class, as the aristocracy, in opp. to the democracy. Accius apud Non. *Primores procerum* provocaret nomine. (v. 346.)

PRIMUS; PRINCEPS; IMPERATOR; CÆSAR. 1. Primus is the first, so far as, in space of time, he makes his appearance first, and others follow him; princeps, so far as he acts first, and others follow his example. (v. 344.) 2. Princeps means the Roman emperor, as holder of the highest civil power, which gradually devolved to him as *princeps senatus;* whereas imperator, as holder of the highest military power, inasmuch as, except him and the members of his family, no one had any longer a claim to the title of *imperator;*

lastly, Cæsar means the Roman emperor, as a member, and from the time of Galba, as a mere successor, of the imperial family and dynasty.

PRINCIPIUM, see *Initium.*

PRISCUS; PRISTINUS; see *Antiquus.*

PRIVUS; PROPRIUS; PECULIARIS. Privus means one's own, in opp. to *alienus*, that which belongs to another, like οἰκεῖος; proprius, that which is exclusively one's own, in opp. to *communis*, that which is common, like ἴδιος; lastly, peculiaris, that which is especially one's own, in opp. to *universalis*, that to which all are entitled. (iv. 344.)

PROBRUM, see *Ignominia* and *Maledictum.*

PROBUS, see *Bonus.*

PROCAX, see *Petulans.*

PROCELLA, see *Ventus.*

PROCERES, see *Primores.*

PROCERUS, see *Altus.*

PROCLIVIS, see *Pronus.*

PROCRASTINARE, see *Differre.*

PROCUL; LONGE; EMINUS; E LONGINQUO. 1. Procul means at a considerable distance, but yet generally within sight, in opp. to *juxta*, Tac. H. ii. 74, like ἄποθεν; whereas longe, at a great distance, generally out of sight, in opp. to *prope*, Plin. Ep. vii. 27, like τῆλε. 2. Eminus means at such a distance as to be in reach only of missile weapons, in opp. to *cominus*, like πόῤῥωθεν; whereas e longinquo, from afar, means from a great distance, in opp. to *e propinquo*, like τηλόθεν.

PRODIGIA, see *Auguria.*

PRODIGUS; PROFUSUS; HELLUO; NEPOS. Prodigus and profusus denote prodigality, as a single feature in a man's character; prodigus (from δέχω?) inasmuch as he regards not the value of money, and neither can nor will carefully put it out to interest, from a genial disposition, as the squanderer; profusus, inasmuch as he thinks nothing too dear, that can minister to his pleasures, from levity of character, as the spendthrift; whereas helluo and nepos denote prodigality as pervading the whole character, which shows itself fully in the quality of prodigality; h e l l u o (from χλιδή) the habitual gourmand and glutton; n e p o s (ἀναπότης) a young and harebrained prodigal, who runs through his own property and that of his parents. (vi. 286.)

PRŒLIUM, see *Pugna.*

PRFERRE, see *Differre.*

PROFICISCI; ITER FACERE; PEREGRINARI. 1. P r o f i c i s c i (from facere, facessere,) denotes only the starting-point of a journey, as to set out, πορεύεσθαι; whereas i t e r f a c e r e and p e r e g r i n a r i, the duration, as to travel, ὁδοιπορεῖν.. 2. I t e r f a c e r e applies to an inland journey, as well as to travelling abroad; but p e r e g r i n a r i, ἐκδημεῖν, supposes that one travels beyond the bounds of one's own country; in which case the *peregrinatio* lasts, even when the point of destination is arrived at, and the *iter* ended. (ii. 133. iv. 69.)

PROFITERI, see *Fateri.*

PROFUGUS, see *Perfuga.*

PROFUSUS, see *Prodigus.*

PROGENIES, see *Stirps.*

PROHIBERE, see *Arcere.*

PROLES, see *Stirps.*

PROLIXI, see *Passi.*

PROLOQUI, see *Eloqui.*

PROMITTERE, s. *Polliceri.*

PRONUNTIARE, s. *Eloqui.*

PRONUS; PROCLIVIS; PROPENSUS. P r o n u s (from πρών, πρηνής,) in its moral meaning denotes inclination in general; p r o c l i v i s, oftener the inclination to something good; p r o p e n s u s, to something bad. (vi. 287.)

PROPALAM, see *Aperire.*

PROPE, see *Pæne.*

PROPENSUS, see *Pronus.*

PROPERUS, see *Citus.*

PROPINQUUS, s. *Necessarius.*

PROPRIUS, s. *Privus.*

PROROGARE, see *Differre.*

PRORSUS, see *Plane.*

PROSAPIA, see *Stirps.*

PROSEQUI, s. *Comitari.*

PROSPER, see *Felix.*

PROTERVUS, s. *Petulans.*

PROTINUS, see *Repente.*

PRUDENS, see *Sapiens.*

PSALLERE, see *Canere.*

PUDENS; PUDIBUNDUS; PUDICUS, see *Castus.*

PUELLA, see *Virgo.*

PUER; INFANS; ADOLESCENS; JUVENIS; VIR; VETUS; SENEX. Puer (from parere, πάϊς,) in a wider sense, is the man in his dependent years, so long as he neither can be, nor is, the father of a family, as a young person, in three periods, as infans, νήπιος, παιδίον, from his first years till he is seven; as puer, in a narrower sense, παῖς, from his seventh year till he is sixteen; as commencing adolescens (from ἄλθειν) a youngster, μειράκιον, νεανίας, from his sixteenth year. Juvenis, in a wider sense, is as long as he remains in his years of greatest strength, from about the time of his being of age to the first appearances of advanced age, as the young man νέος, which also may be divided into three periods;— as ceasing to be adolescens, from his eighteenth year; as juvenis (from ζέω) in a narrower sense, νεανίας, from his four-and-twentieth year; as beginning to be vir, ἀνήρ, from his thirtieth year. Maturus is the man in his ripest years, when the wild fire of youth has evaporated, and may be divided into three periods;— as ceasing to be vir, ἀνήρ, from his fortieth year; as vetus, γέρων, from his fiftieth year; as senex, (ἄναξ) πρεσβύτης, from his sixtieth year. (v. 45.)

PUGIO, see *Gladius*.

PUGNA; ACIES; PRŒLIUM. Pugna (πυκνή, πύξ,) denotes in a general sense, any conflict, from a single combat to the bloodiest pitched battle, like μάχη; acies, the conflict of two contending armies drawn up in battle array with tactical skill, the pitched battle; prœlium (from πρυλέες) the occasional rencounter of separate divisions of the armies, as an engagement, action, skirmish, like συμβολή. (v. 189.) [No: *prœlium* is frequently used of *general* engagements: e. g. illustrissimum est *prœlium* apud Platæas. *Nep.*]

PUGNARE; CONFLIGERE; DIMICARE; DIGLADIARI. 1. Pugnare and confligere mean, to decide a quarrel by force, generally in a mass, in a battle; dimicare and digladiari, to decide a quarrel by arms, and generally in a single combat. 2. P u g n a r e denotes a battle, more with reference to its form, and on its brightest side, as requiring skill and courage; c o n f l i g e r e, as a mere engagement, in consequence of an occasional collision, on its rough side as aiming at slaughter and carnage. Cic. Balb. 9. Qui cum hoste nostro cominus sæpe in acie *pugnavit:* comp. with Off. i. 23. Tenere in acie versari et manu cum hoste *confligere*, immane quiddam et belluarum simile est. Or, Nep. Eum. 4. and 8. 3. D i m i c a r e denotes a fight with weapons agreed upon by the parties, such as swords, spears, lances, clubs, and gives the harmless image of a man who fights in his own defence; whereas d i g l a d i a r i denotes a fight with sword or poniard, and gives the hateful image of a practised gladiator, whose calling and art consist in nothing but fighting and assassinating. Cic. Tusc. iv. 19. Convenit *dimicare* pro legibus, pro libertate, pro patria: comp. with Leg. iii. 9. Iis sicis, quas ipse se projecisse dicit in forum, quibus inter se *digladientur* cives. (v. 187.)

PULCHER, see *Formosus*. PULLUS, see *Ater*.

PULPA, see *Caro*. PULSARE, see *Verberare*.

PULVINAR, PULVINUS see *Culcita*.

PUNGERE; STIMULARE. P u n g e r e means to thrust at with any pointed instrument, in order to inflict a wound or occasion pain; whereas s t i m u l a r e, with a sharp-pointed or penetrating instrument, in order, by inflicting pain, to rouse to watchfulness and activity. (vi. 292.)

PUNIRE, see *Vindicta*.

PURGATIO; EXCUSATIO; SATISFACTIO. P u r g a t i o consists, like justification, in clearing one's self of a suspicion or accusation by proving it groundless; e x c u s a t i o, like making an excuse, is acknowledging something wrong, but with the assertion of, or reference to, subjective innocence; s a t i s f a c t i o, like atonement, is the satisfaction made to the suffering, or injured party, in case of innocence, by *purgatio* or *ex-*

*cusatio*,— in case of guilt, by *veniæ petitio* or by *pœna* (vi. 293.)

PURUS; MUNDUS; MERUS; PUTUS; MERACUS. 1. Purus (ψωρός) denotes purity, as a synonyme of *integer*, and in opp. to *contaminatus*, like καθαρός, Suet. Vesp. 9; whereas mundus, as a synonyme of *nitidus*, and in opp. to *spurcus* or *sordidus*, like κομψός; Senec. Ep. 70. Sall. Jug. 85. Hor. Sat. ii. 1, 65; lastly, merus (from μείρω) as a synonyme of *simplex*, and in opp. to *mixtus*, like ἀκήρατος, ἀκέραιος. Colum. iii. 21. 2. Purus is the general and popular, putus, or usually purus putus, purus ac putus, the technical expression for the purity of gold and silver, that are solid and without alloy. 3. Merus denotes anything unmixed, indifferently, or with praise, as a mixture may be an adulteration; whereas meracus refers especially to unmixed wine, and, figuratively, it is transferred to other objects, and means unmixed in a bad sense, as that which is without its proper ingredients, like the old German word, eitel, thin and poor in quality, in opp. to *temperatus*. Cic. Rep. i. 43. (iii. 204.)

PUS, see *Sanies*. PUSILLUS, see *Parvus*.
PUTARE, see *Censere*. PUTUS, see *Purus*.

## Q.

QUÆRERE; SCRUTARI; RIMARI; INVESTIGARE; INDAGARE. 1. Quærere denotes seeking, in a general sense, as the wish and want to get at something; whereas scrutari, rimari, investigare, and indagare, involve the accessory notion of taking pains. 2. Scrutari and rimari mean to search for something hidden; scrutari (from γρύτη) by rummaging, with evident interest and eagerness; rimari, by digging for, with evident exertion and skill on the part of the searcher; whereas investigare and indagare mean to search after something at a distance; investigare, like the huntsman, who cautiously follows the visible track of the wild animal; indagare (from δέχεσθαι, δήειν,) like the hound who, guided by instinct, follows the scent. Curt. ix. 10. 11. Famem sentire cœperunt, radices palmarum ubique *rimantes:* comp. with ix. 9. 5. *Scrutati* omnia tuguria tandem latentes reperere. Or, Tac. Ann. vi. 3. *Rimans* secreta omnium; that is, what were intentionally kept secret; with xii. 52. Quasi finem principis per Chaldæos *scrutaretur;* which was done without opposition. (v. 121.)

QUÆSTUS, see *Lucrum.*

QUARE, see *Cur.* QUE, see *Et.*

QUESTUS; QUIRITATIO; QUERIMONIA; QUERELA. Questus and Quiritatio are expressions of pain; questus, in single, quiritatio in continued tones of lamentation; whereas querimonia and querela are expressions of indignation; querimonia in the just feeling of the injured person, who will not brook an act of injustice; querela in, for the most part, the blamable feeling of the discontented person, who will brook no hardship. The *Querimonia* is an act of the understanding, and aims at redress or satisfaction; the *querela* is an act of feeling, and aims, for the most part, only at easing the heart. Cic. Cæcil. 3. In populi Romani quotidiana *querimonia:* comp. with Fam. v. 14. Tu non intelliges te *querelis* quotidianis nihil proficere. (v. 310.)

QUIES; TRANQUILLITAS; REQUIES. 1. Quies (from κεῖσθαι?) denotes absolute rest, in opp. to activity in general, like ἡσυχία; tranquillitas, quietness in acting, in opp. to hasty or passionate activity, like ἐκηλία. Sen. Ep. 3. Et *quiescenti* agendum et agenti *quiescendum* est; comp. with Cic. Top. 3. Ut aut perturbentur animi aut *tranquillentur.* Hence is quietus allied in sense with *otiosus, segnis, languidus;* whereas tranquillus with *lenis, placidus, moderatus.* 2. Quies is rest in itself; requies, rest after activity and exertion. Curt. ix. 6. § 2. Ne *quies* corpori invalido adhuc necessaria pulsu remorum impediretur: comp. with § 3. Placuit hic locus ad suam et militum *requiem*. (i. 80.)

Quire, see *Posse*.

Quiritatio, see *Questus*.

Quisque; Quivis; Quilibet; Unusquisque; Omnes; Universi; Cuncti; Totus. 1. Quisque, quivis, and quilibet, denote a totality, which is cut up into several individualities; whereas omnes, universi, and cuncti, denote a combined totality. 2. Quisque means each individual; quivis, any individual you choose, without exception, and with emphasis; quilibet, any individual whatever, without selection, and with indifference, like ὁστισοῦν, synonymously with *primus quisque*, ὁ τυχών. Propert. ii. 6, 26. Templa pudicitiæ quid opus statuisse puellis, si *cuivis* nuptæ *cuilibet* esse licet? apud Lachmann. Cic. Fam. viii. 10. *Quidvis quamlibet* tenue munusculum. 3. Quisque is an enclitic, that is, throws back the accent on the preceding word, and in prose never stands at the beginning of a sentence, like ἕκαστος; whereas unusquisque is accented and emphatic, like εἷς ἕκαστος. 4. Unusquisque denotes each individual, in opp. to some individuals; whereas singuli, individuals, in opp. to the undivided totality, like ἕκαστοι. 5. Omnes (ἅπαντες) denotes all without exception, merely as a totality, in opp. to *nemo*, *unus*, *aliquot*. Cic. Sext. 12, 27. Off. iii. 6, like πάντες; whereas universi, all taken collectively, in opp. to *singuli* and *unusquisque*. Cic. N. D. ii. 17. 65, 66. Off. iii. 6, like σύμπαντες; lastly, cuncti (ξυνεκτοί) all in their combined reality, in opp, to *dispersi*, like ἅπαντες. Liv. vii. 35. Admonitione paventibus *cunctis* quum omnium in se vertisset oculos Decius. Nep. Dat. 5. Qui illum unum pluris quam se *omnes* fieri videbant. Quo facto *cuncti* ad eum opprimendum consenserunt. 6. Totus, solidus, and integer denote that which is originally a whole, but which is liable to fall to pieces by accident, like ὅλος; whereas omnis, universus, and cunctus, denote original individualities, which form a whole by their association, like πᾶς, σύμπας, ἅπας. (iv. 352.)

Quotidie; In singulos dies. Quotidie applies to things that are daily repeated; whereas in singulos dies, to things that, from day to day, are making an advance. Cic. Att. v. 7. *Quotidie* vel potius *in singulos dies* breviores literas ad te mitto. Fam. vi. 4. Catil. i. 2.

## R.

Rabies, see *Amens*.

Radiare, see *Lucere*.

Rami; Ramalia; Virga; Termes; Turio; Surculus; Talea; Sarmentum; Stolo; Virgultum; Fruticetum. 1. Rami and ramalia are the boughs of a tree; rami (from ῥάχος) the living, green boughs, θαλλοί; ramalia, the withered dry boughs. Whereas virga, termes, turio, surculus, talea, sarmentum, and stolo, are only twigs; virga, and the words of rare occurrence, termes olivæ, and turio lauri, without any accessory reference, like κλάδος, κλών, κλῆμα; surculus and talea as members and offspring of the tree, which as scions and shoots should be subservient to the parent-stock, like ὀρσός; sarmentum and stolo, as mere off-shoots of the tree, are set aside, and cast away; sarmentum (from sarpere, ἅρπη,) as a completely useless twig; stolo, as at the same time an injurious sucker. 2. Virgultum is a place grown over with bushes, and not bare; fruticetum (from frutices) a place grown over with shrubs, and not passable. (v. 283.)

Rapina, Raptor, see *Præda*.

Recens, see *Novus*.

RECIPERE, see *Polliceri* and *Sumere*.

RECITARI, see *Eloqui*. RECLUDERE, see *Aperire*.

RECONDERE, see *Celare*. RECORDARI, s. *Meminisse*.

RECUPERARE, s. *Sumere*. RECURVUS, see *Curvus*.

RECUSARE, see *Negare* and *Spernere*.

REDIMERE, see *Emere*. REDIRE, see *Reverti*.

REDOLERE, see *Olere*. REDUNCUS, see *Curvus*.

REDUNDARE, s. *Abundare*. REFELLERE, see *Refutare*.

REFUGIUM, see *Perfuga*.

REFUTARE; CONFUTARE; REFELLERE. 1. Refutare and confutare (from sputare? or φοιτᾶν?) denote a refutation, in whatever manner; refellere (from fallere) on good grounds, and by convincing arguments. 2. The refutans acts on the defensive in refuting the arguments that are opposed to him; the confutans, on the offensive, in exposing their nullity, and cutting them up. Cic. Font. 1. Plus laboris consumo in poscendis testibus quam defensores in *refutandis;* comp. with N. D. ii. 17. Cujus opinionis levitas *confutata* a Cotta non desiderat orationem meam (iv. 43.)

REGALIS, see *Regius*.

REGIO, see *Locus*.

REGIUS; REGALIS. Regius means, what belongs to a king, and descends from kings; regalis, what is suitable to a king, and worthy of him. (iv. 93 v. 48.)

RELIGIO; FIDES. Religio (from ἀλέγειν) is conscientiousness, on the ground of an inward obligation, through the conscience; fides (from πιθεῖν) on the ground of an outward obligation, through a promise. (vi. 268.)

RELINQUERE; DESERERE; OMITTERE; DESTITUERE; DESOLATUS. 1. Relinquere, to leave behind, has reference to an object, to which one stands in a mere outward and local relation of proximity; whereas deserere and omittere, to an object to which one stands in an inward and moral relation as an owner or friend; desertio, like leaving in the lurch, has its ground in cowardice, or other forgetfulness of duty, in opp. to *defensio*, *tutatio;* omissio, like giving up, has its ground in a conviction of being able to dispense with, in opp. to *obtinere*. Tac. Dial. 16. Partes quas intellexerimus te non tam *omisisse* quam nobis *reliquisse*. And 9. *Relinquenda* conversatio amicorum et jucunditas urbis, *deserenda* cætera officia. Cic. Verr. i. 4, 11. *Desertum* exercitum, *relictam* provinciam. 2. Deserere means to forsake, and expose to a possible and remote danger; destituere to an actual and impending danger. Curt. iv. 2, 32. *Desertus*, *destitutus*, hostibus deditus. Liv. vi. 2. Quod defensores suos in ipso discrimine periculi *destituat*. 3. Desertus and destitutus denote, especially, forgetfulness of duty; whereas desolatus, the unmercifulness of the action. Suet. Cal. 12. Deserta, *desolataque reliquis* subsidiis aula. (iii. 290.)

RELIQUI, see *Cæteri*. REMEDIUM, see *Mederi*.
REMINISCI, see *Meminisse*. RENIDERE, see *Ridere*.
RENUERE, see *Negare*. REPAGULUM, see *Sera*.
REPANDUS, see *Curvus*.

REPENTE; SUBITO; EXTEMPLO; E VESTIGIO; ILLICO; STATIM; PROTINUS; CONFESTIM; CONTINUO. Repente and subito denote suddenly; repens means sudden, in opp. to *exspectatus*, expected, Cic. Tusc. iii. 22; to sensim, Cic. Off. i. 33. Suet. Tib. 11, like ἐξαπίνης; but subitus, in opp. to foreseen, ante provisus, Cic. Tusc. iii. 22; meditatus, Plin. Ep. i. 16; paratus, Cic. Or. i, 33, like παραχρῆμα. Extemplo and e vestigio, in opp. to delay; extemplo (ex tempore) in a moment, with reference to time; e vestigio, on the spot, sur-le-champ, with reference to place. Illico and ilicet, in opp. to slowness; illico (in loco) is used in prose, like παραυτίκα; ilicet, by writers of comedy and poets. Statim and protinus, in opp. to, at a future time; statim, immediately, in opp. to *deinde*, Tac. Ann. vi. 3; *postea*, Suet. Cl. 39. A. 51. N. 34, like εὐθύς; protinus, forthwith, like προκα. Confestim and continuo, in opp. to ex intervallo, Cic. Inv. ii. 12. (v. 157.)

REPERE; SERPERE; SERPENS; ANGUIS; COLUBER. 1. Repere means, with small feet and short steps, to move slowly along, to creep; whereas serpere, without feet, by merely twisting the whole body, and without noise to move forward, to creep on the belly. 2. Serpens (ἕρπων) is the general name for whatever creeps like a snake, like ἑρπετόν; anguis (ἔγχος, ἔγχελυς?) is a great formidable snake, ὄφις; coluber (ἀσκάλαφος) a small, spiteful snake, ἔχις, ἔχιδνα. (v. 341.)

REPERIRE, see *Invenire*.

REPETERE, see *Iterum*.

REPREHENDERE; VITUPERARE. Reprehendere has in view the amendment of a fault, and warning for the future, like showing the right path, and μέμψις; vituperare (from vitii πεπαρεῖν) has in view the acknowledgment of a fault, better judgment, shame and repentance, like a rebuke, and ψόγος. Reprehensio is in opp. to *probatio;* for examples, see Cic. Or. 48, 159. Mur. 20, 142. Senec. Vit. B. 1; whereas vituperatio is in opp. to *laudatio;* for examples, see Cic. Fat. 5. Off. iii. 32. Quintil. iii. 7, 1. (ii. 259, iii. 323.)

REPUDIARE, see *Negare*.

REPUDIUM; DIVORTIUM. Repudium is a one-sided putting away of a betrothed bride, or of a married woman; divortium, a mutual agreement, acquiescing in the dissolution of a marriage, or a formal divorce, by which each party was released. The formula of the *repudium* was: Conditione tua non utor:—that of the *divortium:* Res tuas tibi habeto. We say: *Repudium mittere, remittere, renunciare, dicere alicui;* whereas *divortium facere cum aliqua*.

REQUIES, see *Quietus*.

REQUIRERE; DESIDERARE. Requirere denotes requisition as an act of the understanding, which has in view the usefulness of the object; desiderare, as an act of feeling, which surrounds the object with love and sympathy. The *requirens* claims a right, and expects the fulfilment of his claim from others; the *desiderans* harbors a wish, and expects its fulfilment from the course of things, from fortune. Cic. Fam. vii. 26. Magis tuum officium *desiderari*, quam abs te *requiri* putavi meum. (v. 128.)

RERI, see *Censere*. RESERARE, see *Aperire*.

RESPECTUM; RATIONEM HABERE. Respectum habere means, to have regard in thoughts and intentions; rationem habere, in acts and measures. (vi. 304.)

RESTARE; SUPERESSE. Restare means to remain, in opp. to *præteriisse*, *interiisse;* whereas superesse, in opp. to *deesse.* (vi. 304.)

RESTAURARE, see *Instituere*.

RESTIS, see *Laqueus*.

RESTITUERE, see *Instituere*.

RETE; CASSIS; PLAGA. Retia (from ῥῆχος, ἀράχνη,) is the most general expression for fishing and hunting nets; casses and plagæ are implements used in hunting only; casses (from κοττάνη), nets for catching the smaller wild animals; plagæ (from πλέξαι), nets of a stronger texture to get larger animals into one's power by entangling them. Hor. Ep. 2, 32. Aut trudit acres apros in obstantes *plagas*, aut amite levi rara tendit *retia*. (vi. 304.)

RETICERE, see *Silere*. RETUARE, see *Aperire*.

REVERERI, see *Vereri*.

REVERTI; REVENIRE; REDIRE. Reverti and revenire denote properly only momentary actions; reverti, in opp. to *proficisci*, the turning back; revenire, in opp. to *advenire*, the return; whereas redire denotes a more lasting action, which lies between turning back and the return, in opp. to *porro ire*, the journey home. Cic. Att. xvi. 7. p. m. Quam valde ille *reditu* vel potius *reversione* mea lætatus effudit. (iv. 63.)

RIDERE; CACHINNARI; RENIDERE; SUBRIDERE; IRRIDERE; DERIDERE. 1. Ridere and cachinnari denote an audible laugh; ridere, a joyous and temperate laugh, like γελᾶν; cachinnari (from hinnire) an unrestrained and resounding fit of laughter, like καγχάζειν; whereas subridere, and renidere only a visible smile; subridere, as the expression of a waggish or satirical humor; renidere (from nidor, ὄνειδος,) as the expression of a friendly, and also of a dissembling humor, like μειδιᾶν. Cic. Tusc. iv. 31. Si *ridere* concessum sit, vituperatur tamen *cachinnatio.* Verr. iii. 25. Herenn. iii. 14, 25. Ovid, Art. iii. 287. 2. Deridere denotes laughing at, as an act of loftiness and contempt, inasmuch as others are laughed down, like καταγελᾶν; irridere, as an act of insolence and malignant pleasure, inasmuch as others are laughed at before their faces, like ἐγγελᾶν. Cic. Orat. iii. 14. Istos omnes *deridete* atque contemnite; and Verr. v. 92: comp. with N. D. ii. 3. Claudius etiam per jocum deos *irridens;* and Suet. Aug. 36. (iii. 251.)

RIMARI, see *Quærere.*

RIPA; LITUS; ORA; ACTA. 1. Ripa (ῥιπή, ἐρείπω,) is the bank of a river, like ὄχθη; whereas litus, ora, acta, the shores of the sea. Mela. lii. 9. *Oras* ad Eurum sequentibus nihil memorabile occurrit; vasta omnia vastis præcisa montibus *ripæ* potius sunt quam *litora:* and iii. 3, 4. i. 2, 2. Vitruv. ii. 9, 14. Circa *ripam* fluminis Padi et *litora* maris Adriatici. Colum. i. 5. Ovid. Met. i. 42. 2. Litus denotes the shore only as the line which separates the land from the sea, as the strand, like ἠϊών and ῥηγμίν; whereas ora and acta, as the space and tract of land that borders on the sea, as the coast, like ἀκτή and αἰγιαλός; ora (ὤα, οὖρος,) only in geographical reference to the adjacent land, in opp. to the inland country; but acta (ἀκτή) with the accessory notion of being distinguishable by the senses, inasmuch as the coast affords striking views and a pleasant residence. Liv. xxiv. 8. Classem paravimus ut Africæ *oram* popularemur, ut tuta nobis Italiæ *litora* essent. Plin. Ep. v. 6, 2. Gravis et pestilens *ora* Tuscorum, quæ per *litus* extenditur. Hence *litoris ora*, that is, *ora per litus extensa*, Virg. G. ii. 44. Tac. Ann. ii. 78. Appul. Met. iv. p. 92. Avian. Fab. xx. 10. —And Prudent. adv. Symm. iv. 136. Invenit expositum secreti in *litoris acta*. Cic. Fam. ix. 6. Ea tractes quorum et usus et delectatio est omnibus illis *actis* et voluptatibus anteponenda. *Acta* is a foreign word of Greek extraction, which Tacitus (Hist. iii. 76.) expresses by the circumlocution *amœna litorum*. (iii. 207.)

RITUS, see *Consuetudo*. RIVALITAS, see *Imitatio*.
RIXA, see *Disceptatio*. ROBUR, see *Potentia*.
ROBUSTUS, see *Validus*.

ROGARE; ORARE; OBSECRARE; OBTESTARI; PRECARI; SUPPLICARE. 1. R o g a r e and o r a r e denote simply a request as the quiet utterance of a wish; but the *rogans* (ὀργᾶν, ὀρέγεσθαι) feels himself *al pari*, on a par with the person whom he asks, and asks only a courtesy, like αἰτεῖν; the *orans* acknowledges the superiority of the other, and asks a benefit, like δεῖσθαι; whereas o b s e c r a r e and o b t e s t a r i denote a passionate asking, as to conjure; but the *obsecrans* asks urgently, like λιπαρεῖν; the *obtestans* (from θέσσασθαι) in a suppliant manner. Cic. Att. xvi. 16. Igitur, mi Plance, *rogo* te atque etiam *oro*. Pseudocic. p. Red. 16. Pro mea vos salute non *rogavit* solum, verum etiam *obsecravit*. 2. P r e c a r i denotes the calm act of prayer, in which one raises one's hand to heaven, like εὔχεσθαι; but s u p p l i c a r e denotes the passionate act of supplication, in which one throws one's self on one's knees, or on the ground, and wrings one's hands, like ἱκετεύειν. By hyperbole, however, p r e c o r denotes any urgent request; s u p p l i c a r e, any humble request, addressed to a human being. Cic. Parad. v. 3. Noctu venire domum ad eum, *precari*, denique *supplicare*. (v. 232.)

ROGARE; INTERROGARE; PERCONTARI; SCISCITARI. R o g a r e, i n t e r r o g a r e, and q u æ r e r e, denote a simple questioning; r o g a r e (ὀργᾶν, ὀρεγεσθαι), as willing to know; i n t e r r o g a r e, as wishing to know; whereas p e r c o n t a r i and s u s c i t a r i denote urgently asking; p e r c o n t a r i (from γνῶναι) always from a desire of knowledge, with seriousness and calmness; s c i s c i t a r i (redupl. of scitari) often from curiosity, with inquisitiveness, eagerness, or also with cunning, like pumping or ferreting out. (v. 125.)

ROGARE, see *Petere*.

RUDIS, see *Fustis*.

RUINA; STRAGES. R u i n a (from ῥεῦσαι) is the falling down of things raised one upon another, in consequence of the basis giving way; whereas s t r a g e s is the throwing down of bodies standing upright, in consequence of a push from without. Liv. iv. 33. *Strages ruinæ* similis. (vi. 309.)

RUMOR; FAMA. R u m o r (from ῥεῦμα), like report, is the uncertain, dark, often clandestine propagation of intelligence, in opp. to authentic assurance; f a m a (φήμη), like information, is the open and public propagation of intelligence, in opp. to ocular demonstration. The *rumor* interests only by its novelty, is an object of curiosity, and passes away with the generation in which it sprung up; the *fama* interests through its importance, is an object of research, and as a permanent property descends to posterity. (v. 233.)

RUMPERE, see *Frangere*. RUPES, see *Saxum*.

RURSUS, see *Iterum*. RUS, see *Villa*.

RUS; AGER; RUSTICUS; AGRESTIS; RUSTICANUS.

1. R u s (ἄροτον) denotes the country, in opp. to the town or city, the village with what belongs to it; whereas a g e r (ἀγρός) the country, in opp. to the district in general, the open country or fields. Cels. Med 1. Sanum oportet . . . modo *ruri* esse, modo in urbe, sæpiusque in *agro*. 2. R u s t i c u s denotes, like ἀγροῖκος, merely residing in the country; a g r e s t i s, like ἄγριος, growing wild in the fields, like *ferus*, but as a milder expression, for *ferus* (φῆρες) denotes wild-

ness as an inward nature; a g r e s t i s, merely as a mark of the place of residence, or of extraction. 3 In a spiritual sense, r u s t i c u s denotes more an intellectual, a g r e s t i s more a moral roughness; r u s t i c u s, like countrified, has a reference to bashfulness and uncouthness; in its best sense, it is allied to innocence; in its worst, to awkwardness; whereas a g r e s t i s, like boorish, has a reference to shamelessness and vulgarity, is never used in a good sense, but borders on *feritas*, and answers to the German word Flegelei, 'churlishness.' The *rusticus*, in opp. to *urbanus*, violates only the conventional laws of decorum; the *agrestis*, in opp. to *humanus*, the natural laws of decorum also. 4. When Cicero wishes to give to *rusticus* a still milder sense, and secure it from ambiguity, he adopts the word *rusticanus;* so that, according to him, r u s t i c u s is one who actually lives in a country-village, r u s t i c a n u s, one who resembles those who live in country-villages; hence among the *rusticani* the *municipes* may be reckoned, as *rusticorum similes.*

## S.

SABULO; HARENA; SABURA. S a b u l o (from *ψαφαρός*, *ψῆφος*,) and in Pliny s a b u l u m, denote sand, as a sort of light soil; h a r e n a, a r e n a (from *χεράς*), as a dry stony soil, as small or pounded pebbles, in opp. to a fruitful soil; s a b u r a, s a b u r r a, with especial reference to its use, as shipsand, ballast. (vi. 311.)

SACELLUM, see *Templum*.

SACER; SANCTUS. S a c e r (*ἄγος*) denotes that which is sacred, inasmuch as it belongs to the gods, in opp. to p r o f a n u s, like *ἱερός*; whereas s a n c t u s (from *ἁγνός*) inasmuch as it is under the protection of the gods, and, being guarded from profanation, is, in consequence, pure and spotless, in opp. to *pollutus*, like *ὅσιος*. Hence *sanctus* h o m o is a pure, pious man;

sacer, one accursed, devoted to the gods as an expiatory sacrifice. In the same manner sancire means to place under the immediate protection of the gods, as laws and compacts, for example; whereas sacrare means to dedicate to the gods, as temples and altars, for example. (iii. 198.)

SACRAMENTUM, see *Jusjurandum.*

SACRARE; CONSECRARE; DICARE; DEDICARE. Sacrare, consecrare, mean to hallow, with reference to men, with regard to whom the profane use of a thing is withdrawn and forbidden; dicare, dedicare (from δέχεσθαι) mean to dedicate with reference to the gods, to whom the thing is set apart as their property. Hence consecrare may be used in an absolute sense, but dedicare has always a reference to the new proprietors.

SÆPE; CREBRO; FREQUENTER; FREQUENTARE; CELEBRARE. 1. Sæpe denotes often, in opp. to *semel*, Suet. Ner. 33; *nonnunquam*, Cic. Or. 66; *semper*, like πολλάκις; whereas crebro and frequenter, in opp. to *raro*, Rhet. ad Her. iv. 23. Cic. Or. 66; crebro, often, and in quick succession, and rather too often than too seldom, like θαμά; but frequenter (partic. from farcire) often, and not too seldom; for in general creber denotes a multifarious assembly, inasmuch as it is dense and crowded; whereas frequens, inasmuch as it is numerously attended. Consequently, frequens rather implies praise, like *largus;* creber, blame, like *spissus.* And *frequentes senatores* denote the senate, when represented as complete; *crebri senatores*, as wanting room on account of their number, and forced to sit close. 2. Frequentare means to visit a place often, and not neglect it: whereas celebrare, to visit it often, and thereby to enliven it, and to fill it with festive sounds. (i. 17.)

SÆVITIA; CRUDELITAS. Sævitia (from *aî*, *αἰνός*) denotes the blood-thirsty cruelty of the tyrant, who acts like a ravenous beast, that kills and tears its prey, in opp. to *mansuetudo;* whereas crudelitas (from κρύος, crudus) denotes the reckless cruelty of the judge, who enforces the utmost rigor of the law, in opp. to *clementia.* Sen. Clem. 2. Cic. Lig. 3. Att. viii. 9. Plin. Pan. 3.

SÆVUS, see *Atrox.* SALSUS, see *Lepidus.*

SALTUS, see *Silva.* SALUBER, see *Salus.*

SALUS; SANITAS; VALENS; SALUBER; SANUS; SALUTARIS. 1. Salus denotes existence in general, in opp. to *interitus;* whereas sanitas, the health of the person existing, in opp. to *ægritudo;* first of the body, then, in a higher degree, of the soul. 2. Sanus and valens denote health as a temporary state, and are allied in sense with *integer;* whereas saluber and validus denote habitual qualities, and are allied in sense with *robustus.* Hence *salubris oratio* means a speech sound in matter, possessing original strength; *sana*, a temperate and discreet speech. Cic. Brut. 13. 51. Tac. Dial. 25. Plin. Ep. ix. 26. 3. Sanus and saluber represent health, merely as finding one's self well; valens and validus, as possessing strength to act. 4. Saluber in a transitive sense means, what brings *sanitas*, in opp. to *pestilens*, like ὑγιεινός; whereas salutaris, what brings *salus*, in opp. to *pestiferus*, like σωτήριος. Cato, apud Plin. H. N. xviii. 6. Nihil *salutare* est nisi quod toto anno *salubre.* (i. 31.)

SALUS, see *Vita.*

SALUTARIS, see *Salus.*

SALVE, see *Ave.*

SALVUS; SOSPES; INCOLUMIS; INTEGER. Salvus and sospes denote, like σῶς, being safe and sound, in opp. to being killed; salvus is the customary, sospes a select expression; whereas incolumis and integer, like ἀσκηθής, denote being unhurt and untouched; incolumis (from calvere, calamitas, κολούω), in opp. to being wounded, etc.; integer (from tangere) in opp. to being attacked. Tac. Hist. i. 84. Mea cum vestra *salus incolumitate* senatus firmatur;

that is, our safety is assured by the senate not having had a hair touched. And, i. 66. Verba Fabii *salutem incolumitatemque* Viennensium commendantis; *salus* refers to being killed, *incolumitas* to being plundered: comp. with Cic. Orat. iii. 45, 178. Dejot. 15. Sunt tuæ clementiæ monumenta . . . eorum *incolumitates* quibus *salutem* dedisti. (iii. 306.)

SANARE, see *Mederi*.

SANCTUS, see *Sacer* and *Bonus*.

SANGUIS; CRUOR; SANGUINEUS; SANGUINOLENTUS; CRUENTUS. 1. Sanguis denotes the blood circulating in the body, living and supporting life, like *αἷμα*; cruor (*κρύος*) the blood gushing from the body, like *βρότος*. Cic. N. D. ii. 55. *Sanguis* per venas in omne corpus diffunditur: comp. with Rosc. Am. 7, 19. Ut *cruorem* inimici quam recentissimum ostenderet. Tac. Ann. xii. 46. Mox ubi *sanguis* artus extremos suffuderit, levi ictu *cruorem* eliciunt atque invicem lambunt. Sanguis is the condition of physical life; cruor, the symbol of death by slaughter. 2. Sanguineus means, consisting of blood, sanguinolentus, smelling after blood, or blood-thirsty; cruentus, red with blood. (iv. 258.).

SANIES; PUS. Sanies (from *σίσανον*) denotes running, consequently, offensive matter; pus (from *πύθω*), corroding, consequently, pernicious matter. Cels. v. 26, 20. (vi. 316.)

SANITAS, SANUS, see *Salus*.

SAPIENS; PRUDENS; CALLIDUS; SCITUS; SOLERS; CORDATUS; CATUS. 1. Sapiens (from *σήπω*) is the person who chooses right objects, from ennobling views, and pursues them with quietness of mind; prudens and callidus denote the person who chooses right means, and regulates them with circumspection; prudentia is a natural judiciousness, pervading a man's whole nature: calliditas, an acquired knowledge of the world and of men, gained by experience and practice. Cic. Fr. Scaur. 5. Hominis *prudentis* natura, *callidi* usu, doctrina eruditi. 2. Prudens is the person who has accurate practical views, in opp. to *stultus;* scitus, who has tact, mother-wit, and the faculty of combination; solers, who possesses practical genius and inventive power; cordatus, who has his head in the right place, in opp. to *excors;* catus, who discovers and knows secret means and ways. (v. 114.)

SAPOR; GUSTUS; GUSTARE; LIBARE. 1. Sapor denotes objectively the flavor which a thing has, or gives out, in opp. to *odor*, etc.; gustus or gustatus (γεῦσαι) denotes, subjectively, the sensation occasioned by this flavor, or the sense of taste, in opp. to *olfactus*, etc. Sen. Ep. 109. Debet esse optatus ad hujus modi *gustum*, ut ille tali *sapore* capiatur. 2. The libans puts only a small portion of any thing to, or into, his mouth; whereas the gustans has the sense of the effect of what he tastes, and is conscious of its flavor. Ovid, Amor. i. 4, 34. Si tibi forte dabit, quæ *prægustaverit* ipse, rejice *libatos* illius ore dapes. (iii. 125.)

SARMENTUM, see *Rami.*

SATELLES; STIPATOR. Satelles (from στέλλω) denotes an attendant, as a hired servant; stipator (from στῖφος) as a guard. Cic. Rull. ii. 13. Ex equestri loco ducentos in singulos annos *stipatores* corporis constituit, eosdem ministros et *satellites* potestatis. (vi. 318.)

SATIS; AFFATIM; ABUNDE. 1. Satis (from ἄση) denotes, like ἱκανῶς, a sufficient measure, without any accessory reference; whereas affatim and abunde with the accessory notion of rather too much than too little; abunde, like ἅλις, with an objective and absolute reference; whereas affatim, like ἀφθόνως, in a subjective and relative sense. A person may have worked *affatim*, according to his own opinion, and yet not *satis*. Cic. Att. ii. 16. Puto enim me Dicæarcho *affatim satis* fecisse. And, xvi. 1. *Satis* est et *affatim* prorsus. Liv. iv. 22. Frumentum non necessitati *satis*, sed copiæ quoque *abunde* ex ante confecto sufficiebat. 2. Satiare denotes satisfying, as the appeasing of a want generally, of hunger, of a longing, etc.; whereas saturare, as the appeasing of an unnatural craving, of an over-eager longing, or a voracious hunger, of hatred, of the thirst for blood. (i. 109.)

SATIS HABERE; CONTENTUM ESSE; BONI CONSULERE; CONTENTUS; ÆQUUS ANIMUS. 1. Satis habere, that is, to consider as enough, expresses a judgment, and is only a sign of an unimpassioned judgment of the right measure; whereas contentum esse, to be satisfied, expresses a feeling and is a sign of moderation and self-government; lastly, boni consulere, to take in good part, an act of the will, by which a person resigns the realizing of his wish, and acquiesces as becomes a man, in what is inevitable. Satis habere is in construction with an infinitive; contentum esse, generally with an ablative, or with *quod*. Cic. Orat. iii. 19; comp. with Fr. Clod. 6. 2. Contentus animus denotes a relative contentedness, which puts up with and does not murmur at the want of complete success; æquus animus, an absolute contentedness, which feels quite satisfied, and does not wish for a more prosperous state. (v. 343.)

SATISFACTIO, see *Purgatio*.

SATURARE, see *Satis*.

SAUCIUS, see *Vulnus*.

SAXUM; RUPES; CAUTES; PETRA; SCOPULI; LAPIS; CALCULUS; SCRUPULUS. 1. Saxum, rupes, and cautes, are greater; lapis, calx, and scrupus, smaller masses of stone. Plin. H. N. xxxvi. 22. Silex viridis ubi invenitur, *lapis*, non *saxum* est. 2. Saxa (from ψεκάς, ψήχω) are greater masses of stone, in whatever form, like πέτραι; rupes and petræ (πέτραι, from πεσεῖν) are steep and high, like rocks, and therefore difficult to climb; cautes and scopuli are rough and pointed, like crags, and therefore threaten danger; the cautes are smaller, and also not visible in the water, and therefore deceitful; the scopuli (from κόψαι) jutting upwards, threaten and announce danger, like σκόπελοι. 3. Lapis (ἄλιψ) is the most general expression, and denotes the stone only as a material substance, without regard to its form, like λίθος; calculus, is a smooth, generally round pebble; scrupulus, a rough, generally angular pebble; but for this meaning of *scrupulus*, the dimin. of *scrupus*, we have only the authority of grammarians; in authors it has only the figurative meaning of scruple. (v. 191.)

SCANDERE; ADSCENDERE; ESCENDERE; CONSCENDERE; INSCENDERE. Scandere means to mount a steep height, which is connected with exertion, and generally brings both hands and feet into requisition, as to climb; whereas adscendere, escendere, conscendere, and inscendere, mean to mount a height, in a general sense; adscendere, without any accessory notion, merely in opp. to *descendere;* whereas escendere means to mount a height which is fortified, like ramparts, walls, or which confers distinction, as the *rostrum;* conscendere, to mount something in company with others, a ship for instance; inscendere, to mount an enclosed space, a carriage for instance. (iv. 60.)

SCAPHA, see *Navigium*.

SCELESTUS; SCELERATUS; NEFARIUS; NEFANDUS; IMPIUS. Scelestus (from scelus, σκληρός) has reference to the mind, like *ad scelera pronus* and *promptus;* whereas sceleratus, to actions, like *sceleribus pollutus atque opertus.* Hence the epithet sceleratus is applied to things, to *porta*, *campus*, *vicus;* and, in general, things can be called *scelesta* only by personification. In the like manner nefarius and impius as applied to the impiety of the person who acts, only with this distinction, that the *impius* is impious only in mind, the *nefarius* in his actions also; whereas nefandus refers to the horrible enormity of an action. (ii. 149.)

SCELUS, see *Delictum*. SCHOLA, see *Ludus*.
SCIENTIA, see *Cognitio*. SCINDERE, see *Findere*.
SCIPIO, see *Fustis*. SCISCITARI, see *Rogare*.
SCITUS, see *Sapiens*. SCOBINA, see *Lima*.
SCOPULI, see *Saxum*. SCORTUM, see *Pellex*.
SCROBS, see *Specus*. SCROPHA. see *Sus*.
SCRUPULUS, see *Saxum*. SCRUTARI, see *Quærere*.

SCUTUM; CLYPEUS; PARMA. Scutum (σκῦτος) is a larger shield, covering the whole body, σάκος; clypeus and parma smaller shields of a round form, ἀσπίς; clypeus (κλοπιός, καλύψαι) for foot-soldiers; parma (πάλμη) for horse-soldiers also; lastly, pelta (πέλτη) a small shield in the form of a half-moon; cetra, a small leathern shield. Liv. ix. 19. Macedonibus *clupeus* . . . Romano *scutum*, majus corpori tegumentum. Liv. xxxi. 36. Cetratos, quos *peltastas* vocant, in insidiis abdiderat.

SCYPHUS, see *Poculum*. SECESSIO, see *Turbæ*.
SECRETA, see *Arcana*. SECURIS, see *Ascia*.
SECURUS, see *Tutus*.

SEDES; SEDILE; SELLA. Sedes is simply a place for sitting, like ἕδος; whereas sedile and sella are artificially prepared seats; sedile, in any form chosen, as a stool or bench, whether movable or immovable, like ἕδρα; sella, of a particular form, as a chair or throne, like θρόνος.

SEDITIO, see *Turbæ*. SEGNITIA, see *Ignavia*.
SEMITA, see *Iter*. SEMO, see *Numen*.

SEMPER; USQUE. Semper (ἀμπερές) means 'always' and 'ever,' absolutely, without reference to any definite limit; whereas usque only relatively 'always,' within a definite limit, *in* usque dum, etc.; but by the poets it is used without any additional clause, as in Horace, for example, Sat. i. 9. *Usque* sequar te (i. 14.)

SEMPITERNUS, see *Continuus*.

SENECTA, SENECTUS, SENIUM, see *Vetus.*

SENEX, see *Puer* and *Vetus.*

SENSIM, see *Paulatim.*

SENTENTIA; OPINIO; SUFFRAGIUM. 1. Sententia is the view of a subject, resting upon clear perception and acquired conviction, like γνώμη; opinio, an opinion resting upon mere feeling, like δόξα. 2. Sententia is the vote of a senator upon any motion, etc., like γνώμη; whereas suffragium, the simple voting, pronouncing yes or no, or a name, like ψῆφος.

SENTES, see *Dumi.*

SENTIRE, see *Intelligere.*

SEORSUM; SEPARATIM. Seorsum means set apart, in order to prevent a thing being common, with the accessory notion of secrecy; whereas separatim means separated, in order to prevent confusion, with the accessory notion of arrangement.

SEPELIRE; CONDERE; HUMARE. Sepelire and condere denote complete burial, the more or less solemn interment of the remains of a dead person, with or without previous burning; sepelire (Goth. filhan, ἀσπάλαξ) as a proper and technical expression; condere (καταθεῖναι) as a general and softer expression; whereas humare means depositing in the earth, as the last part of burial, in opp. to *cremare.*

SERA; CLAUSTRUM; PESSULUS; REPAGULUM; OBEX. Seræ and claustra are bolts; sera (seruisse, εἴρειν) a movable bolt, that is put on the door; claustrum, a bolt that is fastened to the door; whereas pessuli, repagula, and obices, are merely bars, which supply the place of bolts; pessulus (πάσσαλος) a smaller bar for the *fores*, Plaut. Aul. i. 2, 25. Ter. Heaut. ii. 3, 47; whereas repagulum (from πῆξαι), pangere, a greater bar for the *valvæ*, Cic. Verr. iv. 43. Plin. H. N. xvi. 42, and obex (from objicere) for the *portæ*, Tac. H. iii. 30. Ann. xiii. 39. (v. 292.)

SERIES; ORDO. Series (from serere, εἴρειν) means a

row, as an outward, mechanical, accidental association of things, which, according to their nature, are of the like sort; whereas o r d o (from ἀριθμός, ῥυθμός) an inward, ideal, necessary association of things, which, according to their destination, belong to one another. S e r i e s is a mathematical; o r d o, a moral notion. (vi. 330.)

SERIUS; SEVERUS. S e v e r u s (αὐηρός) means, actively, one who cuts no jokes; s e r i u s, in a neutral sense, what is no subject for joking; and s e v e r e means earnestly; s e r i o, in earnest; whence s e v e r u s is an epithet for persons, s e r i u s for things; Hor. A. P. 105. Decent vultum *severum seria* dictu. Senec. Tranq. 15. Nihil magnum, nihil *severum* nec *serium* quidem ex tanto apparatu putat. S e v e r u s is in opp. to *hilaris*, Cic. Brut. 93, *remissus*, Orat. ii. 17, *luxuriosus*, Quintil. xi. 3, 74; whereas s e r i u s is in opp. to *jucundus*, *jocosus*; and s e r i o to *joco*, *per jocum*. Yet s e v e r u s also supplies the place of *serius*; particularly in *severior*, *severissimus*, and *severitas*, because *serius* does not possess these forms. (i. 75.)

SERMO; COLLOQUIUM; ORATIO. 1. S e r m o (εἰρόμενος) denotes a conversation accidentally arising, or at least carried on without any fixed and serious purpose; whereas c o l l o q u i u m, generally a conversation agreed upon for a particular purpose, like a conference. 2. S e r m o is a natural mode of speaking; o r a t i o, a speech premeditated and prepared according to the rules of art. The *sermo* arises when, in ordinary life, an individual speaks longer than usual, and continues speaking, and is accidentally not interrupted; the *oratio* has a definite extent with an observable beginning, middle, and end, and in it the speaker calculates upon not being interrupted. In the *sermo*, the language of ordinary life predominates, whether in prose or verse, as in the comic poets, and in the *Sermones* of Horace; whereas in the *oratio* the language is select, and in conformity to the rules of rhetoric. Cic.

Q*

Orat. 16. Mollis est *oratio* philosophorum et umbratilis . . . Itaque *sermo* potius quam *oratio* dicitur. Tac. Hist. i. 19. Apud senatum non comptior Galbæ, non longior . . . *sermo*; Pisonis comis *oratio*. (iv. 23.)

SERMO, see *Lingua*.

SERPENS, SERPERE, see *Repere*.

SERVUS; FAMULUS; MANCIPIUM; MINISTER; ANCILLA; SERVITUS; SERVITIUM. 1. S e r v u s, a n c i l l a, f a m u l u s, and m a n c i p i u m, denote a servant who is not free, a slave; m i n i s t e r, one who is free, or only in subordination. Plin. Ep. x. 97. *Ancillæ*, quæ *ministræ* dicebantur; that is, in Christian assemblies. 2. S e r v u s (from εἴρερος) means a slave, in a political and juridical sense, as in a state of subjugation, in opp. to *dominus*, Cic. Verr. iv. 50, like δοῦλος and δμώς; f a m u l u s (χαμαλός?) in a patriarchal sense, as belonging to and part of the family, in opp. to *herus*, Cic. Off. ii. 7, like οἰκέτης; m a n c i p i u m, in an economical sense, as a possession and marketable commodity, like ἀνδράποδον. 3. S e r v a means a female slave, with especial reference to her legal condition; a n c i l l a, in ordinary life, as the feminine of servus. S e r v i t u s denotes slavery, quite indifferently, as a regular, natural, legal state; whereas s e r v i t i u m, either with contempt or compassion, as an irregular, compulsory, ignominious state. Most prose writers, however, use *servitus* merely as the abstract; *servitium*, and especially *servitia*, as the concrete term for *servi*. (v. 136.)

SEVERITAS; GRAVITAS; STRENUITAS. S e v e r i t a s (αὐηρότης) means earnestness, so far as it is seated in the mind; g r a v i t a s (from γεραιός) so far as it makes an impression on others; s t r e n u i t a s (from στρηνής, δραίνω) so far as it shows itself in action. (ii. 129.)

SEVERUS, see *Austerus* and *Serius*.

SICA, see *Gladius*. SICARIUS, see *Homicida*.

SICCUS, see *Aridus*. SIDUS, see *Stella*.

SIGNUM, see *Imago*.

SILERE; TACERE; RETICERE; OBTICERE. 1. Silere (from ἑλλός) means to be still, σιωπᾶν, in opp. to *strepere*, Suet. Aug. 94; whereas tacere (from tegere?) means to be silent, σιγᾶν, in opp. to *loqui*, *dicere*. And the compound word reticere, if a man has something to say, and keeps it to himself, in opp. to *eloqui*, *proloqui;* but obticere, if a man does not speak to one who asks or expects an explanation, in opp. to *respondere*. Cic. Harusp. 28. Sed tamen facile *tacentibus* cæteris *reticuissem*. 2. Tacens and tacitus denote being silent merely as a temporary state; tacens means any one who does not speak; tacitus, one who, when an opportunity for speaking offers, purposely refrains, and observes a significant silence; whereas taciturnus denotes silence as an habitual quality, like close and reserved. (i. 85.)

SILVA; SALTUS; NEMUS; LUCUS. Silva (ὕλη) denotes a wood, in a general sense, merely with reference to the timber, like ὕλη; whereas saltus (ἄλσος) as a wild place, or wood in the midst of mountains, like νάπη; nemus (νέμος) as a pleasant place, as a grove; lucus (λόχμη) as a sacred place, as a grove consecrated to the gods, like ἄλσος, ἄλτις. (ii. 93.)

SIMPUVIUM, see *Poculum*. SIMULACRUM, see *Imago*.

SIMULATIO, see *Imitatio*. SIMULTAS, see *Odium*.

SINERE, see *Ferre*. SINGULARIS, s. *Eminens*.

SINISTER; LÆVUS. Sinister (old Germ. winistra) denotes the left, as a usual and prosaic expression, like ἀριστερός; lævus (λαιός) as a select and poetical expression, like σκαιός. In a figurative sense sinister is the symbol of unpropitiousness and of disaster; lævus, of perverseness and of awkwardness. (vi. 336.)

SINUS, see *Gremium*.

SISTERE; INHIBERE; STATUERE. Sistere and inhibere mean, to make any thing stand still; sistere (ἱστάναι) with reference to a living and running object; inhibere, to a lifeless object, that has merely been put in motion; whereas s t a t u e r e means to make any thing stand fast. (iv. 299.)

SITUM ESSE, see *Cubare.*

SITUS, see *Lutum.*

SOCIETAS, see *Fœdus.*

SOCIUS; SODALIS; AMICUS; FAMILIARIS; PARTICEPS; CONSORS. 1. S o c i i (from sequi) are bound by common interests to act together, as partners, companions, etc.; s o d a l e s and s o c i e n n i, like ἑταῖροι, are bound only by being pleased with each to the common enjoyment of life, as comrades and good friends; but s o d a l i s (from ἔθος, ἠθεῖος,) is the more elevated, s o c i e n n u s, a more comic expression. S o c i u s is generally in construction with an objective genitive, which names the purpose of the *sociatio;* whereas s o d a l i s only with a subjective genitive, which names the other *sodalis*; *socius periculi, culpæ,* but *sodalis meus.* 2. S o d a l i s is a good friend, with whom one stands in a sociable, that is to say, a calm state of intercourse; a m i c u s, a friend, with whom one exchanges the sacred feeling of love and respect; f a m i l i a r i s, a confidant, to whom one is bound, as one heart and soul, in mirth and sorrow. 3. The s o c i u s r e i is considered in the state of a fellow-laborer or fellow-sufferer; the p a r t i c e p s and c o n s o r s as sharers in an enjoyment or in a possession; the p a r t i c e p s, because he voluntarily takes a part in a thing, in opp. to *expers,* like μέτοχος; the c o n s o r s, because, without co-operating, he is entitled to a share, in opp. to *exsors.* Cic. Balb. 28. Fuit hic multorum illi laborum *socius* aliquando; est fortasse nunc nonnullorum *particeps* commodorum. Liv. xxi. 41, and Suet. Aug. 25. The co-regent is *socius imperii,* so far as he shares in the business of government; *consors,* so far as the office is merely honorary. (iv. 208.)

SOCORDIA, see *Ignavia.*

SODALIS, see *Socius.*

SOLEMNIA; FERIÆ; DIES FESTI; FESTA. S o l e m

nia means festivals, so far as they are solemn or regularly returning institutions; feriæ, so far as they are days of rest and recreation; festa, or, in prose, dies festi, so far as they are days of rejoicing, (vi. 339.)

SOLERE; CONSUEVISSE; ADSOLERE. 1. Solere (from ἑλεῖν) is used of events and of actions, like φιλεῖν, to be used; whereas consuevisse only of an action, with reference to a person, like εἰωθέναι, to be wont. In Liv. xxxviii. 17, Hæc quibus *insolita* atque *insueta* sunt Græci timeant! — the word insolitus refers to the frequency of their appearance; insuetus, to the connection of their appearance with the individuality of the subject acting or suffering. 2. Solet is used indifferently; assolet involves praise, and may be resolved into *recte* or *rite solet.* (v. 73.)

SOLERS, see *Sapiens.* SOLICITARE, see *Lacessere.*

SOLICITUDO, see *Cura.*

SOLITUDO; VASTA; DESERTA; TESCA. Solitudo denotes the solitude of a place, indifferently or with praise; whereas vasta, deserta, tesca loca, with blame; vasta loca, as uncultivated wastes, in opp. to *culta;* whereas deserta, as uninhabited deserts, in opp. to *habitata;* and tesca, or tesqua, (from tacere,) as lonely places, where an awful stillness reigns, in opp. to *celebria.* (iii. 226.)

SOLUM; FUNDUS; VADUM; FUNDAMENTUM. Solum, fundus, vadum, denote the natural ground and bottom of a thing; solum, that of the earth, on which one can place a firm foot, in opp. to the movable elements air and water; fundus (from fodere, βυθός,) that of a vessel, in opp. to the remaining space in the vessel; vadum (ἕδος) that of a river, ocean, or sea, in opp. to the water, which flows into it, or to standing water; whereas fundamentum denotes a foundation artificially laid, on which a building, etc. rests, and which, in addition to the *solum*, it particularly needs. Hence the proverbial phrase, *Omnis res jam in vado est;* like a swimmer who has reached the bottom of the water: and *Largitio fundum non habet*, like the vessel of the Danaides. Cic. Brut. 74. Solum et quasi fundamentum oratoris vides. (v. 35.)

SOLUM, see *Tellus*.

SOMNUS; SOPOR; SOMNIUM; INSOMNIUM. 1. Somnus (ὕπνος) denotes sleep, as a usual prosaic expression; sopor (ὕπαρ) as a select poetical expression. In prose sopor has only a causative meaning, a means of producing sleep, but not a deep sleep. 2. Somnium denotes a dream, in prose, like ὄναρ; insomnium, in poetry, like ἐνύπνιον. (v. 278.)

SONITUS, see *Fragor*.

SONS, see *Culpa*.

SORDES, see *Lutum*.

SPARSI, see *Passi*.

SPECIES, see *Figura*.

SOPOR, see *Somnus*.

SOSPES, see *Salvus*.

SPATIARI, see *Ambulare*.

SPECTARE, see *Videre*.

SPECTRUM; MOSTELLUM; MANES; LEMURES. Spectrum denotes the apparition of a departed spirit, as a supernatural appearance; mostellum (dimin. from monstrum) as a horrible apparition; manes (from ἀμενηνὰ κάρηνα) as the apparition of a good spirit; lemures, as that of a hobgoblin. (vi. 344.)

SPECULATOR, see *Explorator*.

SPECUS; CAVERNA; ANTRUM; SPELUNCA; SPELÆUM; FOVEA; SCROBS. 1. Specus and caverna are cavities, whether under-ground, or on a level with the ground, — consequently, a species of *antrum*; spelunca and spelæum, cavities with a perpendicular opening, leading up into a mountain; scrobs, fovea, and favissa, pits with an horizontal opening, leading down into the earth. 2. Specus (σπέος) is a gap, with a longish opening; caverna (from κύαρ) a hole, with a round opening. 3. Spelunca (σπήλυγξ) is a cavity, in a merely physical relation, with reference to its darkness and dreadfulness; antrum (ἄντρον) a grotto, as a beautiful object, with reference to its romantic appearance and cooling temperature; lastly, spelæum (σπήλαιον) is used only by the poets, as the abode and lurking-hole of wild beasts. 4. Fovea (from φύειν) is a pit meant to remain open, or only covered in order to keep in or to catch a wild beast; scrobs, a pit meant to be filled up again, and only dug, in order to bury something, the root of a tree, for instance, or a corpse. (v. 140.)

SPERARE, see *Vereri*.

SPERNERE; CONTEMNERE; DESPICERE; ASPERNARI; RECUSARE; FASTIDIRE; NEGLIGERE. 1. *Spernimus* rejicienda, fugienda ut libidines. *Contemnimus* magna, metuenda ut pericula, mortem. *Despicimus* infra nos posita, ut vulgi opiniones; according to Lambinus. Or, spernere, spernari, aspernari (ἐκπεραίνειν) mean, not to care for a thing, in opp. to *appetere*, *concupisse*, Cic. Fin. ii. 10, 51. Plaut. Mil. iv. 2, 59, something like ἀποβάλλειν; whereas contemnere, poetically temnere (from temere), not to fear a thing, in opp. to *timere*, *metuere*, Cic. Fam. vii. 32. Att. ii. 24. Sen. Prov. 6. Tac. H. ii. 92, like καταφρονεῖν; lastly, despicere, despectare, not to value a thing, in opp. to *suspicere*, *revereri*, *admirari*. Cic. Off. ii. 11, 38. Tac. Ann. ii. 43, like ὀλιγωρεῖν. 2. Spernere denotes despising, as an inward feeling, synonymously with *parvi putare*, *negligere*; spernari, and the more usual word, aspernari, as an utterance of that feeling, synonymously with *recusare*, *abnuere*, *rejicere*, like waving from one. In spernere, the notion of holding cheap predominates; in aspernari, that of aversion or rejection. Spernere refers to an object which is at one's command; aspernari, to something offered to us, or obtruded upon us. 3. Aspernari is confined to the simple avowal of aversion; whereas recusare includes the decided declaration of unwillingness. Curt. vi. 6, 7. Principes *aspernantes* quidem, sed recusare non ausos Persicis ornaverat vestibus. 4. The spernens follows a moral and rational aversion, and acts more or less with a consciousness of his grounds for despising anything; whereas the fastidiens follows a physical and instinctive aversion, whether it be an innate or temporary antipathy, which arises either from an actual loathing, or from what appears like it; lastly, the negligens follows the suggestion neither of reason, nor yet of instinct and feeling, but acts without thought or purpose. (ii. 178.)

SPHÆRA, see *Globus*. SPICA, see *Culmus*.
SPIRITUS, see *Anima*. SPISSUS, see *Angustus*.
SPLENDERE, see *Lucere*. SPOLIA, see *Præda*.
SPOLIARE, see *Vastare*. SPONDERE, see *Polliceri*.

SPONSOR; VAS; PRÆS. Sponsor is a surety in a general sense, who guarantees any thing whatever; whereas vas and præs are sureties in a court of justice; vas (from ἄεθλος) one who gives security for the appearance of one or other party in court; præs, who gives security for a claim of government. (iv. 113.)

SPONTE; ULTRO; SUA SPONTE; VOLUNTATE; LIBENTER. 1. Sponte (πόθος) means voluntarily; whereas ultro, in an over-ready manner; so that sponte refers to the mind of the agent, ultro to the thing itself. Liv. x. 19. Orare ne collegæ auxilium, quod acciendum *ultro* fuerit, *sua sponte* oblatum sperneretur; and Tac. Hist. iv. 79. Suet. Cæs. 6. Sponte accusare means to accuse of one's own accord; whereas ultro accusare means to obtrude one's self into the office of an accuser, when one should be satisfied with not being one's self accused; according to which, ultro accusavit may be resolved into the complete phrase: Haud contentus non accusari ab altero, *ultro* etiam progressus est, ut ipse accusaret alterum, or, *ultro* progressus accusavit alterum. 2. Sponte, from choice, is in opp. to *casu*, or *necessitate*, Colum. ii. 1, 13. Plin. Ep. v. 14. Tac. Ann. vi. 23; whereas sua sponte, quite of one's own accord, like αὐτομάτως, in opp. to *rogatus*, *provocatus*, or *invitatus*. Cæs. B. G. i. 44. Cic. Fam. i. 7. iv. 3. vii. 5. (iii. 103.) 3. Sponte and spontaneus, like ἑκών and ἑκούσιος, paint the voluntary action as an act of the understanding; voluntate and voluntarius, like ἐθελοντής, as an act of the will, in opp. to *invite;* libenter and libens, like ἄσμενος, as an act of feeling, in opp. to *tædio.* (iv. 277.)

Squalor, see *Lutum.* Stagnum, see *Lacuna.*

Statim, see *Repente.* Statua, see *Imago.*

Statuere, see *Destinare* and *Sistere.*

Status, see *Conditio.*

Stella; Astrum; Sidus. Stella (dimin. of ἀστήρ) means any one of the innumerable individual stars, like ἀστήρ; astrum (ἄστρον), any one of the greater bright heavenly bodies, the sun, moon, and principal stars, with their peculiar names, like ἄστρον; sidus (εἶδος), a complication of stars, a constellation, and, by affinity of the notion with number and magnitude, a great star, like τέρας, τείρεα. Astrum and stella denote the stars more in a mere physical relation, as bright heavenly bodies; sidus, more in an astronomical and astrological relation, as portentous and influencing human affairs. Sen. Helv. 9. Dum ortus *siderum*, occasus intervallaque, et causas investigare velocius meandi vel tardius spectare tot per noctem *stellas* micantes liceat. (iv. 409.)

Stercus, see *Lutum.* Stilla, see *Gutta.*

Stimulare, see *Pungere.* Stipator, see *Satelles.*

Stipes; Vallus; Palus; Sudes. Stipes and vallus mean a larger sort of pale or stake, like a pole or the stem of a tree, which must be driven into the earth with a rammer; stipes serves for various uses, in war and upon other occasions; vallus (the dimin of σύαρος?) is chiefly used as a palisade; whereas palus and sudes mean a smaller sort of stake, which may be driven into the earth in the ordinary way; palus (from pangere) serves for various uses, as a hedge-stake, etc., and especially for fastening any thing to it; sudes (from ὄζος?) is also used, on account of its spike, for a palisade, a lance, a javelin. (iv. 324.)

Stipula, see *Culmus.*

STIRIA, see *Gutta.*

STIRPS; GENUS; GENS; PROSAPIA; POSTERITAS; PROGENIES; PROLES; SUBOLES. 1. Stirps, genus, and gens, denote the race usually in an ascending line, as abstract and collective terms, for *majores;* whereas prosapia, progenies, propago, proles, suboles, in a descending line, as abstract and collective terms for *posteri.* 2. Prosapia is an antiquated solemn expression, and only to be used of ancient noble families, Cic. Univ. 11. Quintil. i. 6, 40; posteritas, the usual prosaic, progenies, a select, elevated expression, Cic. Rep. ii. 22; proles and suboles, poetical expressions, Cic. Or. iii. 38; proles denotes children, as fruits destined, as a younger race, to exist with their parents; suboles, as an after-growth, destined to supply the place of the generation that is dying off. 3. Gens (*γενετή*) is a political, genus (*γένος*), a natural race. Gens consists of families, whom the founder of states has united into a community or complex family; genus consists of species and individuals, that by their common properties belong to one and the same class of beings. (v. 307).

STIRPS; TRUNCUS. Stirps (*στέριφος*) denotes the stock as the animating and supporting principal part of a tree, in opp. to the branches and leaves, as growing from it and dependent upon it; truncus, the naked, dry part of the tree, in opp. to the branches and leaves, and even to the top itself, as its ornament; in short, so far as it answers to the trunk of the human body. (iv. 322.)

STOLIDUS, see *Stupidus.*

STOLO, see *Rami.*

STOMACHARI, see *Succensere.*

STRABO; PÆTUS. Strabo (*στραβός*) means, one who squints from nature, or sickness, or bad habit; whereas pætus, one who squints designedly and waggishly. (vi. 350.)

STRAGES, see *Ruina*. STRENUITAS, see *Severitas*. STREPIDUS, see *Fragor*. STRUES, see *Acervus*.

STUDIUM; BENEVOLENTIA; FAVOR; GRATIA. 1. Studium is usually the attachment and dependent feeling of the lower towards the higher, of the soldier towards the general, of the subject towards the ruler, of the scholar towards the teacher, of the individual towards his party; whereas favor is the love and favor of the higher towards the lower, of the public towards the player, of the people towards the candidate, of the judge towards one of the parties, etc.; lastly, benevolentia is love and good-will towards one of equal rank. In Cic. Rosc. Com. 10. Quod *studium* et quem *favorem* secum in scenam attulit Panurgus? the public is first considered as an auditor, then as a judge of the player. Orat. i. 21. Ego qui incensus essem *studio* utriusque vestrûm, Crassi vero etiam amore. 2. Studium, favor, and benevolentia, denote a temporary affection, occasioned by and contracted from external circumstances,— consequently, of a quieter, or entirely latent sort; whereas amor is love deeply rooted in the soul, bordering on passion. Cic. Fam. i. 9. Nihil est quod *studio* et *benevolentia* vel potius *amore* effici non possit. Att. v. 10. *Amores* hominum in te, et in nos quædam *benevolentia*. 3. Favor is, subjectively, the favor which a person entertains towards another, in opp. almost to *invidentia;* whereas gratia is, objectively, the favor in which a person stands with another, in opp. to *invidia*. (iv. 106.)

STUPIDUS; BRUTUS; BARDUS; STULTUS; FATUUS; STOLIDUS. Stupidus, brutus, and bardus, denote a merely negative quality, want of intellect; stupidus (from τύφω, ταφεῖν), that of a human being who comprehends with difficulty, as dull-witted, like ἀναίσθητος; brutus (μαυρωτός), that of beasts, and of men whose organization is like that of beasts, who comprehend nothing, as without reason, like βλάξ; bardus, who comprehends slowly, as without talent, like βραδύς; whereas stultus, fatuus, and stolidus, denote a positive quality of the mind, which has false notions and a perverse judgment; stultus (from τέλλω, ἀτάλλω, ἀταλόφρων), a want of practical wisdom, as folly, like μωρός, in opp. to *prudens;* fatuus, a want of æsthetical judgment, as silliness; stolidus, a want of reasonable moderation, as brutality. Liv. xxv. 19. Id non promissum magis *stolide* quam *stulte* creditum. (iv. 229.)

SUAVIS; DULCIS. Suavis (ἠΰς) denotes, like ἡδύς, a pleasant odor, and, figuratively that which gives a calm pleasure; dulcis, like γλυκύς, a pleasant flavor, and, figuratively, that which gives a lively pleasure; hence dulcis is a stronger expression than *suavis*, in Plin. Ep. v. 8, 10. Hæc vel maxima vi, amaritudine, instantia; illa tractu et *suavitate*, atque etiam *dulcedine* placet. Plin. H. N. xv. 27. *Dulce*, et pingue, et *suave.* (iii. 256.)

SUAVIUM, see *Osculum.* SUBITO, see *Repente.*

SUBLIMIS, see *Altus.* SUBOLES, see *Stirps.*

SUCCENSERE; IRASCI; INDIGNARI; STOMACHARI. Succensere and ægre, graviter, moleste, difficiliter ferre, to take any thing ill, denote a silent, irasci, indignari, and stomachari, a loud displeasure; ira, anger, has the character of a passion, inasmuch as it thirsts after vengeance; indignatio, indignation, that of an awakened or excited moral feeling, inasmuch as it expresses with energy its disapprobation or contempt; stomachatio, a fit of passion, that of a choleric temperament, inasmuch as it suffers the bile to overflow, and gives vent to its irritability by blustering and brawling. The iratus makes his appearance as an enemy, and excites fear; the indignabundus, as a judge, and inspires awe; the stomachans, as a hypochondriac, and is a subject for comedy. (v. 119.)

SUDES, see *Fustis* and *Stipes.*

SUFFRAGIUM, see *Sententia.*

SUFFUGIUM, see *Perfuga*. SULCUS, see *Porca*.

SUMERE; CAPERE; PREHENDERE; ACCIPERE; EXCIPERE; RECIPERE; SUSCIPERE; RECUPERARE. 1. S u m e r e (sub-imere) means to take up any thing, in order to use it, like αἱρεῖν; c a p e r e (from κάπτειν) to lay hold on any thing, in order to possess it, like λαβεῖν; lastly p r e h e n d e r e, p r æ h e n d e r e (from χανδάνειν) to lay hold on any thing, in order, in a mere physical sense, to have it in one's hand. Cic. Phil. xii. 7. Saga *sumpsimus*, arma *cepimus*. 2. A c c i p e r e means to take any thing offered, with willingness, δέχεσθαι; e x c i p e r e, to intercept, or catch any thing that is escaping, ὑποδέχεσθαι; r e c i p e r e, to take any thing that wants protection, with a generous feeling; s u s c i p e r e, to undertake, or take upon one's self any thing burdensome, with self-denial. The a c c i p i e n s usually takes in his hand; the e x c i p i e n s, in his arms; the r e c i p i e n s, in his bosom; the s u s c i p i e n s, on his arm or back. 3. R e c i p e r e means to receive again, without taking pains; whereas r e c u p e r a r e, to regain by one's own exertion. Liv. xiii. 53, urbem *recipit*, by merely taking possession; comp. with xxvi. 39, urbe *recuperata*, by conquest. (iv 131.)

SUMMUS; SUPREMUS. S u m m u s (superl. of sub) denotes the uppermost, indifferently, and with mere local reference, like ἄκρος, in opp. to *imus*. Rhet. ad Her. iii. 18. Cic. Rosc. Com. 7. Vell. P. ii. 2. Tac. H. iv. 47; whereas s u p r e m u s is a poetical and solemn expression, with the accessory notion of elevation, like ὕπατος, almost in opp. to *infimus*. (iv. 357.)

SUMPTUS; IMPENSÆ. S u m p t u s means expense, so far as it diminishes wealth and capital, allied to prodigality; i m p e n s æ, so far as it serves to the attainment of an object, allied to sacrifice. (vi. 357.)

SUPERARE, see *Vincere*.

SUPERBIA; ARROGANTIA; FASTUS; INSOLENTIA. S u p e r b i a, from self-sufficiency, thinks others beneath itself, and considers them only as to the inferiority of their endowments; pride, in opp. to humility, arrogantia would make others, who owe it no homage, sensible of its endowments or privileges, in opp. to modesty; fastus (from σπαθᾶν?) pushes men from itself, as unworthy to stand in connection with it, as a presumptuous, in opp. to a sober, unassuming disposition; insolentia (from salire, insilire,) misemploys its superiority, in a rude manner, to the humiliation of the weaker, as insolence, in opp. to humanity and magnanimity. The superbus would outshine others, the arrogans would encroach upon them; the fastosus despises them; the insolens insults them. (iv. 187.)

SUPERESSE, see *Restare.*

SUPPLEMENTUM, see *Complementum.*

SUPPLICARE, see *Rogare* SUPREMUS, see *Summus*

SURCULUS, see *Rami.* SURRIPERE, see *Demere.*

SUS; VERRES; SCROFA; PORCUS. Sus (ὗς, σῦς,) is the most general name for swine, and that which is used by natural historians, like ὗς; verres, scrofa, porcus, are economical names; verres (from ἔρσης), a boar-pig; scrofa (γρομφάς), a sow kept for breeding; porcus (πόρκος), a young pig, like χοῖρος. With sus is associated the accessory notion of filthiness; with porcus, that of fatness. (v. 335.)

SUSCIPERE, see *Sumere.* SUSPICERE, see *Vereri.*

SUSPIRARE; GEMERE. Suspirare, to sigh, is a deep drawing of the breath and then forcible emission of it, as the immediate consequence of an afflicted heart; whereas gemere (γέμειν), to groan, is more of a voluntary act, in order to give vent to the afflicted heart; hence suspirium is more an expression of uneasiness and distress, gemitus of actual pain. Cic. Att. ii. 21. Cum diu occulte *suspirassent;* postea jam *gemere*, ad extremum vero loqui omnes et clamare coeperunt. (v. 244.)

SUSTINERE, SUSTENTARE, see *Ferre.*

## T.

TABERNA, see *Deversorium*. TABULÆ, see *Axes*.

TACERE, TACITURNUS, see *Silere*.

TÆDA, see *Fax*. TÆDET, see *Piget*.

TÆTER, see *Teter*. TALEA, see *Rami*.

TALIO, see *Vindicta*. TARDARE, see *Manere*.

TARDUS; LENTUS. Tardus denotes slowness, with reference to the great length of time spent, in opp. to *citus*, Sall. Cat. 5; whereas lentus, with reference to quietness of motion, in opp. to *acer*, etc. Quintil. ix. 4. (iv. 218.)

TELLUS; TERRA; SOLUM; HUMUS. Tellus denotes the earth as a whole, as the centre of the universe, as a goddess, in opp. to other bodies in the universe, or other divinities, like *Γαῖα, Γῆ*; whereas terra (τέρσω, torreo,) as matter and one of the elements in opp. to the other elements, like γαῖα, γῆ; *solum* (ὅλον) as a solid element, in opp. especially to water, like πέδον; lastly, humus (χθών, χαμαί), as the lowest part of the visible world, in opp. to the sky, like χθών. Hence the derivative terrenus is in opp. to *igneus;* solidus is in opp. to *fluidus;* lastly, humilis, in opp. to *sublimis*. (i. 173.)

TEMETUM, see *Vinum*. TEMPERATIO, see *Modus*.

TEMPESTAS, see *Ventus*.

TEMPLUM; FANUM; DELUBRUM; ÆDES; SACELLUM. 1. Templum, fanum, and delubrum, denote properly the temple, together with the consecrated environs, like ἱερόν; whereas ædes, the building only, like ναός; lastly, sacellum, a consecrated place without the building, with merely an altar. 2. In a narrower sense, templum denotes a great temple of one of the principal gods; whereas fanum and delubrum, a smaller temple of an inferior god, or of a hero, etc.

TEMPUS, see *Dies*. TEMULENTUS, see *Ebrietas.*
TENEBRÆ, see *Obscurum.*

TENERE; HABERE; POSSIDERE. T e n e r e (from τείνειν) means, to have anything fast in one's hand, and in physical possession; h a b e r e (from σχέω) to have in one's power, and in effective possession; p o s s i d e r e (from ποτί and sedere) to have, as one's own property, and in legal possession, Plin. Ep. i. 16. Tenet, habet, possidet. (vi. 366.)

TENTARE; EXPERIRI; PERICLITARI; PERICULUM; DISCRIMEN. 1. T e n t a r e means, to make an experiment, in order to form a judgment of something, from a desire of knowledge, and with activity; p e r i c l i t a r i, with courage and contempt of the danger associated with the experiment; e x p e r i r i, merely to learn something by actual experiment. 2. P e r i c u l u m denotes danger, as occupying duration of time; d i s c r i m e n, as a point of time, as the critical moment and the culminating point of *periculum.* Liv. vi. 17. In ipso *discrimine periculi* destituat. (v. 263.)

TENUIS, see *Exilis.* TERERE, see *Lævis.*
TERGUM, see *Dorsum.*

TERGUS; CUTIS; PELLIS; VELLUS. T e r g u s and c u t i s denote the outermost covering of the flesh, as merely bare skin; t e r g u s (from στορχάζειν, to enclose), the coarse skin of an animal, which covers the soft and eatable flesh, like δέρμα; c u t i s (κύτος), the finer skin of human beings, which protects the sensitive flesh like χρώς; whereas p e l l i s and v e l l u s denote the flesh together with a covering; p e l l i s (from palla) more bristly, consisting of *pili*, like δορά; v e l l u s (from εἶλαρ? or villus?), more woolly, consisting of *villi*, like μαλλός. Men have *cutis;* elephants, snakes, etc. *tergora;* lions, goats, dogs, etc., *pelles;* sheep, *vellera.* Juven. x. 192. Deformem pro *cute pellem.* (v. 17.)

TERMES, see *Rami.*
TERMINARE, TERMINUS, see *Finire*, *Finis.*

TETER; FŒDUS; TURPIS; DEFORMIS. T e t e r, tæter (ἀταρτηρός) is the ugliness which disturbs the feeling of security, and excites fear or shuddering, like hideous, shocking, βλοσυρός; foedus (ψοῖθος), that which offends natural feelings, and excites loathing and aversion, like μιαρός; turpis (from torpere) that which offends the moral feeling, or sense of decency, and excites disapprobation or contempt, in opp. to *honestus*, *gloriosus*, like αἰσχρός; deformis, that which offends the finer sensations, and excites dislike, in opp. to *formosus*, like δυσειδής. Cic. Off. i. 34. Luxuria cum omni ætate *turpis*, tum senectuti *fœdissima* est. Rep. ii. 26. Tyrannus quo neque *tetrius* neque *fœdius* . . . animal ullum cogitari potest. Vatin. 3. Quanquam sis omni diritate *teterrimus*. Vell. Pat. ii. 69. In Vatinio *deformitas* corporis cum *turpitudine* certabat ingenii. (v. 111.)

TESCA, see *Solitudo*. TETRICUS, see *Austerus*.
TIGNUM, see *Trabes*.
TIMERE, TIMOR, see *Vereri*.
TITUBARE, see *Labare*. TOLERARE, see *Ferre*.
TORMENTUM, s. *Cruciatus*. TORQUERE, see *Vertere*.
TORRIDUS, see *Aridus*. TORVUS, see *Atrox*.
TOTUS, see *Quisque*.

TOXICUM; VENENUM; VIRUS. Toxicum (from taxus) denotes poison, as a mere term in natural history, without accessory reference; venenum, as an artificial poison, of a sweet and tempting flavor; virus (εἶαρ, ἰός), as a noxious and distasteful juice or drink. Liv. ii. 52. Tribuni plebem agitare suo *veneno*, agraria lege; comp. with Cic. Læl. 23. Evomat *virus* acerbitatis suæ. (v. 355.)

TRABES; TIGNUM. Trabes, trabs (τράφηξ) denotes a longer and narrower beam, like a pole; tignum, a shorter and thicker beam, like a block. A raft consists of *trabes*, not of *tigna;* whereas the woodwork of a building, which, as a pillar, is destined to support something, is composed of *tigna*, not of *trabes*, by which the cross-beams only are denoted. Cæs. B. Civ.

ii. 9. Supra eum locum duo *tigna* transversa injecerunt, quibus suspenderent eam contignationem supraque ea *tigna* directo transversas *trabes* injecerunt easque axibus religaverunt. (v. 290.)

TRACTUS, see *Locus*. TRAGULUM, see *Missile*.

TRAMES, see *Iter*. TRANQUILLUS, see *Quietus*.

TRANS; ULS; ULTRA. Trans and Uls, like πέραν, in opp. to *cis*, denote, on the other side, with the character of unaccented prepositions, as a mere geometrical designation of place, like *super;* trans (τρανές) is the usual, uls the antiquated and obsolete expression; whereas ultra (comparative from ollus, ille), like πέρα, in opp. to *citra*, with emphasis and distinction of the relative distance of that which lies on the other side, like *supra*. The separation denoted by ultra is merely that of a boundary; the separation denoted by trans, that of an obstruction. Tac. Germ. 29. Protulit magnitudo populi Romani *ultra* Rhenum *ultraque* veteres terminos imperii reverentiam . . . Non numeraverim inter Germaniæ populos, quanquam *trans* Rhenum Danubiumque considerint, eos, qui decumates agros exercent. Eutrop. vii. 9. Liv. xxii. 43. Tac. Ann. xvi. 17. (iii. 109.)

TRANSFUGA, see *Perfuga*.

TRANSVERSUS; OBLIQUUS. Transversum means, that which crosses a straight line at right angles, like across; obliquum, that which is not perpendicular to a straight line, but forms with it unequal angles, the one acute, the other obtuse, like awry or slanting. (vi. 375.)

TRIBUERE, see *Impertire*. TRISTITIA, see *Dolor*.

TROICUS, TROIUS, see *Achivi*.

TRUCIDARE, s. *Interficere*. TRUCULENTUS, s. *Atrox*.

TRUDIS, see *Fustis*. TRUNCARE, see *Mutilare*.

TRUNCUS, see *Stirps*. TRUX, see *Atrox*.

TUERI; DEFENDERE. Tueri (from στοχάζεσθαι) supposes only possible danger, as to protect, in opp. to *negligere*, Cic. Fin. iv. 14; defendere, an actual attack, as to defend, in opp. to *deserere*. Hence those that are under age have *tutores;* those that are accused, *defensores*. The *tuens* shows more of carefulness and love, as seeking to prevent danger; the *defendens*, more of spirit and strength, as resisting danger. (iv. 307.)

TUMERE, see *Turgere*.

TUMULUS, see *Collis*.

TURBA, see *Caterva*.

TURBÆ; TUMULTUS; SEDITIO; SECESSIO; DEFICERE; DESCISCERE. Turbæ and tumultus denote the civil broils of public life; turbæ (τύρβη) interruptions of public order; tumultus (from tumere) of the public peace; whereas seditio and secessio are political commotions, in consequence of decided, evident differences of opinion, and of conflicting principles; seditio (from se and ire) when concord is first disturbed, and the parties as yet contend with words only; secessio, when the prospect of reconciliation is already given up, and the parties either stand opposite each other, ready to come to blows, or, at least, have broken off all connection with each other. 2. The seditiosi and secedentes are citizens and members of a free community, and only suspend public concord; whereas the deficientes and desciscentes break a compact, because, either as subjected states they rebel, or as allies fall off; deficere, as the most general expression, represents the falling off, in a moral point of view, as a treacherous, fickle, cowardly desertion; desciscere (from scindere) in a political point of view, as an alteration in the constitution and political system. (v. 363.)

TURBO, see *Ventus*.

TURGERE; TUMERE. Turgere (τραγᾷν) denotes being swoln, with reference to actual corpulency and fulness, like σπαργᾶν, σφριγᾶν; whereas tumere (from στόμφος) with reference to concealed nothingness and emptiness, like οἰδᾶν. Hence sails are called *tur-*

*gida*, inasmuch as the wind, which swells them out, is something, and actually fills them; and *tumida*, inasmuch as it is merely air, consequently nothing, and only seems to fill them. (iv. 191.)

TURIO, see *Rami*.

TURPIS, see *Teter*.

TUTUS; SECURUS; INCURIOSUS. 1. Tutus denotes safety objectively, he who actually is safe, like ἀσφαλής; securus (sine cura) subjectively, he who thinks himself safe; hence tutus is used for provident, with reference to foresight; securus is used as a softer expression, for improvident, with reference to the want of foresight. Sen. Ep. 97. *Tuta* scelera esse possunt, *secura* non possunt: and 105. The substantive *securitas*, however, must be used to supply the want of a similar substantive from *tutus*. 2. Securus, securitas, denote freedom from care and anxiety merely as a state of mind, like ἀμέριμνος, in opp. to *sollicitus*, Tac. Hist. iv. 58; whereas incuriosus, incuria, denote the want of carefulness and attention, with a practical reference, like heedless, ὀλίγωρος, in opp. to *cura*. Sen. Ep. 100. Fabianus non erat negligens in oratione, sed *securus*. (iii. 120.)

## U.

UBER, see *Fœcundus* and *Mamma*.

UDUS; UVIDUS; HUMIDUS; AQUOSUS; MADIDUS. 1. Uvidum and udum (ὑάς, vadum, from ὕω, uveo) denote, like ὑγρόν, the wetness which consists entirely of water or other fluid particles, whether actually, apparently, or only by hyperbole, *humore constans;* whereas humidum and humectum (from χυμός) is the wetness which is caused by water soaking through, *humore mixtum*. Senec. N. Q. ii. 25. Dicis nubes attritas edere ignem cum sint *humidæ*, imo *udæ*. Hence is udus (in opp. to *sudus* and *solidus*) used by Tertullian as synonymous with *aquanus;* whereas *humidus* (in opp. to *aridus*) is synonymous with *aquosus*, only that by *aquosus* is meant a separation and juxta-position of wet and dry; by *humidus*, a mixture and association of wet and dry; hence *pratum aquosum* means a meadow with ponds and puddles; *pratum humidum*, a meadow soaked with water. 2. U d u s is only a contracted form of *uvidus;* h u m e c t u s is distinguished from *humidus* only as a sort of participle. Pacuv. ap. Varr. Terra exhalabat auroram *humidam, humectam.* 3. H u m i d u s, h u m e n s, refer, like moist, to the inward quality of a body; whereas m a d i d u s, m a d e n s, like μυδαλέος and dripping, only to the exterior and surface of a body, in opp. to *siccus.* Cic. Phil. xiv. 3. Imbuti sanguine gladii legionum exercituumque nostrorum, vel *madefacti* potius duobus consulum, tertio Cæsaris prœlio; for i m b u e r e, as the causative of *imbibere*, refers to a *humectatio*, a moisture of the inner part; m a d e f i e r i, to a *redundatio*, the cause of which lies in this, that the inner part is so over-full, that nothing further can be forced into it. (ii. 12.)

ULCUS, see *Vulnus.* ULIGO, see *Lacuna.*

ULNA; LACERTUS; BRACHIUM; CUBITUS. U l n a (ὠλένη) is the whole arm, from the shoulder to the hand, which serves as a measure, an ell; l a c e r t u s (ἀλκή) the upper arm; b r a c h i u m (βράγχιον, βραχίων), the under-arm; c u b i t u s, the bending between the two, the elbow. (vi. 383.)

ULS, ULTRA, see *Trans.* ULTIMUS, see *Extremus.*

ULTIO, s. *Vindicta.* ULTRO, s. *Præterea* and *Sponte.*

UMBROSUS, see *Obscurus.*

UNA; SIMUL. *Una* means together, at the same place, like ὁμοῦ; whereas *simul* (ὁμαλῶς) at once, at the same time or moment, like ἅμα.

UNCTUS, see *Delibutus.* UNCUS, see *Curvus.*

UNDA, see *Aqua.* UNICUS, see *Eminens*

UNIVERSUS, UNUSQUISQUE, see *Quisque.*

USQUE, see *Semper.* USURA, see *Fænus.*

USURPARE, see *Uti.*

UTERQUE; AMBO; UTERVIS; UTERLIBET. 1. U t e r q u e denotes 'both,' as two unities, like ἑκάτερος; a m b o, as the halves of a pair, like ἄμφω. Cic. Fin. ii. 7. Hic, qui *utramque* probat, *ambobus* debuit uti. Orat. 6, 21. Terent. Ad. i. 2, 50. Curemus æquam *uterque* partem; tu alterum, ego alterum; nam *ambos* curare propemodum reposcere illum est quem dedisti. Plin. Pan. 90, 4. Vell. P. ii. 66. This difference is palpable from Cic. Mur. 18, 37. Duæ res vehementer in prætura desideratæ sunt, quæ *ambæ* in consulatu Murenæ profuerunt . . . . Horum *utrumque* ei fortuna ad consulatus petitionem reservavit. And Orat. iii. 26. A quibus *utrisque* submittitur aliquid. 2. U t e r q u e and a m b o are copulative, and may be resolved into *unus et alter*, and have their predicate actually in common; whereas u t e r v i s and u t e r l i b e t are disjunctive, and may be resolved into *unus vel alter*, and have their predicate in common only by possibility. Ter. Andr. prol. 10. Qui *utramvis* recte norit, *ambos* noverit. (iv. 349.)

UTI; USURPARE; FRUI; FRUNISCI. U t i and u s u r p a r e denote the mere act of using, by which a person turns a thing to his advantage; but u t i (from οἴω) a permanent use; u s u r p a r e (usui rapere) a single act of using; whereas f r u i and the antiquated word f r u n i s c i (from φρονεῖν), the pleasant feeling of this use, as to enjoy; f r u i is the primitive, f r u n i s c i the inchoative of the verb. Sen. Vit. B. 10. Tu voluptate *frueris* , ego *utor.* Flor. ii. 6. Hannibal cum victoria posset *uti*, *frui* maluit. Cic. Rosc. Am. 45, 131. Commoda, quibus *utimur*, lucem, qua *fruimur*, spiritumque, quem ducimus, a Deo nobis dari. Cic. Cat. iii. 2, 5. Quorum opera . . . assidue *utor;* comp. with Fin. ii. 35, 118. In ea, quam sæpe *usurpabas*, tranquillitate degere omnem vitam. Cic. Orat. 51, 169. Post inventa conclusio est, qua credo *usuros* veteres illos fuisse, si jam nota et *usurpata* res esset. (iii. 134.)

UTIQUE, see *Plane*.
UVIDUS, see UDUS.
UXOR, see *Fœmina*.

## V.

VACARE; OTIARI; FERIARI; CESSARE; NIHIL AGERE. Vacare (from ἧκα? means to have one's time free, in opp. to *occupatio*, which compels one to work; otiari (from αὔσιος, αὔτως), to be at leisure, in opp. to *negotia*, which oblige one to work; feriari, to enjoy a holiday, in opp. to working all day; cessare (from cedere?) or from καθίζειν?), to make a half-holiday, and enjoy a short cessation, in opp. to previous activity; nihil agere, to do nothing, in opp. to activity in general. (vi. 388.)

VACILLARE, see *Labare*.
VACUUS, see *Inanis*.
VADERE, see *Ire*.
VADUM, see *Solum*.
VAFER, see *Astutus*.
VAGARI, see *Errare*.
VALDE, see *Perquam*.
VALE, see *Ave*.
VALENS, see *Salus*.
VALERE, see *Posse*.
VALETUDO see *Æger*.

VALIDUS; FIRMUS; ROBUSTUS. 1. Validus (from ὅλος, οὖλος), means strong, in an active sense, as able to perform something, in opp. to *imbecillis*, Cic. Fam. vii. 1. Plin. H. N. xiv. 21, like σθεναρός; whereas firmus and robustus, in a passive sense, as able to endure; firmum (from φράξαι, φάργνυμι), strong from an immovable position, and, consequently, stedfast, in opp. to *labans*, *vacillans*, and, for want of a corresponding adjective, to *imbecillus*, Cic. Fam. ix. 16. Sall. Jug. 10. Quintil. v. 10, 49, like βέβαιος; robustum (from ἐῤῥῶσθαι) through its compact nature, and its impenetrable and, consequently, durable materials, nearly in opp. to *tenerum*, like ῥωμαλέος and ἰσχυρός. 2. Imbecillitas denotes generally a mental, infirmitas, a bodily weakness, according to Cic. Fin. v. 45. In *infirma* ætate, *imbecillaque* mente:

both are sometimes used in a mental sense, in which case imbecillitas denotes a natural weakness of the head or heart, a want of talent or of spirit; whereas; infirmitas, a moral weakness of character, fickleness and uncertainty, for example: Cæs. B. G. vii. 77. Nolite stultitia ac temeritate vestra aut *imbecillitate* animi omnem Galliam prosternere; comp. with iv. 5. Cæsar *infirmitatem* Gallorum veritus, quod sunt in consiliis capiendis mobiles et rebus plerumque novis student. Or, Cic. Divin. ii. 60, with Fam. xv. 1. Or, Tac. Ann. iv. 8, with Hist. i. 9. (iv. 164.)

VALLUM, see *Agger*. VALLUS, see *Stipes*.

VALVÆ, see *Ostium*.

VARIUS; DIVERSUS; CONTRARIUS; VERSICOLOR; VARIEGARE. 1. Varium (from *αἰόλος*) means, possessing differences in its own texture, varied; whereas diversum, differing from something else, distinct. Catull. 47, 10. Quos longe simul a domo profectos *diverse variæ* viæ reportant; that is, whom various ways, in an entirely different direction, bring home. Tac. Hist. i. 25. Otho postquam *vario* sermone callidos et audaces cognovit pretio et promissis onerat . . . Suspensos cæterorum animos *diversis* artibus (namely, spe et metu) stimulant. 2. The diversa will have nothing in common, and go different or even opposite ways from each other; whereas the contraria confront and stand directly opposite to each other. Hence the following climax in Cic. Divin. ii. 26, 55. *Diversas* aut etiam *contrarias*. Vell. Pat. ii. 75. *Diversa* præsentibus et *contraria* exspectatis sperare. Quintil. v. 10, 26. 3. Varium denotes variegated, as exhibiting different colors at the same time, like *ποικίλον*; whereas versicolor, that which changes its color, according to the light in which it is held, like *αἰόλον*. Propert. iii. 13, 32. Aut *variam* plumæ *versicoloris* avem. Pliny is describing two different properties, xxxvii. 10, when he describes the stone Mithrax, as at the same time *multicolor* and *contra solem varie re-*

*fulgens.* 4. Variare means to give a varied appearance in general; variegare, to give a varied appearance, especially by different colors. (iii. 269.)

VAS, see *Sponsor.*

VASTA, see *Solitudo.*

VASTARE; POPULARI; DIRIPERE; AGERE FERRE; EXPILARE; SPOLIARE; PECULARI. 1. Vastare (from ustus ?) means to lay waste, from rage or from policy to destroy the property of an enemy, like *πέρθειν, πορθεῖν*; whereas populari, diripere, and agere ferre, to plunder for one's own use; populari, on a great scale, for example, to lay waste all the crops, and drive off the herds; diripere, on a small scale, to break into the houses, and break open the closets; agere ferre includes both meanings, like *ἄγειν καὶ φέρειν.* 2. Spoliare and populari mean to plunder, in a state of open warfare; whereas expilare and peculari, depeculari, in a state of peace; expilare (*ψιλόω*) by open force; peculari (dimin. of *πέκω*) by fraud, and by secretly purloining the property of the state. Cic. Parad. vi. 1. Si socios *spolias*, ærarium *expilas.* (iv. 339.)

VATES, see *Canere.*

VATICINARI, see *Divinare* and *Hariolari.*

VECORS, see *Amens.* VEGETUS, see *Vigens.*

VEHEMENS, see *Acer.*

VELLE; OPTARE; EXPETERE; CUPERE; AVERE; GESTIRE. 1. Velle, obtare, and expetere, are acts of calm reason and self-determination; whereas cupere, avere, and gestire, acts of excited feeling and of passion. Senec. Ep. 116. Cum tibi *cupere* interdixero, *velle* permittam. 2. Velle (*ἑλεῖν*) means to wish, and co-operate towards the realization of one's wish, like *θέλειν* and *βούλεσθαι*; optare (from *ποθεῖν*) to wish, and leave the realization of one's wish to others, or to fate, like *ποθεῖν*; expetere, to wish, and apply to others for the realization of one's wish, like *ὀρέγεσθαι.* Sen. Ep. 95. Sæpe aliud *volumus*, aliud *optamus*. Cic. Off. i. 20. Nihil nisi quod honestum sit homines aut admirari aut *optare* aut *expetere* oportet. 3. C u p e r e (κάπτειν) denotes a vehement, passionate desire; g e s t i r e (γηθεῖν), a lively desire, showing itself by gestures; a v e r e (from χαίνειν, χάος), an impatient, hasty desire. C u p i d u s means, being eagerly desirous of something, like ἐπιθυμῶν; g e s t i e n s, rejoicing in anticipation of something, like χρῄζων? a v i d u s, being greedy after something. Cic. Sen. 8. Græcas literas sic *avide* arripui, quasi diuturnam sitim explere *cupiens*; comp. with Att. ii. 18. Intellexi quam suspenso animo et sollicito scire *averes*, quid esset novi. And, iv. 11. Perge reliqua; *gestio* scire ista omnia. (v. 57.)

VELLUS, see *Tergus*.

VELOX, see *Citus*.

VENDERE; VENUNDARE; MANCIPARE. V e n d e r e and v e n u n d a r e denote the selling of any thing as a mercantile act; but in v e n d e r e (ἀναδοῦναι) the disposing of the thing is the principal notion, the price merely secondary, in opp. to emere, like ἀποδόσθαι; in v e n u n d a r e, the previous having for sale, or offering for sale, is the principal notion, as in πιπράσκειν, πωλεῖν, ἀπεμπολᾶν; whereas m a n c i p a r e denotes a juridical act, in consequence of which a thing is alienated, and, with all that belongs to it, transferred to another, in a legal form, as his property. (iv. 118.)

VENDITATIO, s. *Jactatio*. VENENUM, see *Toxicum*.

VENERARI, see *Vereri*. VENIAM DARE, s. *Ignoscere*.

VENTUS; PROCELLA; TEMPESTAS; VORTEX; TURBO. V e n t u s (ἀείς, or ἄντη, Hesiod) is the generic term for wind; p r o c e l l a and t e m p e s t a s denote a violent wind; p r o c e l l a (κέλαδος), a mere squall or gust of wind; t e m p e s t a s, a complete storm, or stress of weather, generally accompanied by thunder and lightning, rain or hail; whereas v o r t e x and t u r b o denote a whirlwind; v o r t e x (vertere), a weaker sort, that merely raises the dust; t u r b o (στρέφω, στροφἄλιγξ), a strong whirlwind that causes destruction, (v. 287.)

VENUDARE, see *Vendere*. VENUSTUS, see *Formosus*.

VEPRES, see *Dumi*.

VERBERARE; ICERE; FERIRE; CÆDERE; PULSARE; MULCARE; PAVIRE; CUDERE. 1. Verberare, ferire, and icere, mean, in a general sense, to strike, whether by throwing, hitting, or pushing; but the *verberans* makes his blow rebound; the *iciens* and *feriens* penetrate and wound, or break to pieces; the *iciens* (resembling in form jaciens) chiefly by throwing, for instance, *fulmine ictus;* the *feriens*, by pushing, for instance, *murum ariete*; whereas cædere, pulsare, and mulcare, denote especially striking, generally with a weapon; cædere, with a weapon that cuts and wounds, a hatchet, sword, whip, rod, strap; pulsare and mulcare, with a hard weapon, stick or fist. Pulsare has any object whatever, man, a door, the ground; mulcare, like to cudgel, only an object that can feel pain, especially man. 2. Verberare, in a narrower sense, denotes a quiet chastisement by the blows of a stick, which is generally appointed, as a formal punishment, by the competent authorities; whereas pulsare and mulcare, a misusage by blows or thrusts, which is administered as mere vengeance by unauthorized persons; pulsare (from pellere) as a slighter misusage with hand or stick, which principally hurts the honor and dignity of the person misused; mulcare (μαλάξαι, malaxare), a rougher misusage, with fists or clubs, which aims principally at physical pain, like a sound drubbing. 3. Pavire (παίειν) means to beat, in order to make a soft mass solid; cudere, in order to widen or extend a solid mass. Fulgere, battuere, and cajare are antiquated or vulgar expressions for beating. (v. 67.)

VERBOSUS, see *Garrire*.

VERBUM; VOCABULUM; VOX; DICTUM; DICTERIUM. 1. Verbum (ἄραβος) is a word, as a part of speech;

whereas vocabulum, as a part of language The *verba* are verbs, the *vocabula* words in general. 2. Verba denote words in general, with reference to their meaning; voces, with reference to their form and their sound. 3. As a grammatical term, vox comprehends all the eight parts of speech; vocabulum, all legitimate words, consequently with the exclusion of interjections or natural sounds; nomen, only the nouns, adjectives, substantives, and pronouns; and verbum, only the verbs. 4. Verbum, in a collective sense, denotes a general notion, that which is said; whereas vox, dictum, and dicterium, are particular expressions; vox (ἠχή), an expression of feeling or passion, like an exclamation; dictum, an expression of wit or intellect, like a *bon mot.* Tac. Hist. iii. 39. Audita est sævissima Vitellii *vox*, qua se pavisse oculos spectata inimici morte jactavit; comp. with Ann. vi. 20. Scitum Passieni *dictum* percrebuit, neque meliorem unquam servum neque deteriorem dominum fuisse. 5. Dictum is the general and popular expression for any pointed saying; dicterium, a select term of later times for a particularly smart *dictum*, which is not merely the product of natural wit, but also of cultivation refined by literature and intercourse with polished society. (iv. 29.)

VERERI; TIMERE; METUERE; SPES; FIDUCIA; TIMOR; TIMIDITAS; IGNAVIA; FORMIDO; HORROR. 1. Vereri (ὁρᾶν?) like *αἰδεῖσθαι*, has its foundation in what is strikingly venerable; metuere and timere, like δεῖσαι; and φοβεῖσθαι, in the threatening danger of an object. The *timens* and *metuens* fear the danger; the *verens*, the disgrace and shame. Cic. Phil. xii. 12. Quid? veteranos non *veremur?* nam *timeri* ne ipsi quidem volunt. Sen. 11, 37. *Metuebant* eum servi, *verebantur* liberi, carum omnes habebant. Liv. xxxix. 37. *Veremur* quidem vos Romani et si ita vultis etiam *timemus.* Afran. ap. Gell. xv. 13. Ubi malunt *metui*, quam *vereri* se ab suis. Senec. Ir. iii. 32. Quibusdam *timeamus* irasci, quibusdam *vereamur.* 2. Metus (*ματᾶν*) is fear, only as the anticipation of an impending evil, and reflection upon it, the apprehension that proceeds from foresight and prudence, like δέος, synonymously with *cautio;* whereas timor (from τρέμω), the fear that proceeds from cowardice and weakness. Or, metus is an intellectual notion; fear, as from reflection, in opp. to *spes;* for instances, see Cic. Verr. ii. 54. Off. ii. 6. Liv. xxx. 9. Suet. Aug. 25. Tac. H. i. 18. Ann. ii. 12, 38. Sen. Ep. 5. Suet. Aug. 5. Cels. ii. 6. Curt. viii. 6:—whereas timor is a moral notion, fear as a feeling, in opp. to *fiducia, animus.* Cic. Divin. ii. 31. Att. v. 20. Rull. i. 8. Sallust. Jug. ii. 3. Tac. Hist. ii. 80. Plin. Ep. v. 17. 3. In the like manner are spes, hope, and fiducia, confidence, distinguished. Sen. Ep. 16. Jam de te *spem* habeo, nondum *fiduciam.* Tac. Agr. 2. Nec *spem* modo ac votum securitas publica, sed ipsius voti *fiduciam* ac robur assumpserit. Suet. Cl. 10. Aliquanto minore *spe* quam *fiducia.* Liv. x. 25. Curt. ix. 4, 25. 4. Timor denotes fear, as a temporary state; timiditas, fearfulness, as an habitual quality, which is connected with *ignavia,* as a more precise expression for the more general feeling. Lactant. iii. 17. Epicurus . . . *ignavum* prohibet accedere ad rem publicam, pigrum exercere, *timidum* militare. Ignavia is inaptitude for any noble action, and particularly for deeds of valor; timiditas is, under certain circumstances, excusable; ignavia is absolutely blamable. 5. Metus and timor have their foundation in reflection, whereby a person is made clearly aware of the object and ground of his apprehension; whereas horror and formido is an immediate feeling, which overpowers the understanding by the dreadful image of the nearness of some horrid object, and can give no account of the ground of its fear; formido (fremere) expresses this state immediately as a state of mind, like ὀρρωδία; whereas horror (χέρσος) as the bodily expression of this state, by the hair standing on end, the eyes wildly staring, etc., like

15

φρίκη. Tac. H. iv. 45. *Metus* per omnes ac præcipua Germanici militis *formido.* (ii. 190.)

VERERI; REVERERI; VENERARI; COLERE; OBSERVARE; ADORARE; ADMIRARI; SUSPICERE. 1. Vereri and revereri mean, to feel reverence; whereas venerari, to show reverence. Tac. Ann. xiv. 13; comp. *venerationem* sui with matris *reverentia.* 2. Vereri (ὁρᾶν?) denotes respect bordering on fear and bashfulness; whereas revereri, fear and bashfulness arising from respect. In *vereri*, fear, in *revereri*, respect is the principal notion; hence verecundia is the dread of exposing one's self before the person respected; whereas reverentia, the calm consciousness that some one is worthy of this reverential feeling. 3. Venerari (ἄντεσθαι?) is used (at least in Cicero) only for demonstrations of reverence towards the gods and sacred things; observare, only for such demonstrations towards men; colere, towards either. Cic. Rep. i. 12. Ut . . . Africanum ut deum *coleret* Lælius, domi vicissim Lælium *observaret* in parentis loco Scipio. And, N. D. i. 42. ii. 28. The venerans seeks only to express due reverence, and by self-humiliation to avert the anger of the gods; the colens (from κόλαξ) seeks by acts of courtesy, of service, and of respect, to win the affection of some one, and the fruits of it, as from a cultivated field. Veneratio shows itself more in prayer; cultus, more in sacrifice: veneratio is more a single, transient act; cultus more a permanent expression of respect. Tac. H. i. 10. Vespasianus . . . Titum filium ad *venerationem cultumque* (ejus) miserat; that is, that he might do homage to the new emperor, and then also remain in his circle of courtiers. 4. Observare (from ἐρύεσθαι) involves a mere negative notion, and denotes having regard for, in opp. to slighting; yet is not, on this account, *colere* a stronger, *observare* a weaker term. Colere, indeed, involves more palpable activity, *operam;* whereas observare, more tender regard, *pietatem;* hence some times the one, sometimes the other, is the stronger expression. 5. Adorare is the most general expression for any sort of worship; whereas veneratio consists more in gestures, precatio in words. 6. *Reveremur validas auctoritates; admiramur raras virtutes; suspicimus excellentia dignitate.* At the same time it appears to me, that the *reverens* is in a state of silent awe; the *admirans* with the expression of loud, or at least visible enthusiasm; the *suspiciens*, under the image of one looking up to another with an humble feeling of his own inferiority. Revereri refers especially to moral; admirari, to intellectual and moral; suspicere, to any, even adventitious, pre-eminences. (ii. 185.)

VERRES, see *Sus*. VERSICOLOR, see *Varius*.

VERSUTUS, see *Astutus*.

VERTERE; TORQUERE; CONVERTERE; INVERTERE; PERVERTERE. Vertere means to turn, that is, to move anything in order to give it another position or situation, like τρέπειν; torquere (from τρέκω, ἀτρεκής), to twist, that is, in order to move a fixed point, like στρέφειν. 2. Convertere means, either to turn in a body, with reference to those acting, as, for instance, Ut pæne terga *convertant;* or, with reference to the action, to turn completely; whereas invertere means, to turn only half round, so that the reverse side of the thing turned is exposed; lastly, pervertere means to turn upside down, so that the thing turned becomes useless, or falls to the ground. (v. 289.)

VERUTUM, see *Missile*.

VESANUS, see *Amans*.

VESTIS: VESTITUS; VESTIMENTUM; AMICTUS; AMICULUM; CULTUS; HABITUS. 1. Vestis (from vas, Goth. wastjan) is the most general expression, and denotes sometimes the whole clothes; vestitus, sometimes only a single article of dress, *vestimentum*. Vestem mutare denotes, to go into mourning; vestimenta mutare, to shift one's clothes. 2. Vestis and vestimentum denote the clothes which cover the body, as necessary or decent; amictus and amiculum (from ambi and jacere) the cloak or mantle which covers the under-clothing, for the sake of warmth or of ornament; amictus, the whole of the over-clothing; amiculum, a single article, as a mantle. Tac. G. 17. Feminæ sæpius lineis *amictibus* velantur, partemque *vestitus* superioris in manicas non extendunt. Curt. v. 1, 38. Sil. It. vii. 447. 3. Cultus and habitus have a wider meaning than *vestis;* cultus (occulere) whatever belongs to dress, girdle, hat, ornaments, arms, etc.; habitus, whatever belongs to the exterior in general, cleanliness, mode of dressing the hair, carriage of the body, etc. Suet. Cæs. 44. Dicam ea, quæ ad formam et *habitum* et *cultum* et mores pertinebant. Cal. 52. *Vestitu* calceatuque cæteroque *habitu.* (v. 209.)

VETARE; INTERDICERE. Vetare means to forbid by virtue of the law, in opp. to *jubere;* whereas interdicere, to forbid, by virtue of official authority, in opp. to *addicere, permittere.*

VETERNUS, see *Antiquus.* VETULA, see *Anus.*

VETUS; SENEX; GRANDÆVUS; LONGÆVUS; SENECTA; SENECTUS; SENIUM. 1. Vetus homo (ἔτος) denotes an old man, from the fiftieth year of his life, in opp. to *juvenis,* a young man, like γέρων; whereas senex (ἄναξ? or ἕνους ἔχων?), an old man from his sixtieth year, with the accessory notion of his being worthy of respect, like πρεσβύτης; lastly, grandævus and longævus denote a very aged man, who has already exceeded the usual duration of life, and who is, consequently, somewhere about eighty or upwards. 2. Senecta denotes old age indifferently, merely as a period of life; senectus, as a venerable and experienced age, that commands respect and indulgence; senium, the infirm and burdensome age, which is to be looked upon as a disease. (iv. 89.)

VETUS, VETUSTUS, see *Antiquus* and *Puer*.

VIA, see *Iter*. VIBRARE, see *Librare*.

VICINUS; FINITIMUS; CONFINIS. Vicini (οἰκεῖοι) are neighbors, in reference to house and yard; whereas finitimi and confines, with reference to the boundaries of the land; finitimi, in a one-sided relationship, as the neighbors of others, who dwell near their boundaries, in a mere geographical sense; confines, in a mutual relationship, as opposite neighbors, who have boundaries in common, with the moral accessory notion of friendship associated with neighborhood. The *finitimi* are *finibus diremti;* whereas the *confines* are *confinio conjuncti.* (v. 181.)

VICISSIM; INVICEM; MUTUO. Vicissim (from εἰκάζω) denotes, like on the other hand, and in hand, and in turn, a successive; invicem and mutuo, like reciprocally and in return, a mutual acting and suffering between two persons or things; invicem, more with reference to reciprocal actions; mutuo, to reciprocal or mutual states. (vi. 402.)

VICTUS, see *Vita*.

VIDERE; CERNERE; SPECTARE; INTUERI; CONSPICERE; ADSPICERE; ADSPECTUS; CONSPECTUS; OBTUTUS. 1. Videre and cernere denote seeing, as perceiving by the organ of sight; videre (ἰδεῖν) as perception in general, in opp. to an obstruction of the view, like ὁρᾶν; cernere (κρίνειν) especially as a clear perception, in opp. to a transient or dim view; whereas spectare, intueri, tueri, and contueri, denote looking, as the dwelling of the eyes upon an object; spectare means, quietly to fix the eye upon an object that interests the understanding, and dwell upon it as upon a theatrical representation, like θεᾶσθαι; whereas intueri (from στοχάζομαι), to fix the eye upon something that strikes the fancy or soul, as to contemplate, θεωρεῖν. Cic. Fam. vii. 1. Neque nos qui hæc *spectavimus*, quidquam novi *vidimus*. 2. Intueri denotes merely to contemplate attentively;

c o n t u e r i, to gaze upon fixedly, keenly, and with eyes widely opened. 3. C o n s p i c e r e means to descry, that is, to get sight of an object of one's self, and generally of an unexpected object; whereas a d s p i c e r e means to look at, that is, to cast one's eye upon an object, whether consciously or not. 4. A d s p e c t u s has an active meaning, as the looking at; c o n s p e c t u s, a passive meaning, as the sight of, that is, the appearance, often also the *field of view*, *sight* [as in *to be* or *come in sight*]; o b t u t u s has a neutral sense, as the look. Suet. Tib. 43. Ut *adspectu* deficientes libidines excitaret; comp. with Cal. 9. Tumultuantes *conspectu* suo flexit; and with Cic. Orat. iii. 5. Qui vultum ejus cum ei dicendum esset, *obtutumque* oculorum in cogitando probe nosset. (iv. 305.)

VIERE, see *Ligare.*

VIGENS; VEGETUS; VIVIDUS; VIVUS; ANIMANS; VITALIS; VIVAX. 1. V i g e n s (*ἀΐξαι*) denotes a man, both in body and mind, fresh and in full strength; v e g e t u s, one, in a mental sense, on the alert and animated; v i v i d u s (from ἠΰς? or from vis?), one, in a moral sense, full of life and energy. Liv. vi. 22. Exactæ jam ætatis Camillus erat . . . sed *vegetum* ingenium in *vivido* pectore *vigebat*, virebatque integris sensibus. 2. V i v u s (Goth. quiws) means living, in opp. to dead; a n i m a n s, possessing life, in opp. to inanimate. 3. V i t a l i s means long-lived; v i v a x, tenacious of life. (iv. 445.)

VIGIL; INSOMNIS; EXSOMNIS. V i g i l denotes the state of being awake as positive, and involves consciousness and will, and the application of vital energy, like *ἄγρυπνος*; whereas i n s o m n i s and e x s o m n i s, only negatively, as sleepless, *ἄυπνος*; but the i n s o m n i s cannot sleep; the e x s o m n i s will not sleep. Tac. Ann. i. 65. Cum oberrarent tentoriis *insomnes* magis quam *pervigiles*. Vell. P. ii. 88. Mæcenas ubi rem *vigiliam* exigeret, sane *exsomnis*. Hor. Od. iii. 7, 6. Frigidas noctes non sine multis *insomnis* lacrimis agit; comp. with 25, 7. Non secus in jugis *exsomnis* stupet Evias; or Virg. Æn. ix. 167, with vi. 556. (iv. 444.

VILLA; FUNDUS; PRÆDIUM; AGER; CAMPUS; RUS; ARVUM. 1. Villa (dimin. of ἕδος) denotes a country-house, usually with a real estate; fundus, a real estate, usually with a country-house; prædium, sometimes a country-house, sometimes a real estate, like landed property. At the same time villla is an architectural term; fundus, an economical term; prædium, a juridical term. Cato, R. R. 3. Ita ædifices, ne *villa fundum* quærat, neve *fundus villam*. 2. Villa, fundus, and prædium, suppose a proprietor, like *portio;* whereas ager, arvum, rus, and campus, are thought of without reference to a proprietor, like *pars*. 3. Ager and campus denote the field, whether cultivated or not; ager (ἀγρός), the open field, in opp. to ground that is built upon, or planted with trees, consequently in opp. to *urbs*, *oppidum*, *vicus*, *hortus*, *silva*, like ἀγρός; whereas campus (κῆπος) denotes the low-lands and plains, like πεδίον, consequently in opp. to the high-lands, *mons* and *collis;* Cic. Div. i. 42. N. D. ii. 60. Colum. i. 2. Herenn. iv. 18. 25. Curt. viii. 1, 4. 4. Rus and arvum denote the corn-field; rus (ἄροτος) in opp. to the village or the town, like ἄρουρα; arvum, in opp. to pasture-lands and plantations, consequently in opp. to *pabulum*, *pascuum*, *pratum*, *olivetum*, Sall. Jug. 95. Cic. N. D. i. 45. Plaut. Truc. i. 2, 47. Hor. Ep. i. 16, 2. like ἄροτος. Cic. Fr. ap. Quintil. iv. 2. *Fundum* habet in *agro* Tiburino Tullius paternum. Orat. iii. 33. De *fundo* emendo, de *agro* colendo. Tac. G. 26. *Arva* per annos mutant, et superest *ager*. (iii. 5.)

VINCERE; SUPERARE; OPPRIMERE. 1. Vincere (εἴκειν? or ἀγκὰς ἀναγκάζειν?) means, to drive an adversary from his place, like νικᾶν; superare to win a place from an adversary, like ὑπερβάλλεσθαι. The vincens has more to do with living objects, with enemies; the superans with inanimate objects, with difficulties. Tac. Ann. i. 25. *Invictos* et nullis casibus *superabiles* Romanos. 2. Evincere denotes especially the exertion and duration of the conflict; devincere, its consequence, and the completeness of the victory. 3. Vincere means to conquer by fighting; apprimere, without fighting, by merely appearing, in consequence of a surprisal, or of a decided superiority of forces. Cic. Mil. 11. Vi *victa* vis, vel potius *oppressa* virtute audacia est: and to the same purport, Muren. 15. Mithridatem L. Murena repressum magna ex parte, non *oppressum* reliquit. (iv. 278.)

VINCIRE, see *Ligare*.

VINCULA; CATENÆ; COMPEDES; PEDICÆ; MANICÆ. Vincula (ἀγκάλη, from nectere) are bands of any sort, as a generic term for *catenæ*, etc., like δεσμοί; catenæ are chains, whether for fettering or for other uses, like ἁλύσεις; compedes (from πέδη), for fettering in general, the hands or the feet; pedicæ, irons for fettering the feet; manicæ, irons for fettering the hands. Tac. Ann. vi. 14. Celsus in *vinculis* laxatam *catenam*, et circumdatam in diversum tendens suam ipse cervicem perfregit. (iv. 284.)

VINDICTA; ULTIO; TALIO; PŒNA; MULCTA; CASTIGATIO; PUNIRI. 1. Vindicta (ἀναδέκτης) is an act of justice, like avenging: ultio (ἀλαλκεῖν, ἀλέξειν), an act of anger, like revenge; talio (τλῆναι), an act of retaliation. 2. Ultio, vindicatio, and talio, take place in consequence of the supreme authority of an individual; punitio, mulctatio, and castigatio, in consequence of the demand of others; pœna (ποινή, πεῖνα, πένομαι), as a punishment which the violated and offended law demands, by any mode of suffering; mulcta (μαλάξαι) as an amercement, which juctice and equity demand, as a compensation for injuries done, especially a fine; castigatio, as a chastisement, which may serve to improve the individual, especially a rebuke. Pœna is for the general good; m u l c t a, for the good of the injured party; c a s t i g a t i o, for that of the guilty party. (v. 249.) 3. P œ n i r e means to punish, according to the principles of justice; whereas p u n i r i, in Cicero, to take vengeance into one's own hands.

VINOLENTUS, see *Ebrietas*.

VINUM; TEMETUM. V i n u m (*οἶνος*) is the general and usual; t e m e t u m (from taminia), the antiquated and poetical name for wine.

VIOLARE, see *Lœdere*. VIR, see *Homo* and *Puer*.

VIRGA, VIRGULTUM, see *Rami*.

VIRGO; PUELLA; VIRAGO. V i r g o is an unmarried woman, whether young or old, in opp. to *mulier*, like *παρθένος*; whereas p u e l l a, a young woman, whether married or not; for instance, Nero's wife, Octavia, twenty years old, in Tac. Ann. xiv. 64, like *κόρη*; v i r a g o, a masculine, strong, heroic, young woman; for instance, the Amazones, *ἀντιάνειραι*.

VIRTUS; INNOCENTIA; HONESTAS. V i r t u s (*ἀρτυτή*) means virtue, as far as it shows itself in becoming and meritorious actions; i n n o c e n t i a, as far as it shows itself in blameless, especially disinterested conduct; h o n e s t a s (*χνοαστός*) as far it shows itself in virtuous and noble sentiments. (vi. 406.)

VIRTUS, see *Ferocia*. VIS, see *Potentia*.

VISCERA, see *Caro*.

VITA; SALUS; VICTUS. 1. V i t a (*οἶτος*) denotes the duration of life, in opp. to *mors;* whereas s a l u s (from *ὅλος* ?), the safety of life, in opp. to *interitus*, *exitium*. 2. V i t a denotes the public; v i c t u s the private life of a man. Nep. Alc. 1. Splendidus non minus in *vita* quam in *victu*. (iv. 448.)

VITALIS, see *Vigens*.

VITIUM; MENDA; MENDUM; LABES; MACULA. V i t i u m (from *αὐάτη*, *ἄτη*), denotes any fault; m e n d a (*μάτη*), a natural fault, especially of the body, a blemish, like *βλάβη*; m e n d u m, a fault committed, especially in writing, a blunder or mistake, like *ἁμάρ-*

τημα; labes (λώβη), a degrading fault, a stain of ignominy, like λύμη; macula (dimin. from μῶκος), a disfiguring fault, a blot, like κηλίς.) (v. 319.)

VITUPERARE, see *Reprehendere.*

VIVAX, VIVIDUS, see *Vivens.*

VIRUS, see *Toxicum.* VIVUS, see *Vigens.*

VIX; ÆGRE. Vix (ἧκα) means scarcely, and refers, like σχολῇ, only to a thing that was near not taking place, in opp. to *omnino non,* Cic. Att. iii. 23; whereas ægre means with much ado, like μόλις and λόγις, and refers to the agent, who is in a state of anxiety as to whether he shall succeed or fail, in opp. to *facile,* Cic. Sen. 20. (iii. 94.)

VOCABULUM, see *Verbum.* VOCARE, see *Nominare.*

VOCIFERARI, see *Clangere.*

VOLUCRES; AVES; ALITES. Volucres (from ἑλίξαι) means whatever flies, including winged insects, like πτηνός; whereas aves and alites mean only birds; avis (ἀετός) as a general term in natural history for any bird, like ὄρνις; ales (from ala) as a select expression only for a larger bird, like οἰωνός, especially the eagle, and alites is used in the language of the augurs as a technical term for those birds whose *flight* must be observed and interpreted, in opp. to *oscines,* or those birds whose *song* and *cry* must be interpreted. Ovid, Art. Am. iii. 410. Jovis in multis devolat *ales aves.* Hor. Od. iv. 2, 2. 4. Virg. Æn. xii. 247. Cic. N. D. ii. 64. (v. 207.)

VOLUNTATE, see *Sponte.* VOLUPTAS, see *Cupido.*

VORAGO; VORTEX; GURGES. Vorago (ὄρηχος) and the poetical word, of foreign origin, barathrum, denote an abyss in water, which may be either in a pool, pond, or sea; whereas vortex and gurges suppose water in motion; vortex moves in a horizontal direction, so that its water turns in a circle, and hinders whatever swims therein from escaping; gurges (from γοργός? or γύργαθος?), in a perpendicular direction, so that it drags down whatever comes into its eddy, into the depth below. Liv. xxviii. 30. Navis retro *vortice* intorta; compare with xxii. 6. Deficientibus animis hauriebantur *gurgitibus*. (v. 155.)

Vox, see *Verbum*.

Vulnus; Plaga; Ulcus; Cicatrix; Saucius. 1. Vulnus and plaga denote a wound from without; vulnus (from lanius?) by means of a weapon, or other cutting instrument; plaga, by means of any instrument carried with intention to injure; whereas ulcus (*ἄλοξ*, *ὦλξ*) means any open or sore place in the body, that has begun to fester, etc.; cicatrix, the scar that is left when a wound is healed. Suet. Vit. 10. Verbera et *plagas*, sæpe *vulnera*, nonnunquam necem repræsentantes adversantibus. Plin. H. N. xvi. 12. Cels. viii. 4. 2. Vulneratus means wounded in general; saucius, so wounded as to be unfit for fighting, and is the proper expression for those that are wounded in battle. Cic. Verr. i. 27. Servi nonnulli *vulnerantur*; ipse Rubrius *sauciatur*. (iv. 255.)

Vultus, see *Facies*.

# INDEX OF GREEK WORDS.

This Index embraces all the Greek words contained in the Latin Synonyms, and will afford valuable aid in elucidating many Greek synonyms. The figures refer to the pages of the book.

U*

# WARREN F. DRAPER,

# PUBLISHER AND BOOKSELLER,

## ANDOVER. MASS.,

Publishes and offers for Sale the following Works, which will be sent, Post-paid, on receipt of the Sums affixed.

---

**HEBREW GRAMMAR.** The Elements of the Hebrew Language. By Rev. A. D. JONES, A.M. 8vo. pp. 163. Price, $1.75.

"The elements of the language are here presented and unfolded in a form so simple and striking, that they cannot fail to be apprehended with a reasonable degree of application. A number of appropriate exercises, selected from different portions of the Old Testament Scriptures, are also given, which furnish ample opportunity for a practical application of the principles previously laid down. The whole is closed with a Clavis to the selections from the Scriptures previously given. The plan of the work is admirable, and happily executed." — *Reformed Church Messenger.*

"The object of the author was to supply a proper elementary book for beginners in the study of Hebrew, and thus prepare the way for the ponderous, complicated, philosophical grammars now in use; and which are more appreciated and useful after having mastered the general principles and facts of the language. We are much pleased with the manner in which the author has accomplished this work for our younger brethren in the ministry." — *Methodist Protestant.*

"Mr. Jones has rendered good service to the cause of education. He says that it is just as easy for young students at school to acquire an elementary knowledge of Hebrew as of Greek and Latin, and that there is no reason arising from the difficulty or disagreeableness of the language why it should not to the same extent enter into the curriculum of early school study. He has accordingly prepared a work which corresponds in general method with the elementary Greek and Latin text-books in current use. He, of course, avoids the refinements of the subject, but by a simple and progressive series of exercise, and by a perfectly plain exposition of the syntax, the student is enabled to take up Hebrew just as he would the *Initia Latina*, and just as easily." — *Publisher's Circular*, Apr. 15, 1870.

**HEBREW PSALTER.** Liber Psalmorum. Text according to Hahn. 32mo. pp. 177. Morocco. $1.00.

"We have here a beautifully clear and eye-comforting edition of the Hebrew Psalter, according to Hahn's text, but arranged in verse mostly according to Rosenmueller..... Every lover of the Hebrew will desire and be grateful for so agreeable a help to his studies and devotions." *Congregationalist.*

"To those who read Hebrew this little volume will be a perfect diamond. We have seen nothing for many a d y which has pleased our fancy more. The paper is excellent, the printing remarkably clear and distinct, and the general appearance of the *booklet* like a gem of the first water — which it is." — *Christian Secretary.*

**HEBREW ENGLISH PSALTER.** The Book of Psalms, in Hebrew and English, arranged in Parallelism. 16mo. pp. 194. $1.50.

"The preacher in expounding to his congregation one of the Psalms of David, will find it very convenient to have the original by the side of the English version. For private reading and meditation, also, such an arrangement will be found very pleasant and profitable. We feel confident that this little volume will be a favorite with Hebrew scholars; and that, when they have once become habituated to it, it will be, to many of them, a *vade mecum.*" – *Bibliotheca Sacra.*

"A handsome edition of the book of Psalms, which will be quite a favorite with clergymen and theological students." — *New Englander.*

A very convenient and admirable manual, and we beg leave to thank our Andover friend for it." — *Presbyterian Quarterly.*

"The volume is beautifully printed, of convenient size for use, and of admirable adaptation to the service of those whose Hebrew has become a dim reminiscence." — *North American Review.*

"A happy design, and beautifully executed in its typography." — *Boston Review.*

**ELLICOTT'S COMMENTARY, CRITICAL AND GRAMMATICAL**, on St. Paul's Epistle to the Galatians. With an Introductory Notice by C. E. STOWE, Professor in Andover Theological Seminary. 8vo. pp. 183 $1.50.

The Commentaries of Prof. Ellicott supply an urgent want in their sphere of criticism. Prof. Stowe says of them, in his Notice: "It is the crowning excellence of these Commentaries that they are exactly what they profess to be, *critical* and *grammatical*, and therefore, in the best sense of the term, *exegetical*. . . . . His results are worthy of all confidence. He is more careful than Tischendorf, slower and more steadily deliberate than Alford, and more patiently laborious than any other living New Testament critic, with the exception, perhaps, of Tregelles."

"They [Ellicott's Commentaries] have set the first example, in this country, [England] of a thorough and fearless examination of the grammatical and philological requirements of every word of the sacred text. I do not know of anything superior to them, in their own particular line, in Germany; and they add, what, alas! is so seldom found in that country, profound reverence for the matter and subjects on which the author is laboring; nor is their value lessened by Mr. Ellicott's having confined himself for the most part to one department of a commentator's work — the grammatical and philological." — *Dean Alford.*

"The *critical* part is devoted to the settling of the text, and this is admirably done, with a labor, skill, and conscientiousness unsurpassed." — *Bib. Sacra.*

"We have never met with a learned commentary on any book of the New Testament so nearly perfect in every respect as the 'Commentary on the Epistle to the Galatians,' by Prof. Ellicott, of King's College, London, — learned, devout, and orthodox." — *Independent.*

"We would recommend all scholars of the original Scriptures who seek directness, luminous brevity, the absence of everything irrelevant to strict grammatical inquiry, with a concise and yet very complete view of the opinions of others, to possess themselves of Ellicott's Commentaries." — *American Presbyterian.*

**COMMENTARY ON EPHESIANS.** 8vo. pp. 190. $1.50.

**COMMENTARY ON THESSALONIANS.** 8vo. pp. 171. $1.50.

**COMMENTARY ON THE PASTORAL EPISTLES.** 8vo. $2.00.

**COMMENTARY ON PHILIPPIANS, COLOSSIANS, AND PHILEMON.** $2.00.

THE SET in five vols., on fine paper, extra cloth, bevelled, gilt tops. $10.00.
THE SET in two vols., black cloth $ 8.00.

**HENDERSON ON THE MINOR PROPHETS.** THE BOOK OF THE TWELVE MINOR PROPHETS. Translated from the Original Hebrew. With a Commentary, Critical, Philological, and Exegetical. By E. HENDERSON, D.D. With a Biographical Sketch of the Author, by E. P. BARROWS, Hitchcock Professor in Andover Theological Seminary. 8vo. pp. 490. $ 3.50.

"This Commentary on the Minor Prophets, like that on the Prophecy of Isaiah, has been highly and deservedly esteemed by professional scholars, and has been of great service to the working ministry. We are happy to welcome it in an American edition, very neatly printed." — *Bib. Sacra.*

"Clergymen and other students of the Bible will be glad to see this handsome American edition of a work which has a standard reputation in its department, and which fills a place that is filled, so far as we know, by no other single volume in the English language. Dr. Henderson was a good Hebrew and Biblical scholar, and in his Commentaries he is intelligent, brief, and to the point." — *Boston Recorder.*

"The American publisher issues this valuable work with the consent and approbation of the author, obtained from himself before his death. It is published in substantial and elegant style, clear white paper and beautiful type. The work is invaluable for its philological research and critical acumen. The notes are learned, reliable, and practical, and the volume deserves a place in every theological student's library." — *American Presbyterian, etc.*

"Of all his Commentaries none are more popular than his Book of the Minor Prophets." — *Christian Observer.*

"This is probably the best Commentary extant on the Minor Prophets. The work is worthy of a place in the library of every scholar and every diligent and earnest reader of the Bible." — *Christian Chronicle.*

**HENDERSON'S JEREMIAH AND LAMENTATIONS.** The Book of the Prophet Jeremiah and that of the Lamentations, translated from the original Hebrew; with a Commentary Critical, Philological, and Exegetical. By E. HENDERSON, D.D. 8vo. pp. 315. $2.50.

"This Commentary, which has been before the public for some years, like that of Isaiah and the Minor Prophets, combines learning and clearness, philological research, critical taste sound judgment, and pure devotion. An introductory dissertation, brief, but luminous and instructive, prepares the reader for an appreciative study of the work. The translation, perhaps, sometimes unnecessarily deviates from the English version. It is printed in the clear and elegant style for which the Andover press is distinguished." — *Evangelical Quarterly.*

"Dr. Henderson is one of the most eminent of modern biblical critics, and is known in this country chiefly by his translations and commentaries on Isaiah and on the twelve Minor Prophets. One of the leading features of his mode of treating Scripture is his happy blending of textual with exegetical comment. His treatise on Jeremiah is well worthy by its elevated scholarship to take a place side by side with the commentaries of Bishop Ellicott and of Professor Murphy, also issued by Mr. Draper." — *Publisher's Circular*, Oct. 1. 1868.

**HENDERSON'S EZEKIEL.** The Book of the Prophet Ezekiel, translated from the original Hebrew; with a Commentary Critical, Philological, and Exegetical. By E. Henderson, D.D. 8vo. pp. 228. Price, $2.00.

"This Commentary treats the greatest, save one, of the Evangelical Prophets after his own spirit. It is full of the fulness of the Gospel. His notes deal freely with the original text, and will be found very helpful to the real student of these sacred symbols." — *Zion's Herald.*

"This Commentary, like that on the Minor Prophets and other books of the Old Testament, by the same author, is very satisfactory. On every page it gives evidence of careful research and critical scholarship. It avoids all fanciful interpretation; its expositions are marked by practical good sense" — *Evangelical Quarterly Review, Pa.*

**MURPHY'S GENESIS.** Critical and Exegetical Commentary on the Book of Genesis; with a new Translation. By JAMES G. MURPHY, LL.D., T.C.D. With a Preface by J. P. THOMPSON, D.D., of New York. 8vo. pp. 535. Price, $3.50.

"The most valuable contribution that has for a long time been made to the many aids for the critical study of the Old Testament, is Mr. Draper's republication of Dr. Murphy on Genesis, in one octavo volume. Dr. Murphy is one of the Professors of the Assembly's College at Belfast. and adds to a thorough knowledge of the Hebrew, and of the science of interpretation, great common sense, genuine wit, and admirable power of expression. Hence his commentary is racy and readable, as well as reliable. No volume will be more useful to those who have been troubled by the Colenso criticisms; and no man has pricked the bubble of that inflated bishop with a more effectual and relieving wound than Dr. Murphy. It is a good deal to say of a commentary, but we say it in all sincerity, that this volume furnishes about as fascinating work for one's hours for reading, as any volume of the day, in any department of literature; while its general influence will be salutary, and effective for the truth." — *Congregationalist.*

**MURPHY'S EXODUS.** 8vo. pp. 385. Price, $3.00.

"Thus far nothing has appeared in this country for half a century on the first two books of the Pentateuch so valuable as the present two volumes". (On Genesis and Exodus.) His style is lucid, animated, and often eloquent. His pages afford golden suggestions and key-thoughts..... Some of the laws of interpretation are stated with so fresh and natural a clearness and force that they will permanently stand." — *Methodist Quarterly.*

"I feel that I am richer for having it on my shelf of Christian armory. I wish every one of my brethren in the ministry had the same joy; and few need be deprived of it, for the books are very cheap." — *Rev. H. C. Fish, D.D.*

"Prof. Murphy's Commentary on Genesis has been published long enough to have secured the highest reputation for scholarship, research, and sound judgment. This volume on Exodus takes it place in the same rank, and will increase rather than diminish its author's reputation among scholars." — *National Baptist.*

"This is the second volume of the ablest Commentary on the Pentateuch that has yet fallen into our hands." — *The Weekly Press.*

"By its originality and critical accuracy is must command the high regard of the scholar and theologian, whilst the ease and grace of its style, the judiciousness with which it selects and unfolds its many subjects of discussion, will be sure to fix and reward the attention of the general student." — *The Lutheran.*

**DÖDERLEIN'S HAND-BOOK OF LATIN SYNONYMES.** Translated by REV. H. H. ARNOLD, B. A., with an Introduction by S. H. TAYLOR, LL. D. New Edition, with an Index of Greek words. 16mo. pp. 267. 1.25.

"The present hand-book of Doderlein is remarkable for the brevity, distinctness, perspicuity, and appositeness of its definitions. It will richly reward not merely the classical, but the general student, for the labor he may devote to it. It is difficult to open the volume, even at random, without discovering some hint which may be useful to a theologian. . . . . From the preceding extracts, it will be seen that this hand-book is useful in elucidating many Greek as well as Latin synonymes." — *Bib. Sacra.*

"The little volume mentioned above, introduced to the American public by an eminent Scholar and Teacher, Samuel H. Taylor, LL. D., is one of the best helps to the thorough appreciation of the nice shades of meaning in Latin words that have met my eye. It deserves the attention of teachers and learners, and will amply reward patient study." — *E. D. Sanborn, late Professor of Latin in Dartmouth College.*

"The study of it will conduce much to thorough and accurate knowledge of the old Roman tongue. To the present edition is appended an 'Index of Greek words,' which embraces all the Greek words contained in the Latin Synonymes, and affords valuable aid in the elucidation of Greek Synonymes." — *Boston Recorder.*

**POLITICAL ECONOMY.** Designed as a Text-Book for Colleges. By JOHN BASCOM, A. M., Professor in Williams College. 12mo. pp. 366. $1.50.

"It goes over the whole ground in a logical order. The matter is perspicuously arranged under distinct chapters and sections; it is a compendious exhibition of the principles of the science without prolonged disquisitions on particular points, and it is printed in the style for which the Andover Press has long been deservedly celebrated." — *Princeton Review.*

"This work is one of value to the student. It treats of the relations and character of political economy, its advantages as a study, and its history. Almost every subject in the range of the science is here touched upon and examined in a manner calculated to interest and instruct the reader." — *Amherst Express.*

"The book is worthy a careful study, both for the views it contains and as a mental training. The author understands himself, and has evidently studied his subject well. The style in which it is put forth also commends it to the reading community." — *Evening Express.*

"This is a valuable work upon a subject of much interest. Professor Bascom writes well, and his book makes an excellent manual. His stand-point in the middle of the 19th century gives it a character quite unlike that of the older works upon the subject." — *Boston Recorder.*

**RUSSELL'S PULPIT ELOCUTION.** Comprising Remarks on the Effect of Manner in public Discourse; the Elements of Elocution applied to the Reading of the Scriptures, Hymns and Sermons; with Observations on the Principles of Gesture; and a Selection of Exercises in Reading and Speaking. With an Introduction by PROF. E. A. PARK and REV. E. N. KIRK. 413 pp. 12mo. Second Edition. $1.50.

"Mr. Russell is known as one of the masters of elocutionary science in the United States. He has labored long, skilfully, and successfully in that most interesting field, and has acquired an honored name among the teachers and writers upon rhetoric. It is one of the most thorough publications upon the subject, and is admirably addressed to the correction of the various defects which diminish the influence of pulpit discourses. It is already an established authority in many places." — *Literary World.*

**HISTORICAL MANUAL OF THE SOUTH CHURCH IN ANDOVER, MASS.** Compiled by REV. GEORGE MOOAR; with a portrait of REV. SAMUEL PHILLIPS, first Pastor of the Church. 12mo. pp 200. $1.25.

"This manual has a value far beyond the promise made in its title-page. Henceforth, whatever may befall the records of the South Church in Andover, or even the Church itself, — though both were blotted from the earth, — its history for a hundred and fifty years is safe. And in that history is embraced an amount of instruction rarely condensed into so small a space. The catalogue of members, numbering 2,177, indicates the date and manner of admission — whether by profession or letter; the date and manner of removal — whether by death, dismission, or excommunication; generally the age of the deceased, and, if females who married during their membership, the names of their husbands." — *Congregational Quarterly.*

**STUDIES IN PHILOSOPHY AND THEOLOGY.** By JOSEPH HAVEN, D.D., Professor in Chicago Theological Seminary. 8vo. pp. 502. Cloth. Price, $2.00.

"This work is divided into two parts. The first part contains Essays having the following titles: Philosophy of Sir William Hamilton; Mill versus Hamilton; the Moral Faculty; Province of Imagination in Sacred Oratory; the Ideal and the Actual. The second part contains Essays on Natural Theology; the Doctrine of the Trinity; Theology as a Science—its dignity and value; Place and Value of Miracles in the Christian System; Sin as related to Human Nature and the Divine Mind; Arianism, the Natural Development of the Views held by the Early Church Fathers.

"Dr. Haven has exhibited much ability and a good spirit in discussing various controverted questions in philosophy and theology. We hope that this volume will tend to increase the interest of the religious public in these important questions. Men who differ from the author in some of his speculations, will be pleased with his distinctness of thought and perspicuity of style."—*Bibliotheca Sacra.*

"Dr. Haven's views in philosophy contravening Mill, and giving a qualified approval of Hamilton, coincide substantially with those of McCosh, Porter, and other able writers of England and America on such topics. As to the foundation of moral obligation he holds that the idea of right is ultimate and inexplicable, and in a condensed Supplementary Note of four pages, ably replies to the criticism of his views by Pres. Hopkins in the 'Law of Love.'.... The theological essays are timely as well as able; opposing rationalizing tendencies, yet defending new school positions; maintaining evangelical doctrine, yet dealing candidly with objectors, both as regards the history and the reason of each case. This is especially true of the author's treatment of the difficult subject of the Trinity, and the development of Arianism."—*The Advance.*

"Professor Haven gives us in this condensed form, the fruitage of his life-thoughts upon the grandest themes that can engage the human attention..... We deem it no more than just to say, that in this volume philosophy and faith blend, each strengthening the other, to a degree unsurpassed in any work of the kind. The wavering will be confirmed by his logic, while those inclined to credulity will be quickened to thought."—*Chicago Evening Journal.*

**POND'S PASTORAL THEOLOGY.** Lectures on Pastoral Theology. By ENOCH POND, D.D., Professor in Bangor Theological Seminary. 12mo. pp 395. Price, $1.75.

"We are glad to notice a new edition of 'Lectures on Pastoral Theology,' by Rev. Dr Pond, of the Theological Seminary in Bangor, Me., first published twenty years ago. These lectures have been almost entirely rewritten, and several of them have been modified in important respects. A valuable feature of the book is its practical character: pastoral duties and relations, and questions which are likely to perplex the minds of young ministers, especially, being treated with minuteness and plainness. Clear common sense—a rare quality—and a correct view of the mutual relations of pastor and people are characteristics of every lecture; and the devout spirit pervading the treatment of the many subjects is what we should naturally expect from the author."—*Congregationalist.*

**THE THEOLOGY OF THE GREEK POETS.** By W. S TYLER, Williston Professor of Greek in Amherst College. 12mo. pp 365. Cloth, bevelled. Price, $1.75.

"Professor Tyler has here produced a work which is an honor to American literature. It is well fitted to be a classic in our Colleges and Theological Seminaries. It furnishes admirable illustrations of the truth of both natural and revealed theology, and suggests original methods for the defence of these truths."—*Bibliotheca Sacra.*

"There are few better Greek scholars in the country than Professor Tyler, who has devoted himself with great earnestness and enthusiasm to the culture and teaching of Greek literature. The chapters which compose the book have all appeared in former years in different Quarterlies. In this way they have attracted the attention of many of our best scholars." Prof. Tyler has done good service to the cause of truth in showing that the Iliad and Odyssey, as well as the dramas of Aeschylus and the tragedies of Sophocles, express ideas and sentiments very much like those we find in contemporary Scriptures."—*Hours at Home.*

"The aim of the author is to detect the analogies between the myths of the Greek drama and epic, and the truths of revelation. The care of the scholar and the enthusiasm of the poet have been given to the work."—*Independent.*

"The book is an important contribution to natural theology. It traces the relation of the theology of the Greek poets to that of Christ. Prof. Tyler does his work with the mind of a master."—*Zion's Herald.*

**ΦΩΚΥΛΙΔΟΥ ΠΟΙΗΜΑ ΝΟΥΘΕΤΙΚΟΝ.** Phocylidis Poema Admonitorium. Recognovit Brevibusque Notis Instruxit. J. B. Feuling, Ph.D., A.O.S.S., Professor Philologiae Compar. in Univer. Wisconsinensi. Editio Prima Americana. 16mo. pp. 32. Paper, 30 cents; gilt edges, 40 cts.

"*Phocylidis Poema Admonitorium*, edited by J. B. Feuling, Professor in the University of Wisconsin, and exquisitely printed. Phocylides was an Ionian poet, contemporary with Theognis and Simonides, say 550 B.C. Suidas says he wrote gnomic poetry and elegies, and calls him a philosopher. Aristotle quotes him, with praise. Only eighteen short fragments of his poems are known to survive, of which two are the elegiac metre, and the rest in hexameters. The didactic poem, here reprinted, in 217 hexameters, has been considered, beyond question, to be a forgery of date since the Christian era. Whenever and by whomsoever written, the little poem is interesting for its style, and for the excellent sentiments which it breathes." — *Congregationalist and Recorder.*

**WHATELY'S ESSAYS ON ST. PAUL.** Essays on some of the Difficulties in the Writings of St. Paul. By Archbishop Whately. 12mo. pp. 397. Cloth extra, gilt tops, $1.50.

"We regard the present volume as, on the whole, the ablest of his theological works. It deserves the faithful study of every clergyman. Dr. Whately is one of those authors who can be as profitably read by those who do not agree with him as by those who do. The religious opinions of a writer who earned so eminent a name in the department of logic and rhetoric, and who had so great skill in the practical affairs relating to the state as well as the church, cannot be without peculiar interest to the theologian." — *Bibliotheca Sacra.*

"The Archbishop's writings are a part of the sterling theological letters of the age, and ought to be possessed by all the studious and thoughtful." — *Journal and Messenger.*

"This book had passed through at least eight editions in England before its publication in this country. Dr. Whately is always entitled to a hearing. Never profound, he is always clear; never very original, he is always instructive; never disgustingly dogmatic, he always seems to feel a serene assurance that he has exhausted the whole subject, and that his verdict is final; always positive and didactic, he is yet never extreme, but always takes the middle and moderate view." — *Watchman and Reflector*

**WHATELY'S ESSAYS ON THE CHRISTIAN RELIGION.** Essays on some of the Peculiarities of the Christian Religion; and Historic Doubts concerning Napoleon. By Archbishop Whately. 12mo. pp. 264 and 48. Bound in one vol.; Cloth extra, gilt tops, $1.50.

**HISTORIC DOUBTS.** Historic Doubts concerning Napoleon. 12mo. pp. 48. Paper covers, 25 cents; cloth, 50 cents.

About the year 1821 Whately published this Essay anonymously. It was designed as an answer to Hume's objections to the credibility of the Christian miracles. Following Hume's method, Whately gravely argued the improbability of the existence of the first Napoleon, and demonstrated that, on Hume's principles, the testimony in relation thereto could not be credited. In the second edition of this Essay, the author humorously assumed the fact of the death of Napoleon, which had then just occurred as a confirmation of his theory, asserting that "the newspapers," finding that his little tract had called attention to their "phantom," had disposed of the tract by killing the phantom.

**THE SHADOW OF CHRISTIANITY,** or the Genesis of the Christian State. A Treatise for the Times. By Prof. Leonard Marsh, author of "The Apocatastasis." 12mo. pp. 167. Price, $1.25.

"One of the topics treated is the characteristic distinction between the Pagan and the Christian civilizations...... Another point which the author discusses in an original way is, the method by which the doctrines of Christ gain ground among men. The spiritual nature of these doctrines is very clearly and forcibly brought out. The clergy will do well to heed this Lay Sermon. It is a good *concio ad clerum*, and will help to brush away a good many crude notions that sometimes get utterance from the pulpit. But not a few readers of the book will be most struck by the chapter in which the author treats of the relations of Capital to Labor; showing how they are founded on the necessary relations of man to nature...... Other topics discussed are: The True Form of Church Organization, as required by the Idea of the Church and the nature of the Christian Religion; the Relation of the Fine Arts to Morals, and especially the Influence on Society and Government of Christianity, as compared with mere climatic and other physical conditions; or the moulding power of moral forces as compared with forces chemical and mechanical." — *Burlington Daily Times.*

**GUERICKE'S CHURCH HISTORY.** Translated by W. G. T. SHEDD, Brown Professor in Andover Theological Seminary. 8vo. pp. $3.00.

This volume includes the period of the ANCIENT CHURCH (the first six centuries. A.C.) or the Apostolic and Patristic Church.

"We regard Professor Shedd's version, now under notice, as a happy specimen of the TRANSFUSION rather than a TRANSLATION, which many of the German treatises should receive. The style of his version is far superior to that of the original." — *Bibliotheca Sacra.*

"The established credit of Guericke's labors in the department of Ecclesiastical History, and the use made of his works by many English writers will make this volume acceptable to a very large class of students and readers." — *London Journal of Sacred Literature.*

**GUERICKE'S CHURCH HISTORY.** A History of the Mediæval Church. 8vo. pp 168. $1.50.

" This portion of Guericke's Church History continues the account down to A.D. 1073, when Hildebrand ascended the Papal chair as Gregory VII.

**DISCOURSES AND ESSAYS.** By PROF. W. G. T. SHEDD. 271 pp. 12mo $1.50.

Few clearer and more penetrating minds can be found in our country than that of Prof. Shedd. And besides, he writes with a chaste and sturdy eloquence, transparent as crystal; so that if he goes DEEP, we love to follow him. If the mind gets dull, or dry, or ungovernable, put it to grappling with these masterly productions. — [Congregational Herald, Chicago.

The striking sincerity, vigor, and learning of this volume will be admired even by those readers who cannot go with the author in all his opinions. Whatever debate the philosophical tendencies of the book may challenge, its literary ability and moral spirit will be commended every where. — *New Englander.*

These discourses are all marked by profound thought and perspicuity of sentiment. — *Princeton Review.*

**LECTURES UPON THE PHILOSOPHY OF HISTORY.** By PROF. W. G. T. SHEDD. 128 pp. 12mo. 75 cents.

CONTENTS. — The abstract Idea of History. — The Nature and Definition of Secular History. — The Nature and Definition of Church History. — The Verifying Test in Church History.

The style of these Lectures has striking merits. The author chooses his words with rare skill and taste, from an ample vocabulary, and writes with strength and refreshing simplicity. The Philosophy of Realism, in application to history and historical theology, is advocated by vigorous reasoning, and made intelligible by original and felicitous illustrations. — *New Englander.*

Professor Shedd has already achieved a high reputation for the union of philosophic insight with genuine scholarship, of depth and clearness of thought with force and elegance of style, and for profound views of sin and grace, cherished not merely on theoretical, but still more on moral and experimental grounds. — *Princeton Review.*

**OUTLINES OF A SYSTEMATIC RHETORIC.** From the German of DR. FRANCIS THEREMIN, by WILLIAM G. T. SHEDD. Third and Revised Edition, with an Introductory Essay by the translator. pp. 216. 12mo. $1.00.

This is a work of much solid value. It is adapted to advanced students, and can be read and reread with advantage by professed public speakers, however accomplished they may be in the important art of persuasion. This edition is an improvement upon the other, containing a new introductory essay, illustrating the leading position of the work, and a series of questions adapting it to the use of the student — *Boston Recorder.*

It is not a work of surface suggestions, but of thorough and philosophic analysis, and, as such, is of great value to the student, and especially to him who habitually addresses men on the most important themes. — *Congregational Quarterly.*

The Introductory Essay which Professor Shedd has prefixed to this valuable Treatise, is elaborate, vigorous, impressive. It excites the mind not only to thought, but also to the expression of thought, to inward and outward activity. The whole volume is characterized by freshness and originality of remark, a purity and earnestness of moral feeling. — *Bib. Sacra,* 1859.

**WINER'S N. T. GRAMMAR.** A Grammar of the Idiom of the New Testament: prepared as a Solid Basis for the Interpretation of the New Testament. By DR. GEORGE BENEDICT WINER. Seventh Edition, enlarged and improved. By DR. GOTTLIEB LÜNEMANN, Professor of Theology at the University of Göttingen. Revised and authorized Translation. 8vo. pp. 744. Cloth, $5.00; sheep, $6.00; half goat, $6.75.

"Prof. Thayer exhibits the most scholarly and pains-taking accuracy in all his work, especial attention being given to references and indexes, on which the value of such a work so much depends. The indexes alone fill eighty-six pages. The publishers work is handsomely done, and we cannot conceive that a better Winer should be for many years to come accessible to American scholars." — *Princeton Review.*

"Prof. Thayer speaks with great modesty of the work as being 'substantially a revision of Professor Masson's translation.' We have carefully compared many paragraphs and pages, and find that the labor performed by him is by no means hinted in his unpretending preface. The improvement in purity, transparency, and accuracy of style, as well as in fidelity, is very noticeable. This edition has the advantage of being brought down to 1866, embodying the labors of one of the ripest scholars of Germany for a life-time, and containing references in cases of textual criticism to the Codex Sinaiticus. There are three elaborate and exhaustive indexes..... The invaluable contents of the volume are thus at once at the command of the scholar..... We are struck with the appropriateness of an expression on the title-page: 'prepared as a *solid basis* for the interpretation of the New Testament.' Clergymen of scholarly habits will find this Grammar, Robinson's New Test. Lexicon, and a critical edition of the the Greek Testament about all the exegetical apparatus they will need. A clear head, patient study, and sympathy with the Divine Spirit will, with such helps, do the work of a Commentator for them better than Commentaries themselves without them." — *Pacific.*

"We trust that this admirable edition of a justly famous and surpassingly valuable work, will gain extensive circulation, and that the study of it will begin afresh." — *Baptist Quarterly.*

"The Seventh Edition of Winer, superintended by Lunemann (Leipz. 1867), we have at last, thanks to Professor Thayer, in a really accurate translation." — *Dr. Ezra Abbott, in Smith's Dictionary of the Bible, American Ed.*

"The translator's preface informs us that after a very considerable portion of the work had been finished, and three hundred pages or more had been stereotyped, the plans which had been formed were largely modified by the publication of the seventh edition of the Grammar in Germany. With a determination to make the work as valuable as possible, the translator resolved to revise the whole in connection with this latest edition. He accordingly retraced his steps to a considerable degree, and prepared his translation in conformity with his modified plan. The result is, that we have before us, in our own language, 'a reproduction of the original work,' in its most perfect form, and with its author's latest additions and improvements. The wisdom, as well as the appreciation of the interests of students of the New Testament, which Professor Thayer has displayed in adopting this course at the cost of long delay and greatly increased labor, entitle him to the favorable regard of the public."—*New Englander.*

"'Without altering the general distribution of matter as it appeared in the sixth edition, he — Winer — constantly improved the book in details, by additions of greater or less extent in more than three hundred and forty places, by erasures and reconstructions, by the multiplication of parallel passages from biblical and from profane literature, by a more precise definition of thoughts and expressions,' etc. Professor Lunemann has added to the seventh edition not only these improvements, but also improvements of his own; and has thus made the seventh edition more full, as well as more accurate, than either of the preceding." — *Bibliotheca Sacra.*

"The work of the American editor is done in a thorough and scholarly manner." — *Congregational Quarterly.*

"The whole appearance of the work as it now stands indicates a careful and thorough scholarship. A critical comparison of several pages with the original confirms the impression made by a general examination of the book. In its present form, this translation may now be recommended as worthy of a place in the library of every minister who desires to study the New Testament with the aid of the best critical helps." — *Theological Eclectic.*

"Great pains also have been taken to secure typographical accuracy, an extremely difficult thing in a work of this kind. We rejoice that so invaluable a work has thus been made as nearly perfect as we can hope ever to have it. It is a work that can hardly fail to facilitate and increase the reverent and accurate study of the Word of God."— *American Presbyterian Review.*

www.ingramcontent.com/pod-product-compliance
Lightning Source LLC
LaVergne TN
LVHW010234110826
845151LV00004B/1290
* 9 7 8 1 4 2 5 5 2 5 1 8 7 *